LET US BE MUSLIMS

Sayyid Abul A'la Mawdudi

EDITED BY
KHURRAM MURAD

THE ISLAMIC FOUNDATION

Editor: *Khurram Murad*
Cover design: *Nasir Cadir*
Cover image: *Batool al-Toma*

Published by
THE ISLAMIC FOUNDATION,

Markfield Conference Centre,
Ratby Lane, Markfield, Leicestershire, LE67 9SY, UK
E-mail: publications@islamic-foundation.com
Website: www.islamic-foundation.com

Quran House, P.O. Box 30611, Nairobi, Kenya

PMB 3196, Kano, Nigeria

Distributed by: Kube Publishing
Tel: +44(1530) 249230, Fax: +44(1530) 249656
Email: info@kubepublishing.com
Website: www.kubepublishing.com

British Library Cataloguing in Publishing Data
Mawdudi, Abul A'la
Let us be Muslims.
1.   Islam
I. Title II. Murad, Khurram
297 BP161.2

ISBN 978-0-860371-57-1

Contents

Introduction by Khurram Murad 13
Preface to the First Edition 43

PART I: IMAN

1. **Knowledge, the First Step** 47
    Allah's Greatest Gift 47
    Is Islam a Birthright? 48
    No Mere Verbal Profession 49
    No Islam Without Knowledge 49
    Dangers of Ignorance 50
    Acquire Knowledge 51

2. **Between Islam and Disbelief** 53
    Muslims or Unbelievers? 53
    Knowledge and Actions 54
    Why Are Muslims Humiliated Today? 56
    Desire For Knowledge 59

3. **How Muslims Treat the Qur'ān** 61
    Irreverence and Misuse 61
    Incomprehensible Contradictions 62
    The Consequences 64
    No Islam Without Submitting to the Qur'ān 65

4. **True Meaning of Iman** 69
    Difference the Kalimah Creates 69

Is Mere Utterance Enough?   70
Meaning of the Kalimah   71
Covenant With Allah   72
Accepting the Prophet's Leadership   73
Obligations of Commitment   74
Our Behaviour   76

5. **Why is the Kalimah Unique?**   77
The Parable   77
Two Kinds of Trees   78
Characteristics of the Kalimah Tayyibah   79
Characteristics of the Kalimah Khabīthah   80
Contrasting Results   81
*Why Are Believers in the Kalimah Not
Flourishing?*   82
*Are Followers of the Kalimah Khabīthah
Prospering?*   83

6. **Why Believe in the Kalimah?**   85
Success in the Hereafter   86
This-world and That-world   86
Success in That-World   87
True Purpose of the Kalimah   88
What Does the Kalimah Teach Us?   89
Actions Must Accord With Knowledge   89

PART II: ISLAM

7. **The False Gods**   93
What is Disbelief and Islam?   93
Islam: Total Surrender   94
Three Reasons for Going Astray   95
*Self-worship — Society and Culture — Obedience
to Human Beings*
Condition of Muslims Today   99

8. **Can We Call Ourselves Muslims?**   103
A True Muslim   103

4

What is Hypocrisy? 104
 Serving the Self — Adherence to Society and
 Culture — Imitating Other People
The True Faith 106
 Abstinence From Alcohol — Confession of Crime
 — Severance of Familial Ties — Giving Up
 Cultural Norms and Customs
The Way to God's Pleasure 109
Muslims of Today 110

9. Are We True Muslims? 111
 Two Types of Islam 112
  Legal Islam — True Islam
 Two Kinds of Muslims 114
  Partial Muslims — True Muslims
 What Kind of Muslims God Desires 115
 Supreme Loyalty to Allah 116
 Where Do We Stand? 117

10. Why Obey God? 119
 Our Well-being 119
 Obeying Others Besides Allah 120
 The Only True Guidance 122
 How to Benefit 123
 No Blind Obedience 124

11. Difference Between Din and Shari'ah 125
 Meaning of Din 125
 Meaning of Shari'ah 128
 Nature of Differences 129
 Juristic Differences Between Muslims 130
 Ignoring the Nature of Differences 131
 Sectarianism 133

12. True Meaning of 'Ibadah 135
 Meaning of 'Ibadah 136
 Misunderstanding 'Ibadah 137
 'Ibadah, Lifelong Service 139

5

PART III: SALAH

13. Meaning and Blessings of the Prayer 145
Remembering God 145
Constant Reminder 147
Sense of Duty 148
God-consciousness 149
Knowledge of God's Law 150
Collective Life 151

14. What We Say in the Prayer 153
Adhan and its Effects 153
Wuḍū': Ablution 155
Niyyah: Intention 155
Tasbīḥ: Glorification 156
Ta'awwudh: Seeking Refuge 156
Bismillah: In His Name 156
Ḥamd: Praise and Thanks 156
The Qur'ān Reading 157
  *Surah al-'Aṣr — Surah al-Mā 'ūn — Surah
  al-Humazah*
Rukū': Bowing Down 160
Sujūd: Prostration 160
At-taḥiyyāt: Salutation 160
Ṣalāt 'ala 'n-nabiy: Blessings Upon the Prophet 161
Seeking Protection 162
Salām: Greetings 162
Du'ā' qunūt 163
Character-building 164

15. Blessings of the Congregational Prayer 165
Private Worship of God 165
Assembling on One Call 167
Purposeful Assembly 167
Fellowship 168
The Sacred Purpose 168
Brotherhood 169
Uniformity in Movements 169

Uniformity in Prayers   170
Leadership   171
Nature and Qualities of Leadership   171
     Piety and Virtue — Majority Representation —
     Sympathy and Compassion — Vacating Office —
     Obedience to Leaders — Criticizing and
     Correcting Mistakes — No Obedience in Sin

16. Has the Prayer Lost its Power?   175
Parable of the Clock   175
Aim of Muslim Ummah   176
Wholeness of Islamic Teachings   177
Abusing the Clock   178
Why Worship Rites are Ineffective   179
Our Deplorable Condition   180

PART IV: SAWM

17. Meaning and Blessings of the Fasting   183
Life of Worship   183
Rituals Lead to a Life of Worship   184
How Does Fasting Develop Us?   184
     Exclusively Private Worship — Sure Sign of Faith
     — Month-long Training — Practising Obedience
     —Communal Fasting
Where Are the Results?   188

18. True Spirit of the Fasting   189
Spirit and Form   189
The Outward Replaces the Real   190
Wrong View of Worship   191
Fasting as a Way to Piety   192
Conditions of True Fasting   192
     Abstention From Falsehood — Faith and Self-
     scrutiny — Shield Against Sins — Hunger for
     Goodness

PART V: ZAKAH

19. Fundamental Importance of Zakah   197
  Meaning of Zakah   197
  Zakah, a Test   198
  Early Practice   198
  Categorical Imperative   200
  The Sign of Faith   201
  Foundation of the Ummah   202
  Conditions for God's Help   203
  Warning to Muslims   203
  Fate of Zakah Defaulters   204

20. Meaning of Zakah   207
  Becoming God's Friends   207
      Wisdom and Understanding — Moral Strength —
      Obedience and Dutifulness — Sacrificing Wealth
  Requirements for Admittance to God's Friendship   210
      Large-heartedness — Magnanimity — Selflessness
      —Purity of Heart — Giving in Adversity —
      Giving in Affluence — Giving for Allah Alone —
      Stressing Benevolence — Amassing Wealth —
      Making Excuses — Spending Reluctantly and
      Resentfully — Considering Spending a Fine —
      Niggardliness
  The Real Test   214

21. Zakah, a Social Institution   217
  Allah's Unique Beneficence   217
  Man's Selfishness   218
  What Selfishness Leads To   219
  Individual and Collective Welfare   220
  What is the Solution?   222

22. General Principles of Spending   223
  Remembrance of God   223
  Spending in the Way of Allah   224
  Essential Prerequisite to Guidance   225
  Spend Only to Please Allah   226

Do Not Stress Your Benevolence 227
Give Only Good Things 227
Give Unobtrusively and Secretly 228
Guard Against Misuse 228
Do Not Harass Debtors 228
Take Due Care of Family 229
Give to the Deserving 229

23. Specific Injunctions of Zakah 231
Produce of the Earth 231
On Wealth and Financial Assets 232
Jewellery
Who Are Entitled to Receive Zakah 234
*Fuqarā': the poor — Masākīn: the destitute and
needy — 'Amilīna 'alayhā: who administer
Zakah — Mu'allafatu 'l-qulūb: who need to be
reconciled — Fī'r-riqāb: freeing from bondage —
Al-gharimīn: overburdened debtors — Fī-sabīli
'llāh: in the way of Allah — Ibnu
's-sabīl: travelers*
Other Important Principles 236
Need For Collective System 238

PART VI: HAJJ

24. Origin and Significance of Hajj 243
Life and Mission of the Prophet Ibrāhīm 243
Ibrāhīm's Times 244
Commitment to the Truth 245
Tribulations and Calamities 246
Migration 247
Raising a New Generation 247
The Greatest of Trials 248
The Universal Islamic Movement 249
*Lūt in Sodom — Ishāq in Palestine —
Construction of the Ka'ba*
Prayers of Ibrāhīm 250

9

25. Restoration of True Hajj   253

Idol Worship Among Ibrāhīm's Descendants   253

How Corrupted Hajj Became   254

 A Yearly Carnival — Perverse Rites — Sacrilege
 of Sacred Months — Self-imposed Restrictions

Restoration of Hajj   256

 Fulfilment of Ibrāhīm's Prayer — Revival of
 Ibrāhīm's Ways — End of Idolatry — Prohibition
 of Indecent Acts — Bragging and Showing Off —
 End of Ostentatious Generosity — Spattering of
 Blood and Flesh Banned — Prohibition of
 Perverse Rites — Changing the Months of Hajj
 Forbidden — Hajj Provisions Made Obligatory —
 Permission to Work During Hajj — End of Other
 Customs — Fixing Boundaries — Ensuring Peace
 and Security

Importance of Hajj   261

26. Renewal of Self   263

The Journey   263

Virtue and Piety   264

Iḥrām and its Conditions   265

Talbiyyah: the Cry of Response   265

Ṭawāf: Walking Round the House   266

Sa'ī: Hurrying Between Ṣafā' and Marwah   267

Wuqūf (Stay) at Minā', 'Arafāt and Muzdalifah   268

Ramī Jimār: Stoning the Pillars   268

The Impact of Hajj   270

Hajj, a Collective Worship   271

27. Renewal of Society   273

Growth in God-consciousness   273

A Season of Reawakening   274

Inspiring Spectacle of Unity   275

Greatest Movement for Peace   276

Centre of Peace and Equality   277

Our Lack of Appreciation   279

Deriving Full Benefit From Hajj   281

PART VII: JIHAD

28. Meaning of Jihad   285
  The Ultimate Objective   285
  Root of All Evil   286
  The First Step   287
  Origin of Corrupt Rule   288
  God's Lordship Over Man   290
  Temptation of Power   291
  Rituals, a Training Course   291
  Governments Run by God-conscious People   292

29. Central Importance of Jihad   295
  Din, Shari'ah and 'Ibadah   295
  Duality of Din   296
  Every Din Wants Power   297
    Popular Sovereignty — Monarchy — British Rule
  Din of Islam   299
  Jihad in Islam   300
  Recognizing True Believers   302
  Change Only Through Struggle   302

Preface to the Eighth Reprint   305
Index of Quranic Verses   309

Introduction

I

Sayyid Abul A'la Mawdudi's *Khuṭubāt,* of which *Let Us Be Muslims* is the new and edited English translation, is no ordinary book.

A collection of ordinary, familiar themes and plain truths, expounded before ordinary, illiterate people in plain words from their everyday language, it has, by the mercy of Allah, stirred more hearts and impelled more lives to alter their course to live in commitment to their Creator than any of his more erudite works. Many, I am sure, would share this impression of mine who like me have been led by his inspiring writings to join the cause of Allah. For who can forget those gatherings where the participants often reminisced about things that had brought them to the Islamic movement. As one person after another rose to tell his story and mentioned Sayyid Mawdudi's writings, I still vividly recollect, one answer overshadowed all others: the *Khuṭubāt.*

To express my own indebtedness to this book, I can do no better than to confess that I have now been reading it for nearly four decades and every time I have found it as fresh and inspiring as ever. Even today, I find myself speaking and writing, without the least embarrassment, words and ideas from the *Khuṭubāt,* as if they were my own.

How did this book come into being? As Sayyid Mawdudi tells in his Preface, soon after migrating to Darul Islam, near

Pathankot (now in the Punjab, India) – on 16 March, 1938 – he started to gather the nearby villagers for the Friday Prayers. To them, in every congregational address (*Khuṭubah*), he tried to explain the essential message, the basic teachings, and the spirit of Islam. Those addresses were collected and published as *Khuṭubāt*.

First published in 1940, since then it has been published in various forms and languages. A popular series has been that of six separate booklets – H*aqiqat-i-Iman*, *Haqiqat-i-Islam*, *Haqiqat-i-Sawm-o-Salat*, *Haqiqat-i-Zakat*, *Haqiqat-i-Hajj*, *Haqiqat-i-Jihad.* Translations in Bengali, Hindi, Tamil, Malayalam, Gujrati, Telgu, Sindi, Pushto and many other subcontinental languages have also been made and published since the early 1950s. The English translation came out thirty-five years later under the title *The Fundamentals of Islam* (Islamic Publications, Lahore, 1975). In all these different forms and languages, it has gone through innumerable reprints and is being constantly reprinted from many places. Many organizations, even individual admirers, have published its parts for mass distribution. Yet its need remains as fresh and its demand as high as ever.

Sayyid Mawdudi's impact on the contemporary Muslim world is not to be measured by the sale of his books, great as they have been. It is doubtful if any other Muslim writer of our day has so many readers, or is so avidly read, but what is important is that his sincere, convincing and passionate voice has left indelible imprints on the minds and lives of his readers. The real measure of his impact, therefore, is the emergence of whole new generations of men and women who have been inspired by him to lead lives of meaningful faith, Iman, in Allah, His Messenger, and His Book, and of dedicated struggle, Jihad, in His cause. No doubt his example in launching and leading a major Islamic movement has played a crucial role in this process, but it is his writings which have made a greater impression, deep and lasting, far and wide.

Of all those writings, Sayyid Mawdudi's words in *Khuṭubāt,* though spoken in the narrow confines of a mosque in a far-flung part of the world, have exercised an influence very far and beyond the time and place in which they were first spoken. They have found a response in the hearts and minds of their readers in true proportion to the sincerity and depth of his message and purpose. They have led many to recognize their inner inconsistencies and make their faith and commitment sincere.

Here, in *Let Us Be Muslims,* then, are the words which have touched many hearts and evoked many responses. What fills them with life and power? What makes this book extraordinary?

For, on the face of it, what Sayyid Mawdudi has said in these addresses is very ordinary and commonplace; indeed so ordinary that many readers might, after one quick look, want to put the book away, without reading any further. Is this not the same stuff, they would say, which we hear, day in day out, from our pulpits? Obey Allah and His Messenger, pray and fast, and everything is going to be alright.

To such readers I would say: let us together explore, at some length, what *Let Us Be Muslims* means to say.

Read the book, and you will find that even ordinary things, once placed in Sayyid Mawdudi's discourse, acquire quite an extraordinary quality, or, at least, in our time, that quality has become extraordinary. This is because he makes those words breathe the same sense and purpose, as against their merely lexical or cultural meanings, which they are given in the Qur'ān. Thus moulded afresh by the Quranic message and burnt in the crucible of his heart, the very things which look so lifeless and irrelevant to life, such as Iman and Islam and the five pillars, acquire a life and revolutionary ardour that they must have had when they were originally proclaimed and instituted. Then, the placid world of our beliefs and practices which we had always taken for granted begins to tumble down. Then, we begin to find the will and courage to 'be Muslims'.

Equally extraordinary is his style, the way he says these things.

Sayyid Mawdudi was not the traditional preacher. His voice did not roar in the air, nor did his body shake on the pulpit. He did not employ racy anecdotes, nor did he chant poetry. Yet his voice, in this book, has the quality which makes it rise from the lifeless, printed pages and penetrate our hearts.

Let us examine more closely, then, both his direct but powerful style and simple but profound message that make this book one of his best.

II

What gives Sayyid Mawdudi's voice the quality that makes it penetrating and irresistible? How does it acquire the power to quicken hearts and galvanize lives?

Obviously the primary force is the nature of his message, its truth and simplicity, and his sincerity and passionate conviction of its relevance to real life. But, no less important is the manner in which he communicates his message. The secret of his persuasive power therefore lies simply in that he has something important and urgent to say and he says it sincerely, clearly and passionately.

Firstly, he speaks to people in their 'language', a language that makes his message lucid and luminous. His language and logic, his idiom and metaphors, all are plain and simple, rooted in the everyday life of his audience. They are not derived from speculative philosophy, intricate logic, or mysterious theology. For, sitting before him were ordinary folk and almost illiterate farmers and servicemen. They knew neither philosophy nor theology, neither history nor politics, neither logic nor rhetoric, nor even the chaste and scholarly Urdu he, until then, always used to write and speak. He therefore uses words which they used in their common life and could understand well, employs a logic which they could easily comprehend, and coins metaphors which could make them recognize reality through their everyday experience.

Sayyid Mawdudi's chief concern is that real Iman which will find acceptance in the sight of Allah, which will bring rewards of dignity and success in this world as well as in the Hereafter. See how with a simple example he is able to demonstrate that such Iman cannot be attained by mere verbal profession, it must be lived by: 'Suppose you are shivering in cold weather and you start shouting "cotton quilt, cotton quilt!" The effect of cold will not be any less even if you repeat these words all night a million times on beads or a rosary. But if you prepare a quilt stuffed with cotton and cover your body with it, the cold *will* stop.'[1]

Nor can it be a birthright, that he establishes with a plain rhetoric question: 'Is a Muslim born a Muslim just as a Hindu Brahman's son is born a Brahman, or an Englishman's son is born an Englishman, or a white man's son is born a white man . . .'[2] Obviously, even an illiterate man would say, No.

Again, look how through an argument which derives its force from the everyday experience of his addressees Sayyid Mawdudi convincingly shows the inextricable link between a life of faith and righteousness in this world and, as its consequence, a life of eternal bliss in the next. As they were farmers, what could serve better as an example than a crop. 'If you sow wheat, only wheat will grow. If thorns are sown, only thorns will grow. If nothing is sown, nothing will grow.'[3] Therefore, 'if you follow his [the Prophet's] way, you will reap a fine harvest in the Hereafter, but if you act against his way you will grow thorns in this world and reap only thorns in the Hereafter.'[4]

Secondly, clear and direct reasoning imparts to Sayyid Mawdudi's discourse a measure of economy and grace which is quite unusual. In very few words he conveys many important themes, all beautifully reasoned. Every word, every argument, every example does its duty; they make his readers use their reason and commit themselves wholeheartedly to the task of 'being Muslims'.

This appeal to reason, *thirdly,* is one of the most outstanding characteristics of Sayyid Mawdudi's discourse. However ordinary and illiterate his addressees may be, for him they are responsible, intelligent, and reasonable people. They are supposed to think for themselves, and they are capable of doing so. That is how God has made them. That is why Sayyid Mawdudi does not treat us as objects to be manipulated by cheap rhetoric and non-rational appeals. Instead, he persistently appeals to our reason with cogent reasoned arguments.

For this purpose, he again and again confronts us with questions rather than dogmatic statements. These questions are artful premises from which we can easily deduce the necessary conclusions, or they reinforce his argument, or they serve as conclusions which, though irrefutable, we are still free to accept. The question-answer style, constantly employed throughout the book, turns his discourse into a dialogue rather than a monologue. Thus we become equal partners in his explorations instead of remaining passive receivers of his findings.

For example: Iman implies the possibility of disbelief. The idea that a Muslim is different from an unbeliever is deeply ingrained in our minds. On the basis of this firmly-held notion Sayyid Mawdudi drives home the true nature of Iman. 'Does it mean that if an unbeliever has two eyes, a Muslim will have four? Or that if an unbeliever has one head, a Muslim will have two? You will say: "No, it does not mean that".'[5] We all think that Muslims will go to Heaven and unbelievers to Hell. But unbelievers, he appeals forcefully to our sense of fairness, which is inherent in every decent human being, 'are human beings like yourselves. They possess hands, feet, eyes and ears. They breathe the same air as you, drink the same water and inhabit the same land. The God who created you also created them. So why should they be ranked lower and you higher? Why should you go to Heaven and why should they be cast into Hell?'.[6]

Obviously, an unbeliever is one because he 'does not understand God's relationship to him and his relationship to God', nor, therefore, does he live by it. But, Sayyid Mawdudi asks us to think, 'If a Muslim, too, grows up ignorant of God's will, what ground can there be to continue calling him a Muslim rather than an unbeliever?'.[7] Now he leaves it to us to answer the unpleasant but crucial and unavoidable question which must follow as its conclusion: 'Now, in all fairness, tell me: if you call yourselves Muslims but in fact are as ignorant and disobedient as a unbeliever, can you in reality be superior to the latter merely on the strength of bearing different names, wearing different clothes and eating different food? Can you on this basis be entitled to the blessings of God in this world and in the Hereafter?'[8]

But, *fourthly*, Sayyid Mawdudi's argument is never the dry bones of rational logic; it is always alive, a piece of flesh and blood, throbbing with emotion and feeling. The power of his discourse is greatly heightened because he combines the plain and simple logic of everyday life with the emotional argument; we find both deeply intertwined at every step of his writing. He suffuses his rationality with passion, which is an equally important constituent of our being. It is not the passion of frenzy, it is the passion which springs from sincerity and truth.

Put simply: his logic has the warmth of emotion, his emotion the force of logic. Cool arguments joined with burning appeals, with ironic contrasts, with charming eloquence, soak into the very depth of our existence. Together they hammer the truth into our minds and provoke us to respond.

His tone, too, is all along personal and intimate. He does not speak as an outsider who is delivering moral sermons from lofty towers. He is part of us. He shares our agonies and difficult decisions. That is why he is also always prepared to lay bare his innermost feelings and thoughts. It is this personal quality that never lets his discourse become wooden, that always accentuates the force of his appeal.

Look how the foolish and ironic inconsistencies of our conduct towards the Qur'ān are exposed in a convincingly reasoned argument that shakes us to our foundations. The fusion of rationality with feeling compels us to reflect upon our situation as well as awakens us to do something about it:

> Tell me: what would you say if somebody got a doctor's prescription and hung it round his neck after wrapping it in a piece of cloth or washed it in water and drank it? Would you not laugh at him and call him a fool? Yet this is the very treatment being given before your eyes to the matchless prescription written by the greatest of all doctors . . . and nobody laughs! . . .

> Tell me: what would you think if someone who was ill picked up a book on medicine and began to read it, believing, thinking that this would cure him. Would you not say that he was deranged? Yet this is how we treat the Book which the supreme Healer has sent for the cure of our diseases.[9]

Or, see how, after depicting the miserable situation in which we Muslims find ourselves today, he appeals to our sense of honour, our sense of justice, and thereby leads us to think about the state of our Islam.

> Is this the blessing of Allah? If it is not – but rather a sign of anger – then how strange it is that it is Muslims on whom it is descending! You are Muslims and yet are wallowing in ignominy! You are Muslims and yet are slaves! This situation is as impossible as it is for an object to be white and black . . .

> If it is an article of faith with you that God is not unjust and obedience to God can never result in disgrace, then you will have to concede that there is something wrong in your claim to be Muslims. Although you may be registered as Muslims on your birth certificates, Allah does not base His judgements on what is written on pieces of paper.[10]

Above all, and *fifthly,* what matters most, what really startles and provokes us, what compels us to choose and respond to the summons of our Creator, is the rhythm of confrontation that permeates Sayyid Mawdudi's entire discourse. His rhythm is not that of narration and exhortation, or even mere persuasion. From a series of kernels of simple truth, he expands his rhythm into one that persistently challenges and confronts us.

The simple truths, in his hands, become the tools with which he makes us expose our inner selves, as well as they provide us with a powerful critique of our society. His purpose is not to preach to us, but to change us. He wants us to think for ourselves and make our own choices. What startles us is the way he lays bare the implications of what we have always so placidly and lazily continued to believe; what provokes us is the way he divulges our inner contradictions and hypocricies, our incongruous, incomprehensible attitudes towards things we claim to value most.

The above examples illustrate how everything that Sayyid Mawdudi says pulsates with the rhythm of confrontation. But nowhere does it stand out so sharply and powerfully as when he calls upon us to compare our lives and conduct with those of Unbelievers:

> Unbelievers do not read the Qur'ān and do not know what is written in it. If so-called Muslims are equally ignorant, why should they be called Muslims? Unbelievers do not know the teachings of the Prophet, blessings and peace be on him, and the straight path he has shown to reach God. If Muslims are equally ignorant of these, how can they be Muslims? Unbelievers follow their own desires instead of the commands of Allah. If Muslims are similarly wilful and undisciplined, setting their own ideas and opinions on a pedestal, indifferent to God and a slave to lust, what right have they to call themselves Muslims? . . .

... [indeed] almost the only difference now left between us and Unbelievers is that of mere name ...

I say 'almost' because there is, of course, a difference between us: we know that the Qur'ān is the Book of God, ... yet we treat it as an Unbeliever treats it. And this makes us all the more deserving of punishment. We know that Muhammad, blessings and peace be on him, is the Prophet of Allah and yet we are as unwilling as an Unbeliever to follow him.[11]

There are many reasons for these paradoxes. But one reason Sayyid Mawdudi explains in his characteristic style: 'You know the damage caused if crops are burnt; you know the suffering which results from failure to earn a livelihood; you know the harm resulting from loss of property. But you do not know the loss of being ignorant of Islam.'[12]

Finally, let us look at one especially exquisite extract from Sayyid Mawdudi's discourse which epitomizes all the distinguishing characteristics of his style. Answering the question, has the Prayer lost its power to change lives, he points to the clock which was in front of his audience and which all of us have, and proceeds to explain why. Note the simple but powerful argument and the beauty and grace of language.

Look at the clock fixed to the wall: there are lots of small parts in it, joined to each other ...

If you do not wind it, it will not show the time. If you wind it but not according to the method prescribed, it will stop or, even if it works, it will not give the correct time. If you remove some of its parts then wind it, nothing will happen. If you replace some of the parts with those of a sewing machine and then wind it, it will neither indicate the time nor sew the cloth. If you keep all its parts inside

INTRODUCTION

its case but disconnect them, then no part will move even
after winding it . . .

Imagine Islam like this clock . . . Beliefs and principles
of morality, rules for day-to-day conduct, the rights of
God, of His slaves, of one's own self, of everything in
the world which you encounter, rules for earning and
spending money, laws of war and peace, principles of
government and limits of obedience to it – all these are
parts of Islam. . .

[But now] . . . you have pulled out many parts of the
clock and in their place put anything and everything: a
spare part from a sewing machine, perhaps, or from a
factory or from the engine of a car. You call yourselves
Muslims, yet you render loyal service to Disbelief, yet
you take interest . . . which un-Islamic gadget is there
that you have not fixed into the frame of the clock of
Islam.

Despite this you expect the clock to work when you wind
it![13]

The parable of the clock not only serves to explain the
'holistic' nature of Islam – which no intellectual discussion
could have explained so lucidly – but it also symbolizes Sayyid
Mawdudi's own contribution to Islamic resurgence: according
each part of Islam its due place, infusing it with its true meaning,
relinking all of them together.

III

What does Sayyid Mawdudi say? He talks, as we noted in
the beginning, about things which are central to Islam: faith and
obedience, knowledge and righteous life, the present world and
the world to come, the Prayer, Fasting, Almsgiving, Pilgrimage

23

and Jihad. But is this not what every religious writer and preacher talks about? So, what is so unique about his discourse? The question is legitimate. Let us see if we can answer it.

No doubt he explains and expounds their meanings and import, too, in a manner which in itself is distinctive and uncommon. But more significantly, and this is central to the importance of this book, he imparts a radical quality to all these elementary everyday themes by renewing their original intent and meaning and by making them relevant to our lives.

How does he do that? Firstly, he restores each part to its rightful place in Islam. Secondly, and this is his unique contribution, he restores the vital links between them which long since have snapped in our minds and lives. Iman and Islam, Dunya and Akhira, Prayer and Fasting, all are there; but each in its own orbit, each in its compartment. Indeed we have become almost habituated to treat each of them as a separate entity. So, even if each part is in its place and is not deformed, even if no foreign part has been fitted to it, to borrow his own metaphor, they do not make the 'clock' of Islam work because they are disconnected. He draws them together and tells us how to link them. Immediately, what was insignificant and irrelevant becomes central, the very destiny of life. Thus, despite his themes being familiar and ordinary, despite their being devoid of elaborate, elegant, oratorial dress, they make an enormous impact.

The richness, strength and range of Sayyid Mawdudi's themes are indeed immense and profound. But we can easily trace seven such vital links which he re-establishes.

First, he links life, and remember the whole of life, with Iman. Iman becomes the *centre* of life, which does not accept anything less than total commitment to the One God. This Iman, for long, we have made irrelevant to real life.

Second, he links our actions with Iman, and therefore, with life. In his understanding, there can be no *true* Iman without actions.

Third, he links acts of ritual worship or *'Ibādāt* – in the sense of five pillars – with Iman as the seed from which they grow and with actions as the branches into which they blossom. They are the stem which *must* grow out of Iman and produce its crop of righteous life.

Fourth, he connects the outward form with the inner spirit; if 'forms' do not yield the desired fruits, they *are* devoid of spirit. Outward religiosity hoisted on empty hearts has no value in the sight of God.

Fifth, he links Jihad with righteous life by emphasizing its position as the pinnacle and culmination of everything God desires of us, the highest virtue – and thus with Iman and life. To be true Muslims, we *must* be Mujahids.

Sixth, he links history with Iman. Iman is no more a mere metaphysical and spiritual force; it is the fulcrum of history, it is the determinant of destiny. Thus history becomes crucial for Iman, and therefore for life. We can no more sit back passively; we must try, actively, to change history, that is, wage Jihad.

Seventh, he links this-world with the Hereafter, as a continuing process. Without striving to fulfil the will of God in the present life, we cannot reap any harvest in the next.

Our previous discussion about Sayyid Mawdudi's style has already shown, to some extent, how he achieves the above task. But let us reflect a little more on some salient features of what he has said.

Iman. The question of Iman lies at the heart of Sayyid Mawdudi's entire discourse here. It is what the whole book is about; on it everything is centred. Indeed the entire contents of this book can be summed up as an echo of just one Quranic Ayah:

O believers, believe (al-Nisā' 4: 136).

25

The meaning of Iman is well-known. What has gone wrong is that it has become irrelevant or peripheral to the actual lives lived by the believers. This has come to pass because of many factors. Iman has come to be taken for granted as a birthright; it has become confined to the mere utterance of the Kalimah; it has been put into a corner of life; it has been made innocuous and 'safe'.

All this Sayyid Mawdudi strongly refutes: Being a Muslim 'is not something automatically inherited from your parents which remains yours for life'.[14] 'Being born in Muslim homes, bearing Muslim names, dressing like Muslims and calling yourselves Muslims is not enough to make you Muslims.'[15]

For, 'no one is an Unbeliever or a Muslim simply because of his name. Nor does the real difference lie in the fact that one wears a necktie and the other a turban'.[16] Similarly, 'mere utterance of six or seven words cannot conceivably transform an Unbeliever into a Muslim, . . . nor can it send a man to Paradise instead of Hell'.[17]

There is no compulsion to recite the Kalimah. But, having recited it, Sayyid Mawdudi stresses, you have 'no basis whatsoever to make claims like "life is mine, the body is mine, wealth is mine". It is absurd . . . You have no right to move your hands and feet against His wish, nor to make your eyes see what He dislikes . . .'.[18] Also, 'you have no right to say, "My opinion is this, the prevalent custom is this, the family tradition is this, that scholar and that holy person say this". In the face of Allah's word and His Messenger's Sunnah, you cannot argue in this manner.'[19]

Sayyid Mawdudi is a great iconoclast, for no idolatry can ever co-exist with true Iman. But his chief concern does not lie with idols of stone, of natural objects. It lies with the idols of self, of society and culture, of human beings which so often become gods in hearts and lives.

What is Islam? 'To entrust yourselves completely to God is Islam. To relinquish all claims to absolute freedom and independence and to follow God's will is Islam ... To bring your affairs under God means to accept unreservedly the guidance sent by God through His Book and His Messengers.'[20] But there are people who 'obey the dictates of their own reason and desires, follow the practices of their forefathers, accept what is happening in society, never bothering to ascertain from the Qur'ān and Sunnah how to run their affairs, or refuse to accept the teachings of the Qur'ān and Sunnah by saying: "They do not appeal to my reason", or "They are against the ways of my forefathers", or "The world is moving in an opposite direction"'. For them Sayyid Mawdudi has this to say: 'Such people are liars if they call themselves Muslims.'[21]

Each of these is a god if obeyed besides God: self; society; family or nation; men, especially the rulers, the rich, and the false thinkers. Against them Sayyid Mawdudi inveighs relentlessly: 'To be slaves of the three idols, I say, is the real *Shirk* (idolatry). You may have demolished the temples of bricks and mortar, you may have broken the stone idols in them, but you have paid little attention to the temples within your own hearts. To smash these idols is the essential precondition to becoming a Muslim.'[22]

Because 'with these idols in your hearts you cannot become slaves of God. Merely by offering Prayers many times a day, by ostentatiously observing Fasts, and by putting on the outward face of Muslims you may deceive your fellow beings – as well, indeed, yourselves – but you will never be able to deceive God.'[23]

Having defined the nature of Iman and idolatry, and the claim of Iman upon the whole person, he tells us plainly: 'If you obey the directions of God in some matters, while in others follow your own self, desires, society or man-made laws, then you are guilty of Disbelief to the extent of your disobedience. You may be half Unbeliever, or a quarter Unbeliever, or less or more.'[24] To claim to be Muslims and to reserve even the tiniest territory in hearts or lives from God is sheer hypocrisy, too.

Such categorical statements may mislead some to think that Sayyid Mawdudi is engaged in the business of excommunicating Muslims. Not at all. Lest there be any misunderstanding, he says: 'Do not for a moment think that I am trying to brand Muslims as Unbelievers. This is not my purpose at all.'[25] His only purpose is to give us the criteria by which each one of us should judge himself, but not others: 'Do not use this criterion to test or judge others and determine whether they are Mumins or hypocrites and Muslims or Unbelievers; use it only to judge your own selves and, if you detect any deficiency, try to remove it before you meet Allah.'[26]

Iman has two levels. Sayyid Mawdudi makes a very sharp and very important distinction between the two: faith at the level of profession – what he calls 'legal Islam', and faith at the level of fidelity and actualization – what he calls 'true Islam', which God desires, which assures us His rewards in this world and the Hereafter. His concern in this book, he makes abundantly clear, is 'true Islam', for it is what counts in life and in God's scale.

But at the same time, he stresses, very wisely, the importance of legal Islam. For faith thus defined forms the basis for membership in the Ummah. By clarifying the important distinction between Din and Shari'ah, he strikes at the very root of sectarianism which results in mutual excommunication. For all his stress on true Islam, and for all his rhetoric – 'You are not Muslims', 'this is sheer hypocrisy' – it must be noted that Sayyid Mawdudi never issued or signed any *fatwa* (edict) of Disbelief against anyone in his entire life.

And he provides us with a breadth of tolerance that is so rare in these days: 'What right has one servant to say that he alone is the genuine servant while the other is not?' One may argue that his understanding is correct, but this does not give him the authority to expel anyone from Islam. 'Anyone who does display such temerity assumes, as it were, the status of the Master. He would seem to be saying, "Just as it is compulsory for you to obey the Master's order, so also it is compulsory for you to accept my way of understanding. If you fail to do that, I shall, with my own power, dismiss you from the Master's service" . . . A person who insists upon such submission to his own interpretation and judgement and assumes such powers of dismissal for himself irrespective of whether God Himself dismisses someone or not, is in fact saying that God alone is not God but that he himself is also a small god.'[27]

Actions: Real Iman, once installed at the centre of life, once lodged in heart, must flourish into a mighty tree of righteous deeds (*as-ṣāliḥāt*). Unfortunately, something which was important for the vitality and true worth of Islam – the relationship between *imān* and *'amal* – became an issue, quite unnecessarily, for the jurists and philosophers. Muslims have no need to assume a prerogative that is God's: to determine any particular person's place in the Hereafter. Or, to engage in the business of excommunication. But they must never lose a vision of Iman which can retain its power only when linked with deeds.

Sayyid Mawdudi's real business is to make Iman real and decisive in actual life. And that, as we see, he does with remarkable vigour and clarity. The Kalimah, he says, 'must be rooted in the heart, it must drive out any belief opposed to it, it should make any actions in contravention of it well-nigh impossible.'[28]

'Ibādāt: Foremost among righteous deeds are the obligatory acts of ritual worship like Salah and Zakah. It is impossible for us to have the seed of Iman in our hearts and yet ignore these basic duties. Sayyid Mawdudi echoes the Qur'ān and Sunnah when he declares that 'only those can be taken to be true believers who perform the Prayers and give the Alms. Those who disregard these two fundamental teachings are not true in their faith.'[29].

On the other hand, acts of worship, if correctly performed, must result in claiming the whole of life for Iman, and bring all of it under God. We only have to read the discourse on 'True Meaning of 'Ibadah' to appreciate fully how forcefully Sayyid Mawdudi argues this important point.

Spirit: If acts of worship do not lead to a life lived in worship, the only reason is that they have been emptied of their true meaning and purpose, their true spirit. 'When the soul departs, what feats can a dead body perform',[30] says Sayyid Mawdudi. The Prayer is meant to restrain us from everything that Allah dislikes. 'If it does *not,* the reason lies in you, not in the Prayer. It is not the fault of soap and water that coal is black!'[31]

Sayyid Mawdudi inveighs heavily against 'religiosity' hoisted on empty hearts and divided loyalties. 'What would you say about a servant', he asks, 'who, instead of performing the duties required of him by his master, just stands in front of him with folded hands and keeps chanting his name?' For example 'his master commands him to cut off the hand of a thief. But the servant, still standing there, recites scores of times in an extremely melodious voice: "Cut off the hand of the thief, cut off the hand of the thief", without ever trying to establish that order under which the hand of a thief may be cut off'. However, when you see a person who 'reads from dawn to dusk the Divine injunctions in the Qur'ān, but never stirs himself to carry them out, chanting instead the name of God on a thousand-bead rosary, praying uninterruptedly and reciting the Qur'ān in a beautiful voice . . . you exclaim "What a devout and pious person he is!", you are misled because you do not understand the true meaning of 'Ibadah'.

Similarly, 'how astonishing that you think the Prayers, Fasting, chanting on rosary-beads, recital of the Qur'ān, the Pilgrimage and Almsgiving of those people are in fact acts of worship, who day and night violate or ignore the laws of God and follow the orders of the unbelievers.'[32]

Jihād: Jihad is firmly linked with Iman in the Qur'ān, and therefore with the whole Muslim life. It is the purpose which calls the Ummah into existence. But, for long, we have come to believe that we do not have to stir ourselves to undertake this vital duty for it makes no difference to our Iman.

This tragic chasm Sayyid Mawdudi spans forcefully and unequivocally.

It is this 'unconcern' with Jihad that, he says, empties all other acts of worship of their spirit. 'But now, I say, you must understand that a heart devoid of any intention to undertake Jihad will find all ritual worship empty of meaning. Nor will those acts bring you any nearer to your God.'[33] For, 'if you believe Islam to be true, you have no other alternative but to exert your utmost strength to make it prevail on earth: you either establish it or give your lives in this struggle'.[34]

Why? His argument is lucid and convincing. *Firstly,* having believed in Allah and the Messenger, and accepted Islam as our Din, we must bring ourselves totally under God's rule. Therefore Muslims 'should rise to bring their King's land under His law, to destroy the power of those rebels among His subjects who have set themselves up as sovereigns, and to free His subjects from the burden of slavery to others. Merely believing in God as God and in His law as the true law is not enough'.[35]

Otherwise, *secondly,* we would be living under two Dins: one, in our minds, or at most in our private lives; the other, in our public lives. For, 'Din without power to govern is just like a building which exists in the mind only. But, it is the building which actually exists, in which you actually live, that is important'.[36]

One cannot follow two Dins, for he can obey only one at a time. 'In reality you are followers only of that being's Din whom you are actually obeying. Is it not then utter hypocrisy to call that being your ruler and to claim to belong to his Din whom you do not obey.' Further, 'is it not meaningless to assert that you have faith in this Shari'ah when all your affairs are conducted in violation of this Shari'ah and in fact you follow another Shari'ah?'[37]

Obviously, *thirdly*, this situation is unacceptable. For 'how can Allah's Din accept to co-exist with any other Din, when no other Din admits of such partnership. Like every other Din, Allah's Din, too, demands that all authority should genuinely and exclusively be vested in it'.[38]

Fourthly, because the lordship of man over man is the root cause of all corrupt rule on earth, it is our duty to 'stand up and fight against corrupt rule; take power and use it on God's behalf. It is useless to think you can change things by preaching alone'.[39]

History: Iman is squeezed out of life once we begin to take history as merely an interplay of material forces. Sayyid Mawdudi puts Iman back at the centre of history, just as he installs it at the centre of heart and life. It becomes the fulcrum by which the scales of destiny are tipped: 'You are Muslims and yet are wallowing in ignominy! You are Muslims and yet are slaves! This situation is as impossible as it is for an object to be black and white.'[40]

Further, 'it is impossible for a people to possess God's word and yet suffer disgrace and ignominy, live under subjugation, be trampled on and kicked around, and carry the yoke of slavery on their necks, being led by the nose like animals'.[41]

How does, then, this come to happen? Sayyid Mawdudi has absolutely no doubt. 'If it is an article of faith with you', he argues, 'that God is not unjust and obedience to God can never result in disgrace, then you will have to concede that there is something wrong in your claim to be Muslims'.[42] In this respect Muslim conduct towards the Qur'ān is very crucial. 'If a people possess Allah's Book and still live in disgrace and subjugation, they are surely being punished for doing injustice to Allah's word. The only way to save yourselves from Allah's anger is to turn back from this grave sin and start trying to render His Book its due.'[43]

Although we had to quote from the text very extensively, it was necessary to show clearly the principal threads that run through Sayyid Mawdudi's discourse in this book. The above discussion clearly demonstrates how they make his contribution distinctive and unique.

These threads underline the crucial and radical importance of Sayyid Mawdudi's discourse summoning Muslims: Let us be Muslims. Everything which has either lost its original meaning or has been emptied of its true intent becomes redefined. But the most remarkable thing, as we said, is that he connects all of them together again. That is why while he says nothing very different from what others are saying, his impact has been tremendous. For, thus connected, Iman regains its original power to change man and his world.

IV

Anyone who reads Sayyid Mawdudi's discourses will find no difficulty in understanding the true intent and purpose of what he embraces and expounds. One may disagree with it, or find it uninspiring, but he cannot deny that Sayyid Mawdudi is talking the same language and conveying the same message as do the Qur'ān and the Prophet, blessings and peace be on him.

But some have taken exception to what he says. He has replied to them in his Preface to the eighth reprint which is included herein. But we may still find it useful to compare his discourses with the Qur'ān and Hadith. For it is their light which radiates through his words.

Let us first look at the Qur'ān.

True Iman which resides in hearts, shapes lives, and finds acceptance with God is always differentiated from outward, legal Iman. 'The Bedouins say, "We believe." Say: you do not believe, rather say, "We have surrendered", for [true] faith has not yet entered their hearts' (al-Ḥujurāt 49: 15). Similarly mere verbal professions of faith, which are contradicted by actions, are rejected. 'O Messenger, let not those grieve you who vie with one another in Disbelieving, from among those who say, "We believe", with their mouths, but their hearts believe not' (al-Mā'idah 5: 41).

Hence even believers are often called upon 'to believe', that is, to attain true faith. 'O believers, believe in God and His Messenger, and the Book He is sending down upon His Messenger, and the Book He sent down before' (al-Nisā' 4: 136). Or, 'Believe in God and His Messenger, and spend out of that in which we have made you vicegerents . . .' (al-Ḥadīd 57: 7).

The link between Iman and actions is clearly manifest in the way both are almost always bracketed together: al-ladhīna āmanū wa 'amilu 'ṣ-ṣāliḥāt (those who believe and do righteous deeds). Or, one only has to read those Ayahs which describe the demands and conditions of true Iman by saying: in kuntum muminīn (if you are believers).

The bond between true faith and ritual worship, on the one hand, and a life lived totally in worship, which leads to justice and compassion in society, on the other, is firmly established in many places: 'Have you seen him who denies Judgement. That, then, is he who pushes away the orphan; and urges not to feed the needy. Woe, then, unto those praying ones who are unmindful of their Prayer, those who want to be seen, and who refuse [even] small kindnesses' (al-Māʿūn 107:1 – 5).

Thus the claim of Iman upon the whole of life, its nature as a bargain, as a total commitment, is fully established. 'O believers, enter wholly into Islam [self-surrender unto God]' (al-Baqarah 2: 208). For 'the only [true] way in the sight of God is Islam' (Āl 'Imrān 3: 19). Therefore 'whoso desires a way other than surrender unto God, it will never be accepted from him' (Āl 'Imrān 3: 85).

Jihad, as Sayyid Mawdudi has argued, now becomes integral to Iman. The Qur'ān makes it the criterion by which the truthfulness of Iman is to be judged. 'The believers are those only who [truly] believe in God and His Messenger, and then they doubt not; and who struggle hard with their wealth and their lives in the way of God; it is they who are the truthful ones' (al-Ḥujurāt 49: 15).

The Akhira as the harvest of what we sow in Dunya is such a recurring and predominant motif in the Qur'ān that it hardly needs to be repeated here.

But that, according to the Qur'ān, history (Dunya, in a sense) itself is a crop of beliefs and actions, of Iman and *taqwā*, of *ṣabr* (steadfastness and patience) and *istighfār* (seeking forgiveness) is not always well understood. 'Had the people of cities believed and been conscious of Us, We would indeed have opened up for them blessings from heaven and earth' (al-A'rāf 7: 96). And, 'Ask forgiveness from your Lord, then turn towards Him in repentance; He will loosen the sky over you in abundance, and He will increase you in strength unto your strength' (Hūd 11: 52). Also, 'Had they established the Torah and the Gospel, and what has been sent down to them from their Lord, they would have partaken of all the blessings from above them and from beneath their feet' (al-Mā'idah 5: 66).

Turning to the Hadith we find there the same themes propounded in the same manner.

We have only to open any collection of Hadith and read through those which include a phrase like *lā yuminu* (he does not believe); *laisa huwa minnā* (he does not belong to us); *lā īmāna lahū* (there is no faith in him); *laisa huwa bi mumin* (he is not a believer). We will immediately realize how categorically the Prophet, blessings and peace be on him, links a wide range of values and actions with Iman.

Just look at some of them.

One among you does not believe unless he loves me more than his father, his children, and all mankind (*Bukhārī, Muslim*).

One among you does not believe until all his desires follow what I have brought (*Sharḥ al-Sunnah*).

What lies between a man and Disbelief is the abandonment of the Prayer (*Muslim*).

The covenant between us and them is the Prayer, so if anyone abandons it he becomes a unbeliever (*Aḥmad, Tirmidhī*).

One who is not trustworthy has no faith; and one who does not keep his promise has no religion (*Baihaqī*).

When one fornicates he is not a believer, when one steals he is not a believer, when one drinks he is not a believer, when one takes plunder which makes men look at him he is not a believer, and when one defrauds he is not a believer (*Bukhārī, Muslim*).

He does not belong to us who does not show mercy to our young ones and respect our old ones (*Tirmidhī*).

By Him in whose hand my soul is, one does not believe till he likes for his brother what he likes for himself (*Bukhārī, Muslim*).

Reviling a Muslim is disobedience to God, and fighting with him is Disbelief (*Bukhārī, Muslim*).

I swear he does not believe, I swear he does not believe, I swear he does not believe. [When asked who, he said,] One from whose injurious conduct his neighbour is not safe (*Bukhārī, Muslim*).

He is not a believer who eats his fill while his neighbour is hungry (*Bukhārī*).

There are three signs of a hypocrite, even if he fasts and claims that he is a Muslim: when he speaks he lies, when he makes a promise he breaks it, and when he is trusted he betrays his trust (*Muslim*).

Flesh which has grown out of the unlawful earnings will not enter Paradise, for Hell is more fitting for all flesh which has grown out of the unlawful (*Aḥmad*).

If anyone knows how to shoot and gives it up he does not belong to us [for he gives up a skill which is essential for Jihad] (*Muslim*).

V

Since this book was first published in 1940, it has been meeting very real and great spiritual, intellectual and cultural needs of all those who have had the chance to read it. Since then it has been evoking faith and commitment in many lives. Its messages, by their acceptance and absorption, by the subsequent development of Muslim thought and society, and by the rising waves of Islamic resurgence, have too now become quite familiar. Some retrospect of time previous to their appearance is therefore necessary to appreciate their original freshness.

The early thirties, when Sayyid Mawdudi spoke these words, were stressful times for the Muslims in India. They were in a cauldron of political and cultural turmoil and uncertainty. The Khilafat movement had collapsed; the brief rule of the Congress ministries had given them a foretaste of what miseries awaited them under Hindu majority in a democratic India. They had no leader, no organization, no purpose.

What Sayyid Mawdudi said then contained the essential substance of the message that he had been writing and communicating at various times since the mid-twenties, which he continued to live for until his death in 1979. This was the message of his first book – *Al-Jihad fil Islam* – which appeared in 1926–27. It is a monumental, unparalleled treatise on the Jihad as an ideal, a process and an institution in Islam. It is also a provoking and convincing discourse on Jihad as the ultimate objective, the very life purpose of the Ummah. The concluding theme of this book echoes the theme of *Al-Jihad*.

The same message he had been propounding through the pages of his monthly journal, the *Tarjumanul Qur'ān*, since 1932. Yearning to do something for what he had so long been writing about compelled him to migrate from Hyderabad, in South India, to Darul Islam, in North India. For, he said, 'I have now concluded that the real battleground is going to be Northern India. There the Muslim destiny will be decided and its effects will overtake the whole of India.'

In coming to Darul Islam he accepted Dr. Muhammad Iqbal's (d. 1938) invitation, too, to collaborate with him in undertaking a reconstruction of Islamic thought. But paramount in his mind, as his many letters show, was the burning zeal and sense of urgency to awaken the Muslim Ummah to its real mission and purpose. One must read all of his other epoch-making writings of the time to understand him fully.

So, in the small mosque in Darul Islam, he had before him simple villagers who did not know much of politics, history, theology. The only things they knew were Iman and Islam and the five pillars. Explaining to them in simple language what he had written earlier was the task that he accomplished in these addresses.

The original freshness of those addresses, despite the passage of time, lingers on; it would not fade away. For the intent and import of God's message is universal. They still leaven, as they leavened then, the hearts of their readers. Their need remains as great as ever.

The need of a good English translation can hardly be overemphasized. English is now the language of millions of Muslims. It is also an international language through which any contents can be easily made available to other Muslim languages. The presently available English version, *Fundamentals of Islam,* is a commendable effort and I must express my debt of gratitude to it for the immense help it has given me in the preparation of this new translation. However, it does not convey fully the real power and charm of the original Urdu. Perhaps no translation can, yet the need to improve further and further remains.

Translation is a difficult art, especially if it has to be effected between languages as disparate as Urdu and English. The task becomes more difficult if one has to translate a subject as unique as Islam into a language whose ethos has no place for it. The problem is further aggravated because of the masterful rhetoric which characterizes Sayyid Mawdudi's addresses. The tone and temper of English and Urdu are different; but the spoken word in Urdu loses much more of its charm once rendered into English.

There was, therefore, no alternative but to resort to editing. The purpose of editing, however, it must remain clear, has not been to omit, add, modify or explain anything unless absolutely necessary. There has been only one limited aim: to improve the readability, to accentuate the power, to deliver the message as forcefully and effectively as does the original. This is not therefore a literal translation, but nor is it liberal. It is as faithful as one could be, while balancing the tension between the conflicting demands of remaining faithful to the original as well as retaining its power and charm. Some minor deletions there are, but only where it was necessary to take out what in English looked cumbersomely repetitive. And some words which would have been totally incomprehensible to an English reader have been either substituted or omitted.

Every temptation to 'modernize' the text, to bring it into conformity with the life and experience of the present-day readers of the English version, has been resisted. For even the most advanced, rational and technological 'man' shares a large and deep world with the most primitive, of which he himself may not be very aware. Hence the simple logic and examples of this book should strike as deep a chord within him as they do among its ordinary readers.

This is something important we must keep in mind. The minds of farmers or servicemen that Sayyid Mawdudi was addressing were not burdened with complex and subtle concepts like state, society, and sovereignty, nor were they well versed in theological debates. Hence his language must be understood in the context of his audience, though its larger implications should not be missed.

For example, for his audience the only reality that ruled was the 'government'. They would have had no idea of the complex differences between concepts like sovereignty, state and government, state and society, individual and collectivity, small and big government. Hence we find Sayyid Mawdudi using, without any reservation, the word 'government' to convey many important and complex messages. Similarly, he unhesitatingly uses the vocabulary of a farmer or a serviceman. For example, the Adhan is likened to 'divine bugle'; the Ummah to 'army of God'. Therefore, let there be no effort to read any more than what is intended in the light of the reader's own difficulties with concepts like regimentation, totalitarianism, or spirituality. Many who have tried to read Sayyid Mawdudi in this perspective have been misled to ascribe to him what he never intended and said. To understand him fully one should read all of his writings.

As the book is addressed primarily to Muslims, the original Islamic terminology in Arabic is retained and is used freely and frequently in the English text, without italicization or accents. A word of explanation is here necessary. I personally feel no hesitation in using 'God' for Allah, both to achieve communication with those who do not know 'Allah' as well as to 'Islamize' the word God. The only way to do so, in my view, is to use such words interchangeably with their Arabic counterparts, so that both vocabularies may finally come to be used without the reader even noticing the change from one to the other. Like 'Allah' and 'Khuda' are used in Urdu.

The same principle has been followed with respect to other key terms like Iman, Disbelief, Kalimah, Mumin, Unbeliever, Din, Shari'ah, 'Ibadah, Salah, Zakah, Sawm, Hajj. I think they need to be made part of the English language, if English is to become, one day, a Muslim language as well. They should attain the same status as Islam, Muslim, Jihad. At the same time, words like Prayer, Fasting, Pilgrimage should also begin conveying the Islamic meanings.

A new title has also been given: *Let Us Be Muslims.* Nothing less than such a direct summons could have done some justice to the spirit of this book. This title at least expresses its basic purpose. For the purpose of the book is to call Muslims to Islam, to be Muslims as God desires them to be. New chapter headings have also been given. Each, too, I feel, reflects the spirit and content better.

This new English version, I hope, now reads much better. I must take this opportunity to thank Mr. Paul Moorman whose editorial help has been invaluable in preparing this edited translation.

After all the labour I am still not satisfied that the English does full justice to the original. Being unequal to the task, I must confess my inadequacy. But, if it can give the readers some sense of the life and power that fill Sayyid Mawdudi's original words, if it can too, in some degree, touch some lives, by the leave of God, then my labour will be more than rewarded. Despite all my failings, I hope and trust that Allah will, by His mercy, make many hearts awaken through it. May He also make it a source of forgiveness and mercy for me in the present life and the life to come, and for all those who contributed something in making me a little better than what my fraility would have allowed, chief among them being Sayyid Mawdudi himself.

Khurram Murad
Leicester
29 Ramadan, 1405
18 June, 1985

References

1 *Let Us Be Muslims,* p. 70
2 Ibid, p. 48
3 Ibid, p. 86
4 Ibid, p. 89
5 Ibid, p. 86
6 Ibid, p. 53
7 Ibid, p. 50
8 Ibid, p. 55
9 Ibid, p. 63
10 Ibid, p. 56
11 Ibid, pp. 57–8
12 Ibid, pp. 59–60
13 Ibid, pp. 175–8
14 Ibid, p. 49
15 Ibid, p. 50
16 Ibid, p. 50
17 Ibid, p. 71
18 Ibid, p. 75
19 Ibid, p. 66
20 Ibid, p. 65
21 Ibid, p. 66
22 Ibid, pp. 99–100
23 Ibid, p. 99
24 Ibid, p. 94
25 Ibid, p. 58
26 Ibid, p. 118
27 Ibid, p. 130–1
28 Ibid, pp. 82–3
29 Ibid, p. 201
30 Ibid, p. 110
31 Ibid, p. 164
32 Ibid, p. 138
33 Ibid, p. 293
34 Ibid, p. 300
35 Ibid, p. 290
36 Ibid, p. 297
37 Ibid, p. 296
38 Ibid, p. 299
39 Ibid, p. 288
40 Ibid, p. 56
41 Ibid, p. 64
42 Ibid, p. 56
43 Ibid, p. 64

Preface
to the First Edition

When, in 1357 A.H. [1938], I first came to the Punjab to live in Darul Islam (near Pathankot, East Punjab), I started to organize the Friday Prayers and explain Islam to the nearby villagers. This collection comprises the congregational addresses which I then prepared. My addressees were farmers; they too from the Punjab, whose mother tongue was not Urdu. I therefore had to adopt a language and expression which could be easily understood by the common man. Thus has come into being this collection which, *inshā'allāh*, should be useful for teaching Islam to the masses.

The fundamental beliefs of Islam I have already explained in some detail in my *Towards Understanding Islam.** The Shari'ah, too, I have briefly dealt with there. This collection now explains, with sufficient detail, two other themes: one, the meaning and spirit of Islam; the other, worship. I hope that those who will read these addresses together with *Towards Understanding Islam* will find, with the grace of Allah, sufficient illumination for their journey on the path of Islam.

When read as a Friday address (*Khuṭubah*), each should be prefaced with the opening words that have come down to

---

*   Islamic Foundation, Leicester, 1978.

43

us from the Prophet, blessings and peace be on him. For the second part any *Khuṭubah* may be used, but it must be in Arabic.

Abul A'la
Lahore
15 Ramadan, [13]59 A.H.
[November, 1940]

PART I
Iman

1

Knowledge, the First Step

Allah's Greatest Gift

Brothers in Islam! We all as Muslims sincerely believe that Islam is the greatest blessing that Allah has given us in this world. We find our hearts filled with gratitude to Him for including us in the Ummah of the Prophet Muhammad, blessings and peace be on him, and bestowing upon us this unique blessing. Allah Himself describes Islam as His most invaluable gift to His servants: 'Today I have perfected your Dīn [way of life] for you, and I have completed My blessing upon you, and I have willed that Islam be the Way for you' (al-Mā'idah 5: 3).

To be truly grateful for this greatest favour, you must therefore render to Allah His due. If you do not do so, you are undoubtedly an ungrateful person. And what ingratitude can be worse than to forget what you owe to your God.

How can we, you may ask, render these dues? Since Allah has been gracious enough to include you in the Ummah of the Prophet Muhammad, blessings and peace be on him, the best way of showing gratitude – and there is no other way – is to become totally committed followers of the Prophet. And, since He has made you a part of the Muslim Ummah, to become true Muslims. If you do not, the punishment for your ingratitude

47

will be as great as the original gift was. May Allah save us all from this great punishment! Amin.

You will now ask: How can we become Muslims in the true sense of the word? This question I shall answer in considerable detail in my forthcoming addresses; but today I want to look at a point of fundamental importance, without which we cannot hope to discover true faith. This, you must understand, is the first essential step on your road to becoming a true Muslim.

Is Islam a Birthright?

But, first, think for a while: What does the word 'Muslim', which we all use so often, *really* mean? Can a person be a Muslim by virtue of his birth? Is a person a Muslim simply because he is the son or grandson of a Muslim? Is a Muslim born a Muslim just as a Hindu Brahman's son is born a Brahman, or an Englishman's son is born an Englishman, or a white man's son is born a white man, or a negro's son is born a negro? Are 'Muslims' a race, a nationality or a caste? Do Muslims belong to the Muslim Ummah like Aryans belong to the Aryan race? And, just as a Japanese is a Japanese because he is born in Japan, is a Muslim similarly a Muslim by being born in a Muslim country?

Your answer to these questions will surely be: No. A Muslim does not become truly a Muslim simply because he is born a Muslim. A Muslim is not a Muslim because he belongs to any particular race; he is a Muslim because he follows Islam. If he renounces Islam, he ceases to be a Muslim. Any person, whether a Brahman or a Rajput, an Englishman or a Japanese, a white or a black, will, on accepting Islam, become a full member of the Muslim community; while a person born in a Muslim home may be expelled from the Muslim community if he gives up following Islam, even though he may be a descendant of the Prophet, an Arab or a Pathan.

Such will surely be your answer to my question. This establishes that the greatest gift of Allah which you enjoy – that of being a Muslim – is not something automatically inherited from your parents, which remains yours for life by right irrespective of your attitudes and behaviour. It is a gift which you must continually strive to deserve if you want to retain it; if you are indifferent to it, it may be taken away from you, God forbid.

No Mere Verbal Profession

You agree that we become Muslims only by accepting Islam. But what does acceptance of Islam mean? Does it mean that whoever makes a verbal profession – 'I am a Muslim' or 'I have accepted Islam' – becomes a true Muslim? Or does it mean that, just as a Brahman worshipper may recite a few words of Sanskrit without understanding them, a man who utters some Arabic phrases without knowing their meaning becomes a Muslim? What reply will you give to this question? You cannot but answer that accepting Islam means that Muslims should consciously and deliberately accept what has been taught by the Prophet Muhammad, blessings and peace be on him, and act accordingly. People who do not so behave are not Muslims in the true sense.

No Islam Without Knowledge

Islam, therefore, consists, firstly, of knowledge and, secondly, of putting that knowledge into practice. A man can be white and have no knowledge; because he is born white he will remain so. Similarly, an Englishman will remain an Englishman though he may have no knowledge, because he has been born an Englishman. But no man becomes truly a Muslim without knowing the meaning of Islam, because he becomes a Muslim not through birth but through knowledge. Unless you come to know the basic and necessary teachings of the Prophet Muhammad, blessings and peace be on him, how can you believe in him, have faith in him, and how can you act according to what he taught? And if you do not have faith in him, knowingly and consciously, as fully as you can, how can you become true Muslims?

Clearly it is impossible to become a Muslim and remain a Muslim in a state of ignorance. Being born in Muslim homes, bearing Muslim names, dressing like Muslims and calling yourselves Muslims is not enough to make you Muslims; true Muslims know what Islam stands for and believe in it with full consciousness.

The real difference between an Unbeliever (who does not accept God's guidance) and a Muslim is not that of a name, that one is called Smith or Ram Lai and the other Abdullah. No one is an Unbeliever or a Muslim simply because of his name. Nor does the real difference lie in the fact that one wears a necktie and the other a turban. The real difference is that of knowledge. An Unbeliever does not understand God's relationship to him and his relationship to God. As he does not know the will of God he cannot know the right path to follow in his life. If a Muslim, too, grows up ignorant of God's will, what ground can there be to continue calling him a Muslim rather than an Unbeliever?

Dangers of Ignorance

Listen carefully, brothers, to the point I am making. It is essential to understand that to remain in possession of, or to be deprived of, the greatest gift of Allah – for which you are so overwhelmed with gratitude – depends primarily on knowledge. Without knowledge, you cannot truly receive His gift of Islam. If your knowledge is so little that you receive only a small portion of it, then you will constantly run the risk of losing even that part of the magnificent gift which you have received unless you remain vigilant in your fight against ignorance.

A person who is totally unaware of the difference between Islam and Disbelief (rejection of God's guidance and ingratitude) and the incongruity between Islam and *Shirk* (taking gods besides God) is like someone walking along a track in complete darkness. Most likely his steps will wander aside or on to another path without him being aware of what is happening. Maybe he will be deceived by the sweet words of the Devil, 'You have lost your way in the darkness. Come, let me lead you to your destination.' The poor traveller, not being able to see with his own eyes which is the right path, will grasp the Devil's hand and be led astray. He faces these dangers because he himself does not possess any light and is therefore unable to observe the road signs. If he had light, he would neither lose his way nor be led astray.

This example shows that your greatest danger lies in your ignorance of Islamic teachings and in your unawareness of what the Qur'ān teaches and what guidance has been given by the Prophet, blessings and peace be on him. But if you are blessed with the light of knowledge you will be able to see plainly the clear path of Islam at every step of your lives. You will also be able to identify and avoid the false paths of Disbelief, *Shirk* and immorality which may cross it. And, whenever a false guide meets you on the way, a few words with him will quickly establish that he is not a guide who should be followed.

Acquire Knowledge

Brothers! On this knowledge, whose absolute necessity I stress once again, depends whether you and your children are true Muslims and remain true Muslims. It is therefore hardly a trivial matter to be neglected. You do not neglect cultivating your land, irrigating and protecting your crops, supplying fodder to your cattle or doing whatever else is essential to the well-being of your trades and professions. Because you know that if you do you will starve to death and so lose the precious gift of life. Why then should you be negligent in acquiring that knowledge on which depends whether you become Muslims and remain Muslims? Does such negligence not entail the danger of losing an even more precious gift – your Iman (faith)? Is not Iman more precious than life itself? Most of your time and labour is spent on things which sustain your physical existence in this life. Why can you not spend even a tenth part of your time and energy on things which are necessary to protect your Iman, which only can sustain your being in the present life and in the life to come?

I am not asking you to become scholars, read voluminous books or spend a large part of your lives in the pursuit of knowledge. It is not necessary to study so extensively to become a Muslim. I only want each one of you to spend about one hour of the twenty-four hours of the day and night in acquiring the knowledge of his Din, the way of life, the Islam.

Every one of you, young or old, man or woman, should at least acquire sufficient knowledge to enable him to understand the essence of the teachings of the Qur'ān and the purpose for which it has been sent down. You should also be able to understand clearly the mission which the Prophet, blessings and peace be on him, came into this world to fulfil. You should also recognize the corrupt order and system which he came to destroy. You should acquaint yourselves, too, with the way of life which Allah has ordained for Muslims.

No great amount of time is required to acquire this simple knowledge. If you value Iman, it cannot be too difficult to find one hour every day to devote to this.

2

Between Islam and Disbelief

Muslims or Unbelievers?

Brothers in Islam! Every Muslim believes, as you too must surely believe, that Muslims are different from the unbelievers; that God likes believers and dislikes those who do not believe; that believers will find God's forgiveness, while unbelievers will not; that believers will go to Heaven and unbelievers to Hell. I want you to consider why there should be so much difference between believers and non-believers.

Unbelievers are as much an offspring of Adam and Eve as you. They are human beings like yourselves. They possess hands, feet, eyes and ears. They breathe the same air as you, drink the same water and inhibit the same land. The God Who created you also created them. So why should they be different from you? Why should you be rewarded and they punished?

Consider carefully. Such vital differences between man and man cannot be simply due to the fact that people have different names and wear different types of clothes and eat different types of food. Allah, Who has created all human beings and Who is the Sustainer of all cannot be so unjust as to decide on such petty grounds.

Where, then, does the real difference lie between Muslims and Unbelievers? The answer is that it lies, simply, in the very nature of Islam and Disbelief. The meaning of Islam is submission to God while the meaning of Disbelief is denial and disobedience of God. Muslims and Unbelievers are both human beings; both are slaves of God. But one becomes exalted and meritorious by reason of recognizing his Master, obeying His orders and fearing the consequences of disobeying Him; while the other disgraces himself by failing to recognize his Master and carry out His orders. This is why Allah is pleased with Muslims and displeased with unbelievers. That is why He promises true Muslims that they will be rewarded with Heaven and warns unbelievers that they will be cast into Hell.

Knowledge and Actions

The two things which separate Muslims and Unbelievers are, therefore, knowledge and actions. That is, you must first know who your Master is, what His orders are, how to follow His wishes, which deeds please Him and which displease Him. When these things are known, the second step is to make yourselves true slaves of your Master by giving up your own wishes in deference to what He desires.

If your heart desires to do a certain act and your Master's order is against it, you should carry out that order. If something seems good to you but your Master says that it is bad, you must accept it as bad. And if something else seems bad but your Master says it is good, then you must accept it as good. If you think a certain action will be harmful but your Master says that it must be done, then done it must indeed be, even though it may entail you in loss of life or property. Similarly, if you expect to benefit from a certain action but your Master forbids it, you must refrain from it even though it might have brought all the worldly treasures.

This is the knowledge and actions by which Muslims become true servants of Allah, on whom He bestows His mercy and whom He rewards with honour and dignity. Conversely, Unbelievers, since they do not possess this knowledge, are Allah's disobedient slaves and are denied His blessings.

Now, in all fairness, tell me: If you call yourselves Muslims but in fact are as ignorant and disobedient as an Unbeliever, can you in reality be superior to the latter merely on the strength of bearing different names, wearing different clothes and eating different foods? Can you on this basis be entitled to the blessings of God in this world and in the Hereafter? Islam is not a race or family in which membership is automatically passed on from father to son. A high caste priest's son will not command respect in the eyes of God, if he does wrong deeds, just because he is born into a priestly home; nor will He look down on the son of a low caste family, disregarding his good deeds, simply because of his birth.

On this point God hās explicitly stated in His Book: 'Indeed the noblest among you in the sight of God is the most God-fearing of you' (al-Ḥujurāt 49: 13). That is, the more you know God and the more you obey His commandments, the more honourable you are in His sight. Ibrāhīm was born into the home of an idolator, but he came to know God and obeyed Him. That is why God made him *Imam* (leader) of the whole world. The son of Nūḥ was born into a prophet's home but he did not understand God and disobeyed Him. Despite his high family connection, God so punished him that the punishment became an object lesson for the world.

Understand, therefore, thoroughly that whatever differences there are in the sight of Allah between man and man depend entirely on the state of their knowledge and actions. Both in this world and the Hereafter, God's blessing is reserved for those who recognize Him, accept the right path shown by Him, and carry out His commandments. Those who do not do these things, whether their names are Abdullah and Abdur Rahman or Kartar Singh, Smith or Robertson, are identical in the sight of God. They are unworthy of His blessings.

Why Are Muslims Humiliated Today?

Brothers! You call yourselves Muslims and you believe that Allah showers His blessings on Muslims. But open your eyes and see if those blessings are in fact descending on you? You cannot know what will happen to you in the Hereafter until after your physical death, but you can most certainly look around you and see your condition here on earth.

There are so many hundreds of millions of you in the world that if each of you were to throw a single pebble they would make a mountain. But even though there are so many Muslims and Muslim governments, the world is in the hands of those who have rebelled against God. Your necks are in their grip, to be turned to whichever side they like; your heads, which should not bow before anybody except Allah, are now bowed before human beings. Your honour, which no one dared to touch, is now being trampled upon. Your hands, which were once always held high, are now lowered and stretched out before your enemies. Ignorance, dependence, poverty and indebtedness have subjected you to ignominy everywhere.

Is this the blessing of Allah? If it is not – but rather a sign of anger – then how strange it is that it is Muslims on whom it is descending! You are Muslims and yet are wallowing in ignominy! You are Muslims and yet are slaves! This situation is impossible as it is for an object to be white and black. If Muslims are the loved ones of God, how can they be treated disgracefully? Is your God (God forbid) so unjust that – while you, for your part, acknowledge His due and obey His orders – He allows the disobedient to rule over you, and punishes you for your obedience to Him?

If it is an article of faith with you that God is not unjust and obedience to God can never result in disgrace, then you will have to concede that there is something wrong in your claim to be Muslims. Although you may be registered as Muslims on your birth certificates, Allah does not base His judgements on what is written on pieces of paper. God prepares his own list of obedient and disobedient servants, and it is in this list that you must search to find your true position.

Allah sent you His Book so that you may know Him and learn how to obey Him. Have you ever tried to discover what is written in it? Allah sent His Prophet to teach you how to become Muslims. Have you ever tried to find out what His Prophet has taught? Allah explicitly informed you which behaviour debases man in this world and the Hereafter. Do you avoid such behaviour? What answers do you have to these questions? If you admit that you have neither sought knowledge from God's Book and His Prophet's life nor followed the way shown by him, then how can you claim to be Muslims and to merit His reward? The rewards you are getting now are in direct relation to how good Muslims you are; and your rewards in the Hereafter will be calculated on the same basis.

We have already seen that the only difference between Muslims and Unbelievers is in the matter of knowledge and actions. Men who call themselves Muslims but whose knowledge and actions are the same as those of Unbelievers are guilty of blatant hypocrisy. Unbelievers do not read the Qur'ān and do not know what is written in it. If so-called Muslims are equally ignorant, why should they be called Muslims? Unbelievers do not know the teachings of the Prophet, blessings and peace be on him, and the straight path he has shown to reach God. If Muslims are equally ignorant of these, how can they be Muslims? Unbelievers follow their own desires instead of the commands of Allah. If Muslims are similarly wilful and undisciplined, setting their own ideas and opinions on a pedestal, indifferent to God and a slave to lust, what right have they to call themselves Muslims? Unbelievers do not distinguish between Halal (what is permitted by Allah) and Haram (what is prohibited by Allah) and make indiscriminate use of everything and anything, irrespective of whether it is Halal or Haram. If Muslims behave the same as non-Muslims, what difference is there between them and Unbelievers?

Put simply: If Muslims are as devoid of knowledge about Islam as Unbelievers, and if a Muslim does all those things which an Unbeliever does, why should he be considered superior to an Unbeliever and why should his fate not be the same as that of an Unbeliever? This is a question on which we must all reflect very seriously.

My dear brothers! Do not for a moment think that I am trying to brand Muslims as Unbelievers. This is not my purpose at all. I ask myself, and implore each one of you similarly to ask his own heart, as to why we are being denied the blessing of God. Why are tribulations of all sorts descending upon us from all sides? Why are we disunited and shedding each other's blood? Why are those whom we call Unbelievers (that is, the disobedient slaves of God) everywhere dominating us? And why are we, who claim to be His obedient slaves, living in servitude in so many parts of the world?

The more I have reflected on the reason for this situation, the more I have become convinced that almost the only difference now left between us and Unbelievers is that of mere name; for we in no way lag behind them in neglect of God, in being devoid of fear of Him and in being disobedient to Him.

I say 'almost' because there is, of course, a difference between us: we know that the Qur'ān is the Book of God, while Unbelievers do not, yet we treat it as an Unbeliever treats it. And this makes us all the more deserving of punishment. We know that Muhammad, blessings and peace be on him, is the Prophet of Allah and yet we are as unwilling as an Unbeliever to follow him. We know that God has cursed liars, has positively declared Hell as the abode of all who give and take bribes, has denounced those who borrow and lend at interest as the worst of sinners, has condemned slander as being as bad as eating a brother's flesh, and has warned that obscene behaviour, pornography and debauchery will meet with the severest punishment. Yet despite knowing all this we freely indulge in all these vices as if we had absolutely no fear of God's displeasure.

This is why we are not rewarded: we are Muslims in appearance only. The fact that those who do not accept God's sovereignty rule over us and subject us to ignominy on every possible occasion shows that we are being punished for ignoring Islam – God's greatest gift to us.

Dear brothers! Nothing I have said today is intended as blame. I have not come to censure. My aim is to kindle the desire in you to recover the treasure that has been lost. Such a desire arises when a man realizes exactly what he has lost and how valuable it was. I have spoken sharp and pungent words only to awaken you and compel you to think.

Desire For Knowledge

To become a real Muslim, as I said, the foremost requisite is knowledge of Islam. Every Muslim ought to know the teaching of the Qur'ān, which ways were shown by the Prophet, blessings and peace be on him, what Islam is, and what those things are which really differentiate Islam from Disbelief. Nobody can be a Muslim without this knowledge. The pity is that you show no desire to acquire this knowledge. This indicates that still you do not realize what a great gift you are being deprived of.

My brothers! A mother does not give milk to her child until he cries and demands it. When a man feels thirsty and he searches for water, God brings him to it. If you yourselves are not conscious of your thirst it will be useless if even a well brimming with water appears before you. You must first understand what a great loss you are suffering by remaining ignorant of Islam. The Book of God is with you but you do not know what is written in it. You do not even know the meaning of the Kalimah (*Lā ilāha illa 'llāh Muhammadu 'r-rasūlu 'llāh* (There is no god but Allah; Muhammad is Allah's Messenger)), by reciting which you enter Islam; nor do you appreciate what responsibilities devolve on you after reciting this Kalimah. Can there be a greater loss than this for a Muslim?

You know the damage caused if crops are burnt; you know the suffering which results from failure to earn a livelihood; you know the harm resulting from loss of property. But you do not know the loss of being ignorant of Islam. When you understand the nature of this loss, you will yourselves come and ask to be spared it. And when you make this request then, *inshā'allāh,* means will be available to restore this greatest of gifts to you.

3

How Muslims Treat the Qur'ān

Brothers in Islam! Muslims are the only people in the world today fortunate enough to possess the word of God preserved in its original form, free from all distortions, and precisely in the wording in which it was sent down upon the Prophet, blessings and peace be on him. Paradoxically, these same Muslims suffer the misfortune of being denied the countless blessings and benefits which the word of God must give to those who believe in it. The Qur'ān was sent to them for them to read it, understand it, act upon it, and, with its help, establish on God's earth the rule of His law. The Qur'ān came to grant them dignity and power. It came to make them true vicegerents of God on earth. And history shows that whenever they acted according to its guidance, it did make them the leaders of the world.

Irreverence and Misuse

But now the Qur'ān's usefulness, for many Muslims, consists only in keeping it in their houses to drive away *jinns* and ghosts, in writing its verses on amulets to hang round their necks or washing those amulets with water and then drinking it, or in reading its contents without comprehending their meaning in the hope of receiving some reward. No longer do they seek guidance from it for their lives. No longer do they ask it to tell them what should be their beliefs, morals and actions, nor how they should conduct transactions, what principles they should observe while dealing with enemies and friends, what the rights are of their fellow beings and of their own selves. Nor do they turn to it to find what is true and what is false, whom they should obey and whom disobey, who their friends are and who their enemies, where honour, well-being and benefit are to be found and where disgrace, failure and loss.

We Muslims have given up looking for answers to these important questions in the Qur'ān. Instead, we now ask Unbelievers, idolators, misguided, selfish people, even our own ego and desires – and follow what they advise. What invariably happens to those who ignore Allah and follow the precepts of others has happened to us too. We are reaping only what we have sown everywhere in the world – in Palestine, the Middle East, Pakistan, Indonesia and many other places.

The Qur'ān is the source of every good: it will give whatever and as much as you ask from it. If you seek from it such trivial, frivolous and spurious things as how to scare away *jinns* and ghosts, how to cure coughs and fevers, how to succeed in litigation and find a job – then you may get them, but only them. If you seek supremacy on earth and the power to rule the world you may get that too. And if you wish to reach near God's Throne (*'Arsh*), the Qur'ān will take you there. If you receive only a few drops from the ocean, do not blame the Qur'ān, blame yourselves. For the whole ocean is there waiting for him who knows how to take it.

Incomprehensible Contradictions

The cruel jokes, brothers, which we Muslims play with the Holy Book of Allah are so inane that if we saw someone else doing such things in any other sphere of life, we would mock them and even brand them as lunatics.

Tell me, what would you say if somebody got a doctor's prescription and hung it round his neck after wrapping it in a piece of cloth or washed it in water and drank it? Would you not laugh at him and call him a fool? Yet this is the very treatment being given before your eyes to the matchless prescription written by the greatest of all doctors to provide a cure for all your ailments – and nobody laughs! No one even reflects that a prescription is not meant to be hung round the neck nor are its words to be washed in water and drunk.

Tell me, what would you think if someone who was ill picked up a book on medicine and began to read it, believing, thinking that this would cure him? Would you not say that he was deranged? Yet this is how we treat the Book which the supreme Healer has sent for the cure of our diseases. We think that just by flicking through all its pages, our diseases will disappear without our following the directions given in them or abstaining from the things which they pronounce harmful. Are we not in the same situation as the man who considers that reading a book on medicine will cure his illness?

If you receive a business letter in a language you do not know, you go to a man who knows the language to find out what it says. You remain anxious and restless until you have found out what the letter says, even though it will bring only some paltry worldly profit. But the letter sent to you by the Lord of the worlds which can bring you all the benefits of this-world and the Eternal Life is carelessly set aside. You do not show any uneasiness at not understanding its contents. Is this not astonishing?

I am not trying to make you laugh. Reflect for a while on these facts and your hearts will tell you that the greatest possible injustice is being done to the Book of Allah. Ironically, the culprits are the very people who proclaim their faith in it and proclaim their readiness to sacrifice their lives for it. No doubt they do have faith in it and love it more than their lives, but the pity is that it is they, more than anyone else, who treat it outrageously. And the consequences of such treatment are quite plain to see.

The Consequences

Understand fully that Allah's word does not come to bring misery, disgrace and suffering to man. 'We have not sent down the Qur'ān upon you that you be wretched' (Ṭā Hā 20: 1–2). On the contrary, the Qur'ān is the source of happiness and success. It is impossible for a people to possess God's word and yet suffer disgrace and ignominy, live under subjugation, be trampled on and kicked around, and carry the yoke of slavery on their necks, being led by the nose like animals. A people meet this fate only when they do injustice to the word of God.

Look at the fate of the Israelites. They were given the *Tawrāh* and the *Injīl,* and were told:

> Had they established the Torah and the Gospel and what was sent down to them by their Lord, they would surely have partaken of all the blessings from above them [heaven] and beneath their feet [earth] (al-Mā'idah 5: 66).

But they adopted a wrong attitude towards these Books of Allah, and reaped the consequences:

> An ignominy and helplessness were laid upon them, and they were laden with the burden of God's anger. That, because they used to disbelieve God's messages and slay the Prophets against all right; that, because they disobeyed and were transgressors (al-Baqarah 2: 61).

If people possess Allah's Book and still live in disgrace and subjugation, they are surely being punished for doing injustice to Allah's word. The only way to save yourselves from Allah's anger is to turn back from this grave sin and start trying to render His Book its due. Until you do, your condition will never change – even if you open colleges in each and every village, all your children graduate from universities, and you amass millions through unscrupulous means.

No Islam Without Submitting to the Qur'ān

Brothers! Two most important things every Muslim must know to do justice to the Book of God: who is truly a Muslim and what the word 'Muslim' means.

Human beings who do not know what humanity is and what the difference is between man and animal will inevitably indulge in behaviour unworthy of the human race and attach no value to being human. Similarly, people who do not know the true meaning of being Muslims and how a Muslim is different from a non-Muslim will behave like non-Muslims and will not be worthy of being Muslims.

Every Muslim, adult or child, should therefore know what it means to be a Muslim, what difference being a Muslim must make to his life, what responsibilities devolve on him, and what limits are set by Islam within which a man remains a Muslim and by transgressing which he ceases to be a Muslim.

Islam means submission and obedience to God. To entrust yourselves completely to God is Islam. To relinquish all claims to absolute freedom and independence and to follow God's will is Islam. To surrender yourselves before the sovereignty of God is Islam. If you bring all the affairs of your lives under God you are Muslims and if you keep any of the affairs in your own hands or entrust them to someone other than God you are not Muslims.

To bring your affairs under God means to accept unreservedly the guidance sent by God through His Book and His Messengers. It therefore becomes necessary to follow only the Qur'ān and the Prophet's Sunnah. Muslims follow no authority other than that of God, whether it be their reason or customs. In every matter they seek guidance from God's Book and His Messenger to find what they should do and what they should not do. They accept without hesitation whatever guidance they get from there and reject whatever they find opposed to it.

Such total surrender to God is what makes. one a Muslim.

By contrast, people are certainly not Muslims who, instead of following the Qur'ān and the Sunnah, obey the dictates of their own reason and desires, follow the practices of their forefathers, accept what is happening in society, and never bother to ascertain from the Qur'ān and Sunnah how to run their affairs, or refuse to accept the teachings of the Qur'ān and Sunnah by saying: 'They do not appeal to my reason', or 'They are against the ways of my forefathers' or 'The world is moving in an opposite direction'. Such people are liars if they call themselves Muslims.

The moment you recite the Kalimah: *'Lā ilāha illa 'llāh Muhammadu 'r-rasūlu 'llāh',* you accept that the only law you recognize is the law of God, only God is your sovereign, only God is your ruler, only God you will obey, and only the things given in God's Book and by His Messengers are true and right. It means that as soon as you become Muslims you must renounce your authority in favour of God's authority.

Consequently, you have no right to say, 'My opinion is this, the prevalent custom is this, the family tradition is this, that scholar and that holy person say this.' In the face of Allah's word and His Messenger's Sunnah, you cannot argue in this manner. You should judge everything in the light of the Qur'ān and Sunnah; accept what is in conformity with them and reject what runs counter to them, irrespective of the people who may be behind them. It is a contradiction in terms to call yourselves Muslims on the one hand, and, on the other, follow your own opinions or the customs of society or some person's words or actions as against the Qur'ān and the Sunnah. Just as a blind person cannot claim to have eyes, nor a deaf person to have ears, so a person who refuses to subordinate the affairs of his life to the dictates of the Qur'ān and the Sunnah cannot call himself a Muslim.

No one who does not want to be a Muslim can be compelled to be one against his will. You are free to adopt any religion you like and call yourselves by any names you like. But, once having called yourselves Muslims, you must fully understand that you can remain Muslims only as long as you stay within the bounds of Islam. These bounds are: to accept the word of God and His Messenger's Sunnah as the ultimate criteria of truth and justice and to consider everything opposed to them as wrong. If you remain within these bounds you are Muslims, but if you overstep them you cease to be part of Islam. To continue, in such circumstances, to consider yourselves and call yourselves Muslims is tantamount to both self-deception and deception of others. 'Whoso judges not according to what God has sent down, they are the unbelievers' (al-Mā'idah 5: 44).

4

True Meaning of Iman

Difference the Kalimah Creates

Brothers in Islam! You become Muslims by reciting a few words called the Kalimah:

Lā ilāha illa 'llāh Muhammadu 'r-rasūlu 'llāh

There is no god but Allah; Muhammad is the Messenger of Allah.

On pronouncing these words a man is supposed to have radically changed. He was an Unbeliever, now he is a Muslim; he was impure in faith, now he is pure. He deserved Allah's displeasure; now he deserves to be loved by Him. He was going into Hell; now the gates of Heaven are open for him.

On a more concrete level, in social life, this Kalimah becomes the basis for differentiating one man from another. Those who recite it constitute one nation, while those who reject it form another. If a father recites it but his son refuses to, the father is no longer the same father, nor the son the same son. The son will not inherit anything from the father, his mother and sisters may even observe *purdah* from him. On the other hand, if a total stranger recites the Kalimah and marries into a Muslim family, he and his children become eligible for inheritance.

The power of the Kalimah is thus so strong that it takes precedence even over blood ties; it can join strangers together into a nation; it can cut members of the same family off from each other.

Is Mere Utterance Enough?

Why should the Kalimah make such a big difference between man and man? What is so special about it? After all, it contains only a few letters like 'L', 'A', 'I', 'M', 'R' and 'S'. Joined together and pronounced, do they somehow have the power to work magic so as to radically change a man? Can merely saying a few words create such an enormous difference?

Brothers! A little reasoning will immediately tell you that merely opening your mouths and uttering a few syllables can never have such an impact. Idol-worshippers no doubt believe that by reciting some formula of holy words mountains can be moved, the earth can be split and fountains can gush out of it, even though they do not know its meaning. This is because they ascribe supernatural powers to letters, and believe that only uttering them is necessary to make their powers work.

This is not so in Islam. The effectiveness of words lies in their meaning. If they do not penetrate deep into your hearts and have an impact powerful enough to effect a change in your thoughts, in your morals, and in your actions, then their utterance is meaningless and ineffectual.

A simple example will illustrate this point. Suppose you are shivering in cold weather and you start shouting, 'cotton, quilt! cotton, quilt!' The effect of cold will not be any less even if you repeat these words all night a million times on beads or a rosary. But if you prepare a quilt stuffed with cotton and cover your body with it, the cold *will* stop. Or suppose you feel thirsty and shout the whole day, 'water, water'; your thirst will not be quenched. What you need to do is to get some water and take a mouthful. Or again, suppose you are suffering from cold and fever and you decide the best remedy is to chant the name of medicines used to cure these illnesses. You will not get better; but if you actually take these medicines, cold and fever will disappear, *inshā'allāh*.

This is exactly the position of the Kalimah. Mere utterance of six or seven words cannot conceivably transform an Unbeliever into a Muslim, or an impure person into a pure one, or a damned person into a favoured one, nor can it send a man to Paradise instead of Hell. This transformation is possible only after you have understood the meaning of these words and made it penetrate your hearts and change your lives.

So, when you recite these words, you should be conscious what an important commitment you are making to your God, with the whole world as your witness, and what a great responsibility you are taking on as a result of your commitment. Once you have made the affirmation consciously, the Kalimah must inform all your thoughts and reign supreme in your whole lives: no idea contrary to it should form part of your mental furniture. Whatever runs counter to the Kalimah you must always consider false and the Kalimah alone true. After affirming this Kalimah you are not at liberty, as are the unbelievers, to do as you like. You have to follow what it prescribes and renounce what it forbids.

If you recite the Kalimah in this manner, only then can you become true Muslims, only then is created that overwhelming difference between man and man that we have just been discussing.

Meaning of the Kalimah

What, let me tell now, is the meaning of the Kalimah. What do you in fact pledge through it?

The literal meaning of the Kalimah is simple: there is no God but Allah; and Muhammad, blessings and peace be on him, is the Messenger of Allah.

Covenant With Allah

The word *'ilāh'* found in the Kalimah means God. Only that being can be our God who is the Master, Creator, Nourisher and Sustainer, who listens to our prayers and grants them, and who alone is worthy of our worship and obedience.

Saying *Lā ilāha illa 'llāh* means two things. *First,* you have acknowledged that the world has neither come into being without a God nor has many gods. God is there; He alone is God, and there is no other being except Him which possesses divinity. *Second,* you have accepted that this same God is your Lord and Master as well as of the whole universe. You yourselves, and each and every thing that you have or is found in the world, belong to Him alone. He is the Creator and the Provider. Life and death are under His command. Both trouble and comfort come from Him. Whatever one receives is really given by Him; whatever is taken away is taken away by His command. He alone should be feared. From Him alone should we ask any and everything. Before Him alone should we bow our heads. He alone is worthy of worship and service. We are slaves or servants of nobody save Him, nor is anyone else our Master or Sovereign. Our duty is to obey Him and abide by His laws – and His alone.

This is the covenant which you make with Allah as soon as you recite *Lā ilāha illa 'llāh,* and while so doing you make the whole world your witness.

If you violate this covenant, your hands and feet, the tiniest hair on your bodies and every particle on earth and in the heavens, all that witnessed you breaking your pledge, will testify against you in God's court. You will find yourselves in such a hopeless position that not a single witness will be found to aid you. No barrister or trial lawyer will be there to plead your case. In fact, barristers and trial lawyers who in the courts of this world are themselves all too often guilty of bending the law to their own ends, will themselves be standing there, like you, in the same hopeless position. That court will not acquit you on the basis of forceful pleading, false witnesses, or forged documents. You can hide your crimes from the police in this world, but not from God's police. The police here may be bribed, but not there. A witness in this world can give false evidence, but not Allah's witness. The judges of this world can do injustices, but God can never be unjust. And there is no escape from the jail to which Allah sends the guilty.

It is a great folly – the greatest of all follies – to enter into a false covenant with Allah. Before making the covenant, think it through thoroughly and then scrupulously adhere to it. You are under no compulsion to give a mere verbal pledge; but empty words shall not profit you.

Accepting the Prophet's Leadership

After Lā ilāha illa 'llāh, you recite Muhammadu 'r-rasūlu 'llāh (Muhammad is the Messenger of Allah). This means that you accept Muhammad, blessings and peace be on him, as the man through whom Allah has sent you His guidance. If we acknowledge Allah as Master and Sovereign, it is essential to know what His will is. What deeds should we perform that would please Him and what deeds should we refrain from that would displease Him? What laws should we follow to receive His forgiveness and avoid His punishment? To explain all this to us, God appointed Muhammad, blessings and peace be on him, as His Messenger; for this very purpose through him He sent His Book.

The Prophet, blessings and peace be on him, having lived according to God's guidance, showed us the way we should lead our lives. So, when you say Muhammadu 'r-rasūlu 'llāh, you pledge to follow the way and law given by him and to reject anything which runs counter to it. If, after making this pledge, you abandon the code of life brought by the Prophet, blessings and peace be on him, and follow different and conflicting laws, however widely they may be accepted, there can hardly be any worse liars and more dishonest people than you.

For you enter Islam only by solemnly affirming that you accept the code of life brought by him as the only true law and that you will faithfully follow it. It is on the basis of this affirmation that you become brothers unto Muslims, become eligible for inheritance from your Muslim fathers; on the same basis you were married to Muslim women, your children became legitimate and you secured the right to ask Muslims to help you, to give you alms and to be responsible for the protection of your lives, property, honour and dignity. Nothing can be more dishonest if, in spite of all this, you break your pledge.

If you make the pledge of *Lā ilāha illa 'llāh Muhammadu 'r-rasūlu 'llāh* with a full understanding of its meaning, then it is inconceivable that you will not comply with the laws of God even though no police or court forcing you to do so is visible in this world. To anybody who thinks that it is easy to break the laws of God because God's police, army, court and jail are unseen, and that it is difficult to break earthly laws because of the undoubted presence of the police, army, court and jails of the Government, I would clearly say: Your affirmation of *Lā ilāha illa 'llāh Muhammadu 'r-rasūlu 'llāh* is simply not truthful. You are trying to deceive your God, the whole world, all Muslims, and your own selves.

Obligations of Commitment

Brothers and friends! Now that we know the meaning of this Kalimah I wish to draw your attention to the obligations that result from it.

What does it mean to say that Allah is the Master of everything? It means that your lives are not your property; they belong to God. Your hands are not yours, nor do your eyes, your ears or any limb of your bodies belong to you. The lands you plough, the animals who work for you, the wealth and goods you derive benefit from – none of these is your own. Each and every thing belongs to God, and has been given to you as a gift.

You therefore have no basis whatsoever to make claims like 'life is mine, the body is mine, wealth is mine'. It is absurd to claim ownership after having accepted some other being as the real owner. If you sincerely believe that God is the Owner of all these things, then two things automatically follow.

First, since God is the real owner and you are merely trustees of things owned by Him, you must use these things strictly as He has told you. If you do otherwise, you are abusing your trusteeship; this would amount to cheating God. You have no right to move your hands and feet against His wish, nor to make your eyes see what He dislikes. You may not stomach anything contrary to His command. You possess no rights over lands and properties against the wish of the Master. Your wives and children, whom you assume belong to you, are yours only because they have been given to you by your Master. Even they, therefore, must be treated not as you desire but as directed by Him. If you contravene His directions, you make yourselves usurpers. Just as you call people dishonest who seize other people's belongings, you, too, will be dishonest if you look on the gifts of God as your own property, and utilize them according to your own wishes or according to the wishes of someone other than God.

If you suffer hardship by acting according to the wish of your Master, so be it. If lives are lost, bodies are injured, families are broken or money and property destroyed in the process, why should you be grieved? If the Owner Himself decrees loss of His things, it is perfectly within His right. Of course, if you act against the wish of the Master and suffer hardship, you will undoubtedly be guilty because you will have damaged His property. For example: you do not own your lives. If you give away your lives according to your Master's wishes you will only be rendering His due. Giving your lives while working against Him, however, would be criminal.

Second, you do no favour to your Master nor to anyone else, if you spend something given by Him in His cause. You may give away anything, do any duty, or even sacrifice your lives – which to you are very dear – but you are not doing Him a favour. The most you have done is to have rendered His due for His favour done to you. Is this an achievement to boast about, to demand acclaim for? Should people be praised just because they have repaid a favour? Remember that a true Muslim never gets puffed up for spending something in his Master's cause or for doing his duty to Him. On the contrary, he remains humble. Boasting and pride destroy good acts. Anyone who seeks praise, or does good work in order to earn praise, loses his right to receive any reward from God: 'He has sought reward in this world and has already received it here.'

Our Behaviour

Brothers! Imagine the extraordinary kindness shown you by your Master! He asks you for things which really belong to Him and yet promises that it is a purchase He will pay you for. What unbounded generosity this is! 'God has bought from the believers their lives and their possessions in return for Paradise' (al-Tawbah 9: 111).

Such is the kindness of your Master. Now look at your conduct. You re-sell things to others which were given to you by your Master and which He had bought back from you. And what a paltry price you accept for your precious things! The 'buyers' make you work against the wishes of the Master. You serve them as if they are your sustainers. You sell them your brains and your bodies – indeed, everything that these rebels of God want to buy. Can anything be more immoral than this? To sell a thing already sold is a legal and moral crime, even in this world. Those guilty of such crimes are tried in courts for cheating and fraud. Do you think you will escape trial in the court of God?

5

Why is the Kalimah Unique?

Brothers in Islam! Let us consider further the meaning and essential implications of the Kalimah; for it is the very foundation of Islam. Believe it and you enter Islam on its strength; understand it fully and mould your lives in accordance with it and you become true Muslims. Without it you can neither enter nor remain in Islam.

The Parable

Allah calls it Kalimah Tayyibah, a good, pure and wholesome 'word', and thus defines it:

> Are you not aware how God sets forth the parable of kalimah tayyibah? It is like a good tree – firmly rooted, its branches reaching into heaven. It gives its fruits every moment by the permission of its Lord. So God sets forth parables unto men that they may bethink themselves. And the parable of *kalimah khabīthah* (evil word) is like a corrupt tree – uprooted from the earth, having no permanence. God grants firmness unto those who have believed in the firm word, in the present life and in the world to come, and the wrongdoers He lets go astray, for God does whatever He wills (Ibrāhīm 14: 24–7).

Kalimah Tayyibah is here likened to a noble tree, whose roots are firmly fixed in the earth and whose branches reach to the sky; and all the while it continues to yield abundant fruit, as commanded by its Lord. Set against it is the *kalimah khabīthah,* that is, an evil or corrupt word, a false belief and a baseless saying, which may be likened to a self-seeded plant growing in poor, shallow earth and easily plucked out with a single pull because its roots have no firm base.

So striking and beautiful is the parable that the more you reflect on it the more you will come to absorb the lessons that can be learnt from it.

Two Kinds of Trees

Consider examples of the two kinds of trees.

Look at an oak tree. How firmly it is rooted, to what great height it reaches, how extensively its branches spread, what fine foliage it bears! How did this tree acquire such strength and magnificence? From the nature of its fruit, the acorn. Its seed has an inherent right to become a great tree. And this right was so self-evident that when it made its claim, the earth, the water, the air, the warm day and the cool night, in fact, all the elements concerned, acknowledged it, and whatever it demanded from them was given to it.

Thus by merit it developed into a great tree; by yielding beneficial fruit and by the nobility of its dimensions it continued to demonstrate that it deserved to become a tree of mighty stature and that the help given it by the combined forces of earth and heaven was totally justified. More! It was the *duty* of the elements to give such help because the power that is possessed by the earth, water and air and other elements to nourish, develop and mature trees is precisely meant for the purpose of helping trees of noble species.

But what about wild, self-seeded plants? Where are *their* strengths and virtues? Their roots are so shallow they can be pulled up by a child. They are so weak they wither away in the wind. If you touch them you may well be pricked by thorns. If you taste them they may well be bitter and harmful. God, only, knows how many of these sprout every day, and wither away. Why are they as they are? The reason is that they do not possess the intrinsic right to grow that the acorn does and which allows the growth of the mighty oak.

When there are no trees of noble species to grow, the earth, which by its nature cannot remain fallow, tolerates the growth of shrubs and weeds. Water does give nourishment, and some energy is supplied by the air, but none of the elements accepts the right of existence of these plants as they do of the oak. That is why neither the earth allows their roots to spread themselves within itself, nor is water willing wholeheartedly to give nourishment, nor is the air inclined to help them flourish. So when, with this poor subsistence, these plants grow unhealthy, tasting bad, often bearing thorns and poisonous fruits, it is conclusively demonstrated that earth and heaven are not created to help the growth of such plants.

Keep these two examples before you and then think over the difference between the *Kalimah Tayyibah* and the *kalimah khabīthah*.

Characteristics of the kalian Tayyibah

Kalimah Tayyibah is a true 'word'; so true that there cannot possibly be anything truer in the entire world; that the God of the whole universe is Allah alone. Each and every thing on earth and in heaven bears witness to this. Human beings, animals, trees, stones, particles of sand, flowing streams, the bright sun – is there a single thing out of all these which has been created by anybody but Allah, which can survive through anyone's care and sustenance but Allah's, which can be destroyed by anybody but Allah?

The whole universe has been created by Allah and its life and sustenance depend on His mercy; Allah alone is its Master and Ruler. So when you declare: 'In this world god hood and sovereignty belong to none but the One God', everything on earth and in heaven cries out: 'You have told the truth. We all bear witness to it.' When you bow before Him, everything in the universe bows with you because all things are obedient to Him. When you obey His commandments, everything in the universe does likewise. When you walk along His path, you are not alone. In fact, the countless hosts of heaven and earth will be with you: from the sun in the sky to the smallest particle of dust, everything is following the path He has laid down. When you trust Him, you are not putting your trust in some insignificant power but in that greatest power which is the Master of the universe.

All the forces of earth and heaven, you can now understand, will support anyone who has faith in the Kalimah Tayyibah and moulds his life in accordance with it. He will grow and prosper throughout his life on earth and on into the world to come. Not for a single moment will failure or defeat touch him. This is exactly what Allah has stated in the Ayah quoted in the beginning: this Kalimah is like a tree whose roots are firmly embedded in the earth and whose branches are spread over the heavens bearing fruit perpetually, by the command of Allah.

Characteristics of the Kalimah Khabīthah

In contrast to this, what does *kalimah khabīthah* mean? Only that either there is no God or that there is someone else in addition to Him exercising Divine power. Just think! Can there be a more false and empty proposition? Is there anything in the world which lends credence to it? The atheist says there is no God, but everything on earth and in heaven denounces him as wrong: 'Together with all of us, you have been created by God, this very God has given you the tongue with which to utter this falsehood.' The idolator says that there are partners in His Divine powers; they too provide sustenance, they too have power over things; they too can determine our fates; they too can benefit or harm us; they too can listen to prayers and grant wishes; they too deserve to be feared and trusted; their writ too runs on God's earth and their commands and laws too should be obeyed alongside those of God. Yet everything on earth and in heaven refutes this claim as an absolute lie and totally against reality.

Now consider how a person who believes in such a false proposition and leads a life in conformity with it can ever prosper in this world and in the Hereafter. Allah has, in His mercy, allowed them freedom for a certain duration and promised them sustenance. The elements of nature will therefore provide nourishment to them for a while, but they will not concede it as their right. They will be like the self-seeded shrubs and weeds I have just spoken of.

Contrasting Results

The same contrast is to be found between their fruits. Kalimah Tayyibah produces sweet fruits: it establishes peace in the world. Goodness, truth and justice predominate and people benefit accordingly. But what branches can you grow from an evil root like the *kalimah khabīthah?* The more it grows the more it shoots out thorny branches; poison runs in its very arteries. And what fruit can grow on such branches as these? Only such as are continually bitter and poisonous.

See with your own eyes what is happening in the world where Kafr, idolatry or secularism prevail: man is bent on destruction of his fellow beings. Preparations for war are constantly being made. Nuclear weapons and poisonous gases are being manufactured. Nations are set on destroying each other. The powerful subjugate the weak simply to snatch away their bread. The weak are cowed by the armies and police and threats of jail and execution. They can find no escape from the oppression of the strong.

And what of individuals? Their morals are so depraved that even Satan would be ashamed. Human beings are committing acts which even animals would hesitate to do. The rich suck the blood of the poor through exploitation and usury and force the poor to work as if they were slaves born just to serve them. Human dignity and rights are being trampled upon. Abortion is rife because people do not want their physical pleasures to be interrupted. Even wife- swapping is practised.

Little wonder that whenever a plant has grown anywhere from this *kalimah khabīthah*, it is full of thorns, and whatever fruit it produces is bitter and poisonous.

After giving the two parables, Allah says:

> Thus God grants firmness unto those who have believed in the firm word in the present life and in the world to come, and the wrongdoers He lets go astray (Ibrāhīm 14: 27).

Thus Allah will grant strength and endurance in this world and in the Hereafter to those who have faith in the Kalimah Tayyibah. Conversely, He will set at nought all the endeavours of those wrongdoers who put their faith in the *kalimah khabīthah*. They will not do anything good which will bear fruit in this world or the next.

Why Are Believers in the Kalimah Not Flourishing?

You have heard, brothers, the difference between the kalimah Tayyibah and the *kalimah khabīthah* and their results. You will now surely ask: We believe in the Kalimah Tayyibah. Then how is it that we do not flourish and why are the unbelievers prospering?

I should answer this question, and I shall. But, rather than just becoming angry at my words, look into your hearts to see if I am speaking the truth.

In the first place, your claim that you believe in the Kalimah is not true. Believing in the Kalimah does not consist in its mere utterance. It must be rooted in the heart, it must drive out any belief opposed to it, it should make any actions in contravention of it well-nigh impossible.

Tell me, brothers, in the name of God, is this true of you? Are not hundreds of idolatrous and polytheistic beliefs prevalent among you – ideas totally opposed to the Kalimah Tayyibah? Are not the heads of Muslims being bowed before objects other than God? Are not Muslims afraid of forces other than Him? Do they not expect succour from sources besides Him? Do they not take others as their providers? Do they not sometimes put the laws of God aside and follow other laws instead without any qualms? Do they not sometimes openly state in the courts that they do not abide by the Shari‘ah but by custom and usage? Are there not people among us who do not hesitate to violate the law of God for the sake of trifling material benefit? Are there not those who dread the anger of unbelievers but not the wrath of God? And those who are ready to go to any lengths to carry the favour of Unbelievers but are unwilling to do anything to secure God's favour? And those who take the supremacy of Unbelievers to be real but the rule of God as imaginary?

Tell me, for the sake of God, if all this is not fact? And if it *is*, what justification have you for complaining that you are not prospering despite believing in the Kalimah Tayyibah? First you should become true believers in the Kalimah Tayyibah, and model your lives on the pattern it lays down. If even then your lives do not become like trees which have firm and deep roots in the earth and which spread their luxuriant branches up to the sky, then (I crave Allah's pardon) you may consider your God a liar for having made you false promises.

Are Followers of the Kalimah Khabīthah Prospering?

Again, your contention that believers in the *kalimah khabīthah* are prospering in this world is not correct. In the true sense, these people have never before prospered nor are they prospering now. You judge by their excessive wealth, their abundance of luxury goods and their outward trappings of splendour. Material prosperity is not real prosperity. Let their inner selves speak: how many of them have peace of mind? They are laden with luxury but their hearts are fiery furnaces which keep them anxious and restless. How has disobedience to the law of God turned homes into hell? How rampant is suicide in Europe and America? How widespread is divorce? How, through genocide, birth control and abortions, is the human race being diminished? How are drugs and alcohol destroying the lives of many thousands of people? What a terrible struggle for markets and economic prosperity is raging among different nations and classes? How are jealousy, malice and enmity making men fight each other? How has the mad race for possessions made life bitter for so many people? And today's huge and magnificent cities, which look like paradise from a distance, contain thousands and thousands of people who are wallowing in misery. Do you call this prosperity? Is this what you are seeking so enviously?

Remember, my brothers, that the word of God can never be untrue. There is no Kalimah except the Kalimah Tayyibah by following which man may achieve glory in this-world and happiness in the world-to-come. Seek as you will, you will never be able to find any fault with it.

6

Why Believe in the Kalimah?

Brothers in Islam! Why should we believe in the Kalimah, what benefits shall accrue to us by it? Let us try to find an answer to this important question.

Whatever work we do is done with some purpose or some benefit in view. We never do anything without some objective, goal or need. Why do you drink water? Because it quenches your thirst. If you were to discover that drinking water failed to quench your thirst, you would not waste your time doing it the next time you were thirsty. Why do you eat food? Simply because you want to satisfy your hunger and keep your strength to live. If it made no difference whether you ate food or not, you would naturally feel that it was a useless activity. Why do you take medicine when you are ill? Because you want to get rid of your illness and regain your health. But you soon stop taking medicines which do not work. Why do you work so hard cultivating land? So that crops, fruits and vegetables may be produced. But if nothing grew after you had sown the seeds, you would not again exert yourselves to plough the field, to sow the seed and water the ground.

Thus, whatever work you undertake always has an end in view. If the end is achieved, you consider the work fruitful, and if not, you say it was pointless.

Success in the Hereafter

Bearing this in mind, let us now ask: Why should the Kalimah be recited? The obvious answer is: to draw a distinction between an Unbeliever and a Muslim. But what is the nature of this distinction? Does it mean that if an Unbeliever has two eyes, a Muslim will have four? Or that if an Unbeliever has one head, a Muslim will have two? You will say: No. It does not mean that; it means that there should be a difference between the end result of a Muslim's life and an Unbeliever's life. The end result of an Unbeliever's life is failure: he will be deprived of God's mercy in that-world, in the Hereafter, and be totally wretched; while that of a Muslim's is success: he will win the pleasure of God and be happy and honoured there.

This-world and That-world

Your answer is correct. But now tell me: What is the nature of that-world? And, what is the meaning of being a failure in the Hereafter? What does it mean to be successful and honoured there?

We need not delay ourselves working out the answer to the first question, for it has already been given by the Prophet, blessings and peace be on him: 'This-world is the cultivating ground of the Hereafter.'

This-world and the Hereafter are not two separate entities, but a continuous process. This process begins in this-world and ends in the Hereafter. The relationship between the two is the same as that between cultivation and crop. You plough the land, sow the seeds, irrigate and tend the field till such time as the crop is ready. When you have reaped the harvest, you feed yourselves from it throughout the year.

You will naturally reap whatever you have sown in the land. If you sow wheat, only wheat will grow. If thorns are sown, only thorns will grow. If nothing is sown, nothing will grow. Whatever mistakes and errors you make in the course of ploughing, sowing irrigating and tending your fields, the effect will become apparent at the time of reaping the crop. But if you have carried out all the necessary preparations properly, you will get your reward at the time of reaping.

This is exactly the position in respect of this-world and that-world. This-world is like ground to be tilled. Man has been sent into this field for the purpose of raising a crop for himself by his own efforts and hard work. He has been allotted a specific time – from birth till death – to do this task. Whatever type of crop he sows will be reaped in his life beyond the grave, and that produce will be the mainstay of his life in the Hereafter. If you have sown good seed in the field of this-world throughout your lives and have nourished it with water and careful supervision, you will find the fruits of your labours ready in the next life in the shape of beautiful gardens. You will be able to live happily on the fruits of the garden you have cultivated so assiduously throughout your earthly lives; you will not need to do any further hard work. This is Paradise, this is the success, the state of gratification in the Hereafter.

In contrast to this, if you sow thorns and grow bitter and poisonous plants during your lives on earth, you will reap a similar crop in the next life. You will not be given a second chance to grow a good crop and will have no choice but to sustain yourselves on the bad crop. You will have to lie on the bed of thorns which you have nurtured, and eat the bitter, poisonous fruits you have grown. This is what is meant by being wretched and unsuccessful in the Hereafter.

Success in That-world

The same meaning of the Hereafter as I have described is given in the Qur'ān and the Hadith. This shows that the success or failure of a man in the life after death depends on whether his knowledge and actions have been correct during his life on earth.

From the above it follows that the difference between Muslims and Unbelievers in the Hereafter is determined by the difference which existed between them in the patterns of their lives on earth. Unless there is a difference between the knowledge and actions of a Muslim and an Unbeliever in this-world there can be no difference between their ultimate states in the Hereafter. It is impossible that the knowledge and actions of a Muslim be the same as those of an Unbeliever without him suffering the fate that is destined for an Unbeliever.

True Purpose of the Kalimah

You said earlier that the purpose of reciting the Kalimah was to differentiate between the end results of an Unbeliever and a Muslim. Now, having discussed further the nature of the end result and of the Hereafter, we will have to rephrase your answer. Now you will have to say that the purpose of reciting the Kalimah is to set right man's knowledge and actions here in this-world so that ultimately he attains happiness in that- world. This Kalimah teaches us to plant that garden whose fruits we will pick in the Hereafter. If we do not believe in the Kalimah how can we plant the garden and from where will we pick its fruits in the Hereafter? And if we merely utter the words of the Kalimah without it correcting our knowledge and if our actions too remain the same as those of Unbelievers, the result will be the same as if we had not uttered it.

Would you, then, not agree that it is pointless to utter the Kalimah without letting it change our thoughts and deeds? There is no reason why our fates in this case should be different from those of Unbelievers. We do not put God under any obligation by merely uttering the Kalimah. If we do not learn how to plant a garden, and instead sow thorns all our lives, we cannot expect to inherit a flourishing garden with fruits in the next world. Several examples are before you to show that it is meaningless to do something if an identical outcome would result if you had done nothing. Medicine is not medicine if a patient's condition remains the same after using it. In the same way, if a Kalimah reciter's knowledge and actions remain the same as those of a non-reciter, such a recital is meaningless. If no difference exists between the lives of Unbelievers and Muslims on earth, how can there be any difference between their lives in the Hereafter?

What Does the Kalimah Teach Us?

What, then, is the nature of the knowledge which the Kalimah Tayyibah imparts to us? And what difference takes place between the actions of a Muslim and an Unbeliever after acquiring this knowledge?

One: Submission to Allah. The first thing that you learn from this Kalimah is that you are slaves of Allah, and of Allah alone. Fully understand this profound truth, and you will be automatically led to the realization that, in this world, you must live according to the will of that Being whose slaves you are. Because not to do so will be tantamount to rebellion against your Master.

Two: Obedience to the Prophet. The second thing that you learn from the Kalimah is that Muhammad, blessings and peace be on him, is the Messenger of Allah. Having learnt this, it immediately becomes self-evident that, to grow flowers and fruits in this world instead of thorns and poisonous plants, you have to plant your gardens as he has taught you. If you follow his way, you will reap a fine harvest in the Hereafter; but if you act against his way, you will grow thorns in this world and reap only thorns in the Hereafter.

Actions Must Accord With Knowledge

When you have acquired this knowledge it is essential that your actions should be in conformity with it. If you believe that you have to die one day, that after death there is another life, and that in that life you will have to sustain yourselves solely on that crop which you produced in this world before leaving it, then it is scarcely possible for you to deviate from the path shown by the Prophet, blessings and peace be on him. Why do you cultivate your fields in this world? Simply because no crops will grow unless you do and that without a crop you will die of starvation. If you had not been certain of this, if you had thought that a crop could grow without cultivation, or that you could satisfy your hunger without crops, you would never have laboured to cultivate the fields. In other words, your actions accorded with your knowledge.

Judge your position with respect to the Kalimah in like manner. You assert that you accept God as your Master and Muhammad, blessings and peace be on him, as God's Messenger. You also affirm belief in life after death. Why should, then, your actions run counter to Quranic teachings and the Prophet's Sunnah? Such undoubtedly is the result of weak faith. If you really have faith that your fate in the Hereafter depends on your behaviour in this life, you would never risk being negligent in living as God wills you to live. Only someone who does not *really* believe that what he is sowing will produce thorns and that these thorns will cause him harm would do such a thing. You never pick up embers in your hand knowingly because you know that they will burn you. Only children put their hands in the fire because they do not know what will happen.

PART II
Islam

7

The False Gods

Brothers in Islam! Come, let us now try to establish the minimum conditions you should fulfil and the least you should do so that you can be called Muslims.

What is Disbelief and Islam?

You must, first of all, recollect one important thing: What is Disbelief and what is Islam? Disbelief means refusal to obey God, and Islam means total submission to God alone and refusal to accept any ideas, laws or commandments which contravene the guidance received from God.

This contrast between Islam and Disbelief has been clearly described in the Qur'ān. Allah says: 'Whoso judges not by what God has sent down they are the unbelievers' (al-Mā'idah 5: 44). 'Judging' does not refer here to merely legal matters or court judgement. It applies to all those decisions which we all have to make every day in our lives. You are all the time having to ask yourselves whether to do a certain thing or not, and how to act in varying circumstances.

One way to reach a decision in every eventuality has been laid down in the Book of God and in the Sunnah of His Messenger; other ways are prompted by your desires, by your culture and society, or by man-made laws. If you ignore or reject the way laid down by God, if you decide to conduct your lives according to some other way, you are, then, following the path of Disbelief. If you do this always and in every portion of your lives, you are totally Unbelievers. And if you obey the directions of God in some matters, while in others follow your own self, desires, society, or man-made laws, then you are guilty of Disbelief to the extent of your disobedience. You may be half Unbeliever, or a quarter Unbeliever or less or more. Put simply: Disbelief exists in proportion to the extent of rebellion against the law of God.

Islam: Total Surrender

Islam is nothing but man's exclusive and total submission to God. He is not a servant of his self, or of his ancestors, or of his family and nation, or of any ruler, general, leader, Mulla, Shaikh or any other person. He is a servant of God alone. Says Allah:

> Say [O Prophet]: 'People of the Book! Come to the creed common between us and you, that we serve none but God, and that we associate none with Him, and none of us takes others as Lords, apart from God.' But if they turn away, say, 'Bear witness that we are Muslims' (Āl 'Imrān 3: 64).

And further:

> What! Do they seek a Din other than God's, whereas unto Him surrenders whoso is in the heavens and on earth, willingly or unwillingly, and unto Him all must return? (Āl 'Imrān 3: 83).

One fundamental principle has been clearly and forcefully propounded here. True religion means total obedience and submission to God. Worshipping God does not mean merely that you bow before Him five times a day. It means that His commandments should be carried out at all times. You should abstain from what He has forbidden and do what

He has commanded. In every particular find out what the commandment of God is. Never judge the right and wrong by what your own hearts desire, what your intellects suggest, what your forefathers used to do, what your families and relations prefer, what your society approves, what religious scholars tell you, what a particular person orders or would be pleased by. If you follow any other person's orders or suggestions in preference to God's commandment, you are making that person a partner in Godhood. It would mean you were giving him that status which exclusively belongs to God. 'Authority [to lay down what is right and what is wrong] belongs to God alone' (al-An'ām 6: 57).

Worthy of worship is He alone who has created you and who keeps you alive. Everything in the heavens and on earth obeys Him. No stone obeys another stone, no tree obeys another tree, no animal obeys another animal. Are you then worse than animals, trees and stones, which obey only God, that you obey human beings like yourselves in preference to God? This is the central message of the Qur'ān, simple and emphatic.

Three Reasons For Going Astray

Why do people disobey God and go astray? According to the Qur'ān, there are three main reasons.

Self-worship

The *first* is love of one's own desires:

> And who is more astray than he who follows his own likes and dislikes without any guidance from God. Surely God guides not the wrongdoers (al-Qaṣaṣ 28: 50).

Thus, more than anything, it is man's own wishes and desires which lead him astray. For, the one who becomes a slave to his own desires can never become a true slave of God. He will always have only one consideration before him: what will bring him more worldly profit, what will bring him fame and honour, what will give him pleasure and gratification, and what will provide him with comfort and ease. He will therefore do whatever is necessary to achieve his ends, irrespective of whether God has forbidden the kind of thing he is doing. And he will never do anything which will not help achieve these ends, even though God may have ordered him to do so. The god of such a person is his own self – *nafs* – or his own desire, his like and dislike – *hawā* – and not Allah. How, then, can he benefit from God's guidance, asks the Qur'ān:

> Have you seen him who makes his own desire his god? Will you be a guardian over them? Or do you think that most of them hear or use their reason? Nay, they are but as the cattle; nay, but they are further astray from the way (al-Furqān 25: 43–4).

To be a slave of one's desires is worse than being a beast of the field. No animal will overstep the limits set by God. Every animal eats what has been fixed by God for it; it performs only those functions which are allotted to it. But such an animal is man that when he allows his desires to take over, he commits acts as would make Satan himself shudder.

Society and Culture

The *second* reason for going astray is following blindly the customs and practices, beliefs and notions, rites and ceremonies of society and regarding them as superior to God's guidance. Such a person, when reminded of God's commandments, insists that he should follow only what society approves and continue the traditions of his family or country. How can one who is suffering from such a disease be a servant of God? His gods are society, family and nation. What right has he to claim that he is a Muslim? The Qur'ān warns him thus:

> And when it is said to them, 'Follow what God has sent down', they say, 'No, we will follow [only] what we found our fathers doing.' What! Even if their fathers did not use their reason at all, nor were guided? (al-Baqarah 2: 170).

And, further:

> And when it is said to them, 'Come now unto what God has sent down, and unto the Messenger', they say, 'Enough for us is what we found our fathers doing.' What! Even if their fathers had no knowledge and no guidance? O believers! You are responsible for your own souls. Those who are astray can do you no harm, if you are rightly guided. Unto God shall you all return, and then He will tell you what you were doing (al-Mā'idah 5: 104–5).

In every age, the people who refused to follow the Truth have been suffering from this disease. Always it has prevented them from accepting the guidance brought by the Messengers of God. When Mūsā invited people to submit to God's law, they said:

> Have you come to us to turn us from what we found our fathers practising? (Yūnus 10: 79).

When Ibrāhīm tried to dissuade his fellow citizens from associating gods with God, they said:

> We found our fathers worshipping them (al-Anbiyā' 21: 53).

People have, in all ages, made this same excuse to every prophet, 'What you say is contrary to the practice of our forefathers and this is why we cannot accept it.'

> And even so We never sent a warner before you to any people but its men who lived in the pursuit of pleasures said, 'We indeed found our fathers following a certain way, and it is their footsteps that we are following.' He said, 'What! Though I should bring you a better guidance than you found your fathers upon?' They said, 'In what you are sent with, we disbelieve.' So We inflicted Our retribution upon them; and behold how was the end of them that gave the lie [to the truth]! (Zukhruf 43: 23–5).

Allah tells people that they can either follow their forefathers, their society and culture, or His commandments. They cannot do both. If you want to be Muslims you must give up all things apart from God and obey what He has commanded:

> And when it is said to them, 'Follow what God has sent down', they said, 'No, but we will follow what we found our fathers doing.' What! Even though Satan was inviting them unto the punishment of the blazing flame. And whosoever submits his will to God, and is a doer of good, he indeed has taken hold of the most firm handle. And with God rests the outcome of all affairs. And whoso disbelieves, let not his belief grieve you. Unto Us they shall return, and We shall tell them what they did (Luqmān 31: 21–3).

Obedience to Human Beings

The *third* reason is obeying other human beings in preference to God. How does this happen? When we mistakenly believe that the person concerned is a great thinker whose word must be true. When we imagine that he controls our livelihood, having the power to withhold it from us or give us whatever he desires. When we think that he has the authority over us to do as he wishes. Or, when we subscribe to the notion that he can ruin us by laying his curse upon us or take us to Paradise with him if he is obeyed. Or, when we conclude that we must follow the ways of certain nations because they are progressive and modern and have made great advances in the world. If we behave in any of these manners, the door of Divine guidance is closed:

> If you obey most of those on earth, they will lead you astray from the path of God (al-An‘ām 6: 116).

We can be on the right path only when we have faith in one God, and follow His guidance only. How can we find that path when we have invented numerous gods, sometimes obeying this one and sometimes that one.

The three main causes of going astray are now before you: self-worship or unrestrained gratification of one's desires; social conformity or blind following of the customs of society, family and nation; and servitude to human beings in general, especially rulers of the time, rich and false religious thinkers.

If you want to become true Muslims you must first break these three formidable idols who claim to be your gods. For with these three idols in your hearts you cannot become slaves of God. Merely by offering Prayers many times a day, by ostentatiously observing Fasts, and by putting on the outward face of Muslims, you may deceive you fellow beings – as well, indeed, yourselves – but you will never be able to deceive God.

Condition of Muslims Today

To be slaves of the three idols, I say, is the real *Shirk* (idolatry). You may have demolished the temples of bricks and mortar, you may have broken stone idols in them, but you have paid little attention to the temples within your own hearts. To smash these idols is the essential precondition to becoming a Muslim.

This applies to all Muslims thoughout the world. Whatever sufferings you are going through, I am sure, are the result of worshipping these idols. But because I am facing my Punjabi brothers here, I have particularly to tell them that the root of all their misery and humiliation is again precisely these three things. There are more than fifteen million of us in this land. But despite this we have no weight of our own. Some communities numerically far smaller carry much more weight.* And what is the reason? It is solely by being slaves to our own selves, to family customs and to other human beings in preference to God, that our strength has been sapped from within.

Let us look at ourselves. We have created among us many castes, like Rajputs, Gakhars, Mughuls, Jats and many others. Islam asked all these ethnic groups to become one Ummah, to be brothers and to unite harmoniously like a solidly-built wall of cemented bricks. But we are still clinging to the old pagan ideas. Just as there are separate castes among Hindus, so are we also split. We do not intermarry as Muslims should. There is no trace of brotherhood and fraternity between us. Verbally, we call each other Muslim brothers, but in reality we observe all those distinctions which were prevalent before Islam.

It is these distinctions which have prevented us from becoming a strong wall. Each and every brick in the wall is disjointed. We can neither rise together nor face any adverse situation together. If we are asked, in accordance with Islamic teaching, to break these barriers and become one again, what is our answer? Just the same as the opponents of all the Prophets gave: We cannot go against the customs which have come down from our forefathers. And, what answer was given by

---

* This was said, it should be kept in mind, in 1938 when the Punjab was one province and formed part of British India.

God to this obduracy? Only this: You do not have to break these customs and you do not have to give up following the rites of Hindus. But We shall break you into pieces and shall put you to disgrace and dishonour in spite of your large numbers.

Look further: Allah has commanded that your sons and daughters are both entitled to inheritance. What is your answer? 'No, for according to the custom of our forefathers, only sons and not daughters are entitled. We will follow the way of our forefathers in preference to the law of God.' Tell me, in the name of God, is this Islam? When you are asked to break this ancestral custom you say that you will break it only when others too break it. When asked why, you say because if others did not give a share to their daughters and we did, then we would be at a disadvantage when our sons took wives. Just consider what this reply means. Are we to obey the law of God only on condition that others obey it first? We shall be saying next: If others commit adultery, we shall also do it; if others commit theft, we shall also steal. In short, till such time as others give up sinning, we shall continue to commit sins.

In following your caste system and inheritance customs in such a manner all the three false idols we have been discussing are being worshipped. There is slavery to the self, to society, and to Disbelieving nations. And at the same time, while serving all these idols, we still claim that we nonetheless somehow belong to Islam!

These are only two examples. We need only look at the situation with open eyes to see countless others. And in all these we will find that sometimes there is worship of one idol, sometimes of two, and sometimes of three. While these idols are being worshipped alongside the claims of allegiance to Islam and God, how can we expect Allah to shower His blessings on us – blessings which have been promised only to true Muslims?

8

Can We Call Ourselves Muslims?

Brothers in Islam! You now understand that, according to the Qur'ān, men go astray in three ways. The *first* is to ignore the guidance of God and become slaves of desire. The *second* is to give precedence to family, culture, society, customs and the ways of forefathers over the law of God. The *third* is to ignore the way enunciated by God and His Messenger and follow the ways either of so-called important people or of other civilizations and cultures.

A True Muslim

A true Muslim should be free from these three ailments. Only someone who is a slave of none but God and a follower of none but His Messengers can be truly called a Muslim. A Muslim sincerely believes that the teaching of God and His Messenger is absolute truth, that whatever runs counter to it is false, and that it contains all that is good for man in this world and in the Hereafter. A Muslim who has complete faith in these truths will, at every step in his life, look only to God and the Messenger to guide him and submit to whatever they require. Such a person will never feel troubled in his heart about obeying God's commandments, or be concerned if members of his family or his society upbraid him, or if the entire world opposes him. In each case his response will be unequivocal: I am God's slave, not yours; I have faith in His Messenger, not in you.

What is Hypocrisy?

Serving the Self

On the other hand, a person may say, 'This may be the directive of God and the Messenger, but it is difficult for me to accept it because it seems to be harmful. So I shall act according to my own opinion as against the guidance of God and the Messenger.' Obviously, no faith can be alive in the heart of such a person. He is not a true believer (Mumin) but a hypocrite (Munāfiq). While he verbally claims to be a servant of God and a follower of the Messenger, in reality he is a slave of his own self and a follower of his own opinions.

Adherence to Society and Culture

Similarly, a person may say that whatever the injunctions of God and the Messenger may be, a certain practice cannot be given up because it has been followed since the times of his forefathers. He, too, must then be reckoned among the hypocrites, however prominent the mark on his forehead traced by prostration in endless prayers and however pious his face. The spirit of Islam has not entered his heart. Islam does not consist merely in bowing (rukū'), prostration (sujūd), Fasting (Ṣawm) and Pilgrimage (Ḥajj); nor is it found in the face and dress of a man. Islam means submission to God and the Messenger. Anyone who refuses to obey them in the conduct of his life-affairs has a heart devoid of the real Islam – 'faith has not yet entered their hearts'. His Prayers, his Fasting and his pious appearance are nothing but deception.

Imitating Other People

Again, someone may, in defiance of the Book of God and the Messenger's directions, urge thus: Such and such ideas and practices should be adopted because they are prevalent in the West; this particular behaviour must be accepted because other nations are making progress because of it; this point should be conceded because an important person is advocating it. Such a person is in grave danger of losing his faith. This attitude is irreconcilable to Iman.

If you are Muslims and want to remain Muslims, then cast overboard every suggestion which is contrary to the injunctions of God and His Messenger. If you cannot, it ill behoves you to claim to be following Islam. To assert that you believe in God and the Messenger but to ignore their injunctions in the conduct of your lives in favour of other people's thoughts and practices is neither Iman nor Islam. It is sheer hypocrisy.

Allah leaves no doubt about the ridiculous nature of such conduct:

> Indeed We have sent down revelations clearly showing the truth, but God guides whomsoever He will to a straight path. They say, 'We believe in God and the Messenger, and we obey.' Then, after that, a party of them turn away; they are not [true] believers. And when they are called unto God and His Messenger that he may decide between them, behold, a party of them turn away; but if they are in the right, they will come unto him submitting willingly. What! Is there in their hearts sickness? Or are they in doubt? Or, do they fear that God and His Messenger may be unjust towards them? Nay, it is they who are doing wrong. All that the believers say, whenever they are called unto God and His Messenger that he may judge between them, is that they say, 'We hear, and we obey.' It is they who are the successful. Whoso obeys God and His Messenger, and fears God, and has awe of Him, it is they who shall triumph (al-Nūr 24: 46–52).

Reflect on the definition of Iman set out here. What is Iman? It consists in submitting yourselves, willingly and totally, to the Book of God and the guidance given by His Messenger. Whatever guidance and commandments are received from these sources you must implicitly obey and no arguments against them should be listened to, whether they come from your own minds, or from members of your families, or from outsiders. You can only be a Muslim if you develop this attitude. If you do not, you are no more than a hypocrite.

Compare, now, yourselves with those who had real and true Iman in their hearts and see how they obeyed Allah and the Messenger.

The True Faith

Abstinence From Alcohol

You know how widespread the drinking of alcohol was in Arabia. Men and women, young and old, all loved to drink. They sang songs in its praise and were totally addicted to it. You also know how difficult it is to give up drinking after becoming addicted to it. An alcoholic would rather give up his life than stop drinking. If he cannot get alcohol he becomes worse than a physically-ill person.

Yet what happened when the prohibition order was given through the Qur'ān? Those same Arabs who loved alcohol more dearly than their lives broke with their own hands the containers they were drinking from. Alcohol flowed like water in the streets of Madina. One group of people, with drinking vessels in their hands, heard the proclamation of the Prophet, blessings and peace be on him, prohibiting alcohol; those who had vessels close to their lips put them away before a drop could enter their mouths.

Such is the strength of true Iman. This is one of the finest examples of submission to Allah and the Messenger.

Confession of Crime

You know what severe punishment Islam has prescribed for adultery – one hundred strokes on the bare back. The very thought makes a person shudder. And if a married person is involved, the punishment is stoning to death – one trembles at the very mention of such terrible punishment. But have you heard the story of the man who committed adultery at the time of the Prophet, blessings and peace be on him, and had the strength of faith to face its consequences?

There were no witnesses. There was nobody to take him to court, nobody to report him to the police. Yet the Iman in his heart admonished him: As you have gratified your desire in contravention of the law of God, you must undergo the punishment prescribed by God for it. So this person presented himself, of his own accord, before the Prophet, blessings and peace be on him, and said: 'O Messenger of Allah, I have committed adultery. Please give me my punishment.' On hearing these words the Prophet turned aside as if he had not heard the man, but he moved in front of him and repeated his request. The Prophet, blessings and peace be on him, again turned aside, and again the man went and stood in front of him and made the same request for the third time.

Such is the power of true Iman! For one who has such Iman in his heart it is easy to be punished with a hundred strokes on his bare back, or even be stoned to death, but it is difficult to go before God as a disobedient servant.

Severance of Familial Ties

You also know that in this world nobody is dearer to us than our relatives. Fathers, brothers and sons, particularly, are so dear that we are willing to sacrifice everything for them. But now think of the battles of Badr and Uhud and see who fought against whom. A father, in the Muslim army, was drawn against his son, who was in the army of the Unbelievers; or the son was on this side and his father was on the other side. One brother was on this front and another brother on the other front. Close relatives confronted each other and fought as if they were strangers. It was not for the sake of money or chauvinism or personal enmity that men fought against their own flesh and blood; it was for the sake of God and the Messenger that they had the strength and courage to sacrifice the love for their fathers, sons, brothers and whole families.

Giving Up Cultural Norms and Customs

You know, too, that Islam demolished practically all the ancient customs prevalent in Arabia. The greatest evil of all was idol-worship, which had been practised for hundreds of years. Islam told people to give up this evil as well as alcohol, adultery, gambling, theft and armed robbery – all of which were rampant at that time. Women used to walk about unveiled; Islam enjoined them to observe *purdah*. They were not entitled to a share in inheritance; Islam decreed that they should have one. Indeed, no ancient custom was left untouched.

But do you know in what manner did those who truly believed in God and the Messenger submit to all this? The idols which had been worshipped for centuries and at whose altars sacrifices had been offered for long they broke with their own hands. Family customs which had been passed down from generation to generation they totally abolished. Objects which had been considered sacred they trampled under their feet, when ordered to by God. At His command, too, things which had been regarded as prohibited became permissible; what had been considered clean suddenly became unclean and the unclean became clean. Practices which provided profit or pleasure during the days of Disbelief were given up for the sake of God. On the other hand, injunctions laid down by Islam, no matter how hard it was to obey them, were gladly accepted.

This is what true Iman means, this is what is called true Islam. Suppose the people of Arabia had at that time said: 'We do not accept this thing because it will harm our interests and we cannot give up that thing as it profits us greatly, we shall continue following this particular practice since it is what our forefathers did and our society approves, while we like certain ideas of the Romans and will adopt them and certain practices of the Iranians which appeal to us.' Had they in this way rejected all tenets of Islam, there would, as you can imagine, have been no Muslims in the world today.

The Way to God's Pleasure

Brothers! The Qur'ān says:

Never shall you attain true piety unless you spend [in the way of God] out of what you love (Āl 'Imrān 3: 92).

Herein lies the essence of Iman; this is the real spirit of Islam: that you must be prepared to sacrifice for the sake of God, if necessary, whatever is dear to you.

In many affairs of your lives God's commandments beckon you in one direction while your own desires urge you in another. God commands you to do a certain deed but you think that it will cause trouble and loss. God forbids you from a certain action but you consider it to be pleasant and beneficial. On one side is God's pleasure and pitted against it is almost everything in this world. At every step in life you are faced with two paths. One is the path of Islam, and the other of Disbelief and hypocrisy.

By giving up the things of this world and bowing to the commandments of God, you adopt the path of Islam. By rejecting God's commandments in order to satisfy the desires of your hearts and the temptations of the world, you take the path of Disbelief and hypocrisy.

Muslims of Today

So many Muslims today are all too ready to accept whatever is convenient in Islam but all too quick to change direction when conflict arises between Islam and Disbelief. This weakness is found even among some of those claiming to be the greatest champions of Islam. They will shout 'Islam! Islam!' and sing many songs praising it until their mouths are dry. They will be seen doing some work for Islam. But if they are told, 'Let us now implement the law of Islam which you are praising so highly', they will at once say, 'There are some difficulties and obstacles, it is better to leave things as they are for the time being.'

What they mean is that Islam is a beautiful toy, to be displayed on a shelf and praised from a distance, but to be strictly avoided if the question is raised of enforcing its laws to govern ourselves, our families and relations and our businesses and the general conduct of our lives. This is the attitude of even some so-called religious people today.

As a result, neither Prayer nor Fasting nor reciting the Qur'ān nor outward adherence to the Shari'ah is effective. When the soul departs, what feats can a dead body perform?

9

Are We True Muslims?

Brothers in Islam! Who are true Muslims? Let us see what Allah and His Messenger have to say about their lives and hearts:

> Say: My prayers and my sacrifices, and my living and my dying are for God alone, the Lord of all the worlds. No partner has He. Thus I have been commanded, and I am foremost among those who surrender [themselves unto Him] (al-An'ām 6: 163–4).

The same theme is elucidated by the Prophet, blessings and peace be on him:

> One who loves for the sake of Allah alone and hates for the sake of Allah alone; and whatever he gives, gives for the sake of Allah alone, and whatever he withholds, withholds for the sake of Allah alone – indeed, he perfects his Iman (*Abū Dā'ūd*).

The Qur'ān makes clear what Allah demands of you. You should devote yourselves wholly to the service of Allah, you should live for Him alone, you should die for Him alone. You, and the world around you, entirely belong to Allah; let nobody have a share in what belongs to Allah. That is to say, you should not serve anyone but Him, nor live or die for anyone but Him.

The Prophet, blessings and peace be on him, explains what the Qur'ān has said. To be a true believer your love and enmity for everything, all your affections, all relations and transactions in your lives, should have only one purpose: to seek Allah's pleasure. Without this your Iman itself will not be complete; the possibility of rising higher in the sight of God does not arise. The greater the deficiency in this respect, the more defective the Iman.

Some people think that these qualities are required only to reach higher spiritual stations and are not essential to Iman and Islam. In other words, even without these qualities a person can be a good Mumin and a Muslim. This mistaken notion has arisen because people in general do not differentiate between legal Islam and true Islam which alone is truly authentic in the sight of Allah.

Two Types of Islam

Legal Islam

Under legal Islam, on which jurists and states must base their dealings, what lies in your hearts and minds is not taken into account, nor can it be. Your verbal affirmation and those essential signs which must flow out of that affirmation are accepted as sufficient evidence of your Islam. Anyone who affirms by word of mouth belief in Allah, the Messenger, the Qur'ān, the Hereafter and other articles of faith, and who also fulfils those necessary conditions which provide proof of his affirmation, is considered part of Muslim society and all dealings with him are to be conducted as with a Muslim.

This definition provides the legal and cultural basis on which Muslim society is organized. Its purpose is no more than that all those who enter into the Muslim Ummah are recognized as Muslims: nobody from among them can be called an Unbeliever; every one of them must have the same mutual legal, moral and social rights; they should be entitled to marry among Muslims; they should be eligible to receive their share in inheritance; all other civil relations should be established with them.

True Islam

However, in the world-to-come, you cannot be judged as a Muslim and a Mumin on the basis of this legal affirmation, nor on this basis will God accept you as one of His chosen servants. What will count then is having faith in hearts, and willingly and wholly submitting lives to God. Whatever is verbally affirmed is meant for courts and for the common man and the Muslim society. For they can only see the exterior, but Allah sees deep into your hearts and knows precisely the degree of your Iman.

How will He judge a man? Allah will see whether he lived and died for Him alone, whether his loyalties to Him superseded all other loyalties, whether his obedience and his service, indeed his entire life, were devoted only to Him. If they *were* solely for Allah then he will be adjudged a Mumin and a Muslim, but if they were for someone else, then he will not be adjudged a Muslim nor a Mumin. Whoever falls short of this criterion will, to the extent he falls short, be lacking in Iman and Islam, irrespective of how important a Muslim the world may judge him and of any high positions he may hold. With Allah only one thing matters: whether or not you have given away in His way all that He has given you.

If you have, you will be granted the reward which is reserved for those who are loyal and render the service that is due. But if your submission has been less than total, if you spare any part of your life from His service, your claim to be Muslims, which implies that you have wholly given up yourselves to God, will be a deceptive claim. Although you may be able to mislead the world and persuade the Muslim society to grant you its membership and all the rights of Muslims, God cannot be deceived into assigning a place for you among His faithful.

Reflect on the differences between legal Islam and true Islam and you can see that their consequences will vary greatly, not only in the Hereafter but also in this world; the life pursuits, character and disposition of a true Muslim will be totally different from one who merely parades the outward trappings of faith. You will always encounter these two types of Muslims.

Two Kinds of Muslims

Partial Muslims

Some Muslims profess faith in God and the Messenger and declare Islam as their religion; but then they confine this Islam to only a part of their lives. To the extent of this part, they express great attachment to Islam, extensively perform worship rituals like Prayers, use of the rosary, remembrance of God's name. They are very particular in conforming to outward piety in matters like food, dress and other external social, cultural customs. Thus they are fully 'religious'.

But beyond these conventions their lives are not ruled by God. If they love, they love for the sake of their own selves, their country, their nation, or for anything else, but not for Allah. If they become displeased, are angry, hate someone, make enemies, or wage war, it too is for the sake of some worldly or selfish interest. Their relations with their businesses, their wives and children, families, societies – will all be to a great extent unaffected by Islam and based on secular considerations. As landlords, traders, rulers, soldiers, professional people – in all spheres they will behave as if they are autonomous, having no connection with their position as Muslims. When such people establish cultural, educational and political norms and institutions, these have nothing to do with Islam, even though they may seem Islamic.

True Muslims

The second kind of Muslims are those who completely merge their personalities and existences into Islam. All the roles they have become subordinate to the one role of being Muslims. They live as Muslims when they live as fathers, sons, husbands or wives, businessmen, landlords, labourers, employers. Their feelings, their desires, their ideologies, their thoughts and opinions, their likes and dislikes, all are shaped by Islam. Allah's guidance holds complete sway over their hearts and minds, their eyes and ears, their bellies, their sexual desires, their hands and feet, their bodies and souls. Neither their loves nor their hatreds are formed independently of Islamic criteria. Whether they fight or make friends, it is purely for the sake of Islam. If they give anything to anybody, it is because Islam requires it to be given. If they withhold anything from anybody, it is because Islam wants it to be withheld.

And this attitude of theirs is not limited to personal lives; their public lives, their societies are also based entirely on Islam. Their collectivity exists for Islam alone; their collective behaviour is governed by the precepts of Islam alone.

What Kind of Muslims God Desires

The above two kinds of Muslims are significantly different from each other, even if, legally, both are included in the Ummah and the word 'Muslim' is applied to both equally. Historically the first kind of Muslims have made no achievement which may be worthy of mention or which merits our being proud of it. Nothing these 'Muslims' have done has left an Islamic imprint on the pages of world history. The world has received no benefit from their existence; indeed, Islam has suffered decay because of them. Because of the preponderance of such 'Muslims' in Muslim society, power and world leadership largely passed into the hands of rebels against God. For these 'Muslims' have been content merely with ensuring that they enjoy the freedom to live religiously within the narrow confines of their private lives.

God never desired to have such 'Muslims'. Nor did He send His Prophets or reveal His Books to create them. Indeed it is the second kind of Muslims who are desired by God. Only they can ever accomplish anything worthwhile from the Islamic point of view.

Supreme Loyalty to Allah

This is not a phenomenon peculiar to Islam. In fact, no way of life can ever prevail in the world if its followers accord their faith and commitment a subordinate position in their lives. Or, if they live and die for causes other than their faith. We see even today that only those are considered real and true followers of a creed or ideology who are loyal to it with their hearts and souls. Every creed in the world desires such adherents and no creed can prevail in the world except through such followers.

However, there is an important difference between Islam and other creeds and ideologies. Although others demand from men total loyalty and dedication, they in fact have no such right upon him, their claims are entirely unjustified. The objects they place before men are not the kind of objects for which a human being should sacrifice anything. But the God for whom Islam demands the sacrifice of life has a right upon us. Everything must be given in His way, for whatever exists in heaven and on earth belongs to Allah. Man himself, whatever he possesses, and whatever lies within him, all belong to Allah. It is therefore in perfect harmony with justice as well as reason that whatever belongs to Allah must be reserved only for Him. Whatever sacrifice man makes for others or for his own benefit or to gratify his desire is indeed a breach of trust unless it be with the permission of Allah. And whatever sacrifice is made for Allah is in reality a payment of what is due.

But, one lesson Muslims must learn from those who are sacrificing everything for the sake of their false ideologies and false gods: how strange it is that, while such unimaginable dedication, sacrifice and fidelity is being shown for false gods, not even a thousandth part of it is shown for the True God by those who profess faith in them.

Where Do We Stand?

Let us examine our lives by the crucial criteria of Iman and Islam as laid down by the Qur'ān and the Prophet, blessings and peace be on him.

If you claim that you have accepted Islam, have you oriented your living and your dying towards God only? Are you living for His cause alone? Are your hearts and minds, your bodies and souls, your time and efforts, being devoted to the fulfilment of Allah's wishes? Is that mission being accomplished through you which He wants to be fulfilled by the Muslim Ummah? And, again, do you obey and serve only God? Have you eliminated from your lives subservience to selfish desires and obedience to family, brotherhood, friends, society and state?

Have you made your likes and dislikes totally subordinate to the wishes of Allah? If you love somebody, is it really for the sake of Allah? If you dislike somebody, is that too for the sake of Allah? Is no element of selfishness involved in this? Do you give and withhold only for the sake of God? Are you spending on your own selves and giving wealth to other people, or withholding the same, because that is what God wants? Is your motive nothing but to gain His pleasure?

If you find such a state of faith and submission within yourself, you should thank God that He has bestowed upon you the blessing of Iman in its fullness. And if you feel any deficiency, you must give up every other concern and worry and concentrate wholly on remedying this deficiency. For on its removal depends your well-being in this world as well as your success in the Hereafter. Whatever success you may enjoy in the present life will not compensate you for the loss you will suffer in the Hereafter due to this deficiency. But if you make up for this deficiency, even if you gain nothing in this world, you will benefit immensely in the life to come.

Do not use this criterion to test or judge others and determine whether they are Mumins or hypocrites and Muslims or Unbelievers; use it only to judge your own selves and, if you detect any deficiency, try to remove it before you meet Allah. How a *muftī* (religious jurist) or a court judges you should be of least concern to you; it is only the judgement of the Supreme Ruler and answer of the seen and unseen which matters. Do not become happy merely on seeing your names registered as Muslims, but remain anxious about how and where your names are entered in the Register of God.

Real success consists in your being judged as Mum ins and not hypocrites, obedient and not disobedient, faithful and not unfaithful, by that God who is the final Judge.

10

Why Obey God?

Brothers in Islam! I have frequently emphasized that 'Islam' means total surrender to Allah and the Messenger, and that no one can become truly Muslim unless he gives up obedience to anyone or anything apart from God.

But why is so much stress laid on obedience to God and His Messenger? You may ask: Does God need our obedience so badly that He has to demand it so insistently from us? Is He, too, like the rulers of the world so power-hungry that He has to insist His rule cannot be sustained without subjugating us?

Let us try to examine these questions.

Our Well-being

Essentially, the demand for obedience to Allah is intended for the well-being and betterment of man himself. He is not like the rulers of the world. They subjugate people to benefit themselves, but Allah needs nothing from anybody. He is not in need of taxes from you, nor does He require to build mansions, buy cars and amass luxury articles at your expense. He is not dependent on anyone for anything. Whatever is in the world belongs to Him alone and He alone is the Master of all treasures.

He demands obedience from you only because He does not want man – that creation of His whom He has declared to be the noblest – to be the servant of another man like him, or of Satan or bow his head before unworthy things. He does not desire that His vicegerents on earth grope in the darkness of ignorance and, like animals, become slaves to their desires and thus degrade themselves to the level of the lowest of the low. Therefore He urges: You obey Me and walk by the light I have sent through My Messengers. You will find the straight path. By walking on it you will receive dignity in this world as well as in the Hereafter.

> No coercion is there in religion. Distinct has become the right way from [the way of] error. So whosoever rejects false gods and believes in God has indeed taken hold of the most firm handle which shall never break. God is All-hearing, All-knowing. God is the Friend of those who have faith; He brings them out of darkness into the light. And the disbelievers – their friends are false gods that bring them out of the light into darkness; those are the inhabitants of the Fire, therein to abide forever (al- Baqarah 2: 256–7).

Obeying Others Besides Allah

Why will a man plunge into darkness by obeying others besides Allah and why is it that only by obeying Allah can his life be illumined? Let us look into this important question.

Our lives are made up of countless relations and transactions. Our first relationship is with our own bodies: these hands, these feet, these eyes, these ears, this tongue, this heart, the mind, this belly – all these have been entrusted to you by Allah to serve you. You have also been given freedom to decide to what end to employ them.

What to put in your bellies, and what to avoid. What to make your hands do, and what to keep them away from. Where to let your feet walk, and when to hold back. What to let your eyes see and ears hear, and what to refrain from. What to allow your tongues to say, and when to fall silent. What kind of thoughts to make your hearts and minds reflect upon, and what to shun.

These servants of yours you can make do good work or bad, as you choose. In return, they can make you ascend great heights or plunge you into abysmal depths.

Then you have relationships with the members of your family – with your fathers, mothers, sisters, brothers, wives, children and other relatives with whom you have to deal continuously. You have to decide how to behave with these people, what rights you have over them, and what rights they have over you. Your comfort, your happiness and your success in this world as well as in the Hereafter depend very much on how correctly you behave with them. If you behave wrongly, you will make this world a Hell for yourselves. And in the Hereafter, too, you will have to answer to God.

You have relationships with many other people. They are your neighbours, friends and enemies. There are also many who work for you in various ways. To some you have to give something and from others you have to receive something. Some entrust you with their works while you entrust your works to others. You are in command over some people and others are in command over you. In this world, your happiness, your honour and your good names – all depend entirely on your ability to maintain these relationships properly.

In the Hereafter, too, you can acquire places of honour near God only by scrupulously avoiding abusing the rights of others and doing them injustices. There, let no one charge you with having ruined his life or having illegally harmed his honour, life or property. You therefore have to maintain these relationships in a proper manner; actions which may spoil or disrupt these relations should be avoided.

Now consider: in order to maintain proper relationships with you own bodies, with the members of your families and with all other people, you need the light of knowledge at every step. You have to know what is right and what is wrong; what is true and what is false; what is just and what is unjust; what rights you have over others and what rights others have over you; in what there is real benefit and in what lies real harm.

If you try to find this knowledge with the help of your reason and feelings alone, you will not find it. Because your self is overpowered by the urge to immediate gratification of desires. Your reason and feelings are therefore ruled by physical pleasure and immediate temptations. They will tempt you to earn money by doing illegal things, drink alcohol and commit adultery. They will lead you to usurp the rights of others and withhold things due to them on the grounds that such behaviour will profit you: take everything and give nothing. They will also make you exploit others to serve your ends while avoiding the doing of any service to anybody, arguing that this will make life easy and comfortable.

If you allow yourselves to be led by a self which gropes in such darkness, it will drag you down to the level of selfish, depraved, and corrupt persons and your lives both on earth and in the Hereafter will be ruined.

Alternatively, instead of following the self, you may rely on other human beings like yourselves, and place yourselves in their hands to take you in whichever direction they like. The dangers in such a course are obvious: selfish persons may make you slaves of their own desires, and ignorant men, who have themselves gone astray, may mislead you also. Tyrants may use you to perpetrate oppression and injustice on others.

From human beings like yourselves, too, you cannot get that light of knowledge which can guide you to distinguish between right and wrong, between good and bad, and direct you on the right path.

The Only True Guidance

In the final analysis there remains only one source of truth: that one Supreme Being from whom you can get the necessary light. God is All-knowing and All-seeing. He knows the inner reality of all things. He alone can tell you precisely what is to your benefit and what is to your detriment. He alone can lay down which actions are right for you and which are wrong. He has no vested interests and no axe to grind. He has no need to secure any benefit by deception. Therefore, whatever directions that Holy and Self-subsistent Being gives you will be without any ulterior motive and will be intended exclusively for your benefit.

Allah is also the ultimate dispenser of justice. There is not the slightest element of injustice in that Holy Being; His commandments are based totally on truth and justice. In following them there is no danger of you doing any injustice to yourselves or to other people.

How to Benefit

Two things are necessary in order to benefit from the light given by God. *First*, you must believe sincerely in Allah and his Messengers, through whom this light has been transmitted. This means that you should be absolutely certain that whatever guidance the Messenger has brought from God is right and true, whether at a particular time you understand the wisdom behind it or not. *Second*, after you have believed, you should follow that guidance, because without obedience nothing can be achieved.

Suppose a man tells you not to eat a certain thing because it is poisonous and you say, 'You are undoubtedly right, it is poisonous and fatal'. Then, despite acknowledging this truth, you eat that thing. The result will obviously be the same as if you had eaten it unknowingly. So what is the point of just knowing something without acting on your knowledge?

You can achieve real benefit only when you obey Allah after affirming faith in Him, when you obey His commandments and not merely utter your belief in their truth. Similarly, you should not simply promise verbally to abstain from things which have been forbidden, but in fact abstain from them. That is why Allah repeatedly urges: 'Obey Allah and obey the Messenger' (al-Mā'idah 5: 92). And: 'If you obey him, you will be guided' (al-Nūr 24: 54). And: 'So let those who go

123

against His command beware, lest a trial befall them, or there befall them a painful punishment' (al-Nūr 24: 63).

No Blind Obedience

Let there be no misunderstanding about one thing. By saying that only Allah and the Messenger should be obeyed I do not mean that you should refrain from listening to anyone else. No. The only thing is that you should not follow anybody unthinkingly: you should always examine whatever a person tells you to see if it is in accordance with the guidance given by Allah and the Messenger or not. If it is, you should accept what he tells you because you will in fact be obeying not him but Allah and the Messenger. If it is not, you should reject him because no one has a right to be obeyed as against Allah and the Messenger.

You understand that Allah does not Himself appear before man and deliver His guidance. Whatever guidance He has to give He has conveyed through His Messenger. The Prophet, blessings and peace be on him, too, left this world for his heavenly home about fourteen centuries ago. The commandments given by Allah through him are preserved in the Qur'ān and Hadith. But the Qur'ān and Hadith cannot in their nature come before you and give orders to do certain things and not to do other things. It is men who will help you conduct yourselves according to the Qur'ān and Hadith. There is therefore no other course of action open but to obey the teachings of men.

What is essential is that you do not follow people with closed eyes. As I have just told you, you should first see whether they are advising you according to the Qur'ān and Hadith or not. If they are, then it is incumbent on you to obey them. But if they want to lead you on to an opposing course, then it is forbidden to obey them.

11

Difference Between Din and Shari'ah

Brothers in Islam! When talking of Islam we often hear and use two particular words: one is Din and the other is Shari'ah. But very few understand the true meaning of Din and Shari'ah. Not only the illiterate, but even reasonably educated people, and many religious scholars too, do not fully grasp the important distinctions between the two concepts. Due to this ignorance, Din and Shari'ah are often confused with each other, creating serious malaises.

Meaning of Din

The word 'Din' is used in several meanings. The first is sovereignty, power, lordship, kingship, or rulership. The second is the opposite of this, i.e. submission, obedience, service or slavery. The third is to bring to account, to judge, or to dispense reward and punishment for actions. All those three uses are found in the Qur'ān.

Allah says:

> The only [true] Din in the sight of God is [man's] selfsurrender [to Him] (Āl 'Imrān 3: 19).

Here, Din is that way of life in which we recognize Allah alone as the possessor of all power and majesty and surrender ourselves to Him. We must not abase or humble ourselves before anybody save Him. We must regard only Allah as Master, Lord, and Sovereign, and must not be slaves or servants to anybody but Him. We must accept only Allah as the Lord of reward and punishment. We should covet no reward, fear no punishment, except His. Islam is the name of this Din.

False Din arises when you ascribe real powers to anyone besides Allah, when you take anyone as a real ruler and master, as a dispenser of real reward and punishment, when you bow your heads before him in humility, when you serve him and obey his orders, when you covet his reward and fear his punishment more than Allah's. This kind of Din Allah never accepts because it is totally contrary to reality.

No other being in the whole universe except God possesses any power and might, nor does anybody else's sovereignty and kingship exist. We have not been created to be servants and slaves of anyone or anything but God, nor is there anyone else except that real Master who can judge us and award reward and punishment. In many places in the Qur'ān these facts have been explained.

> And whoso seeks a Din other than Islam, it will not be accepted from him (Āl 'Imrān 3: 85).

Thus, anyone who disregards the sovereignty and kingship of God, acknowledges someone else as his master and ruler, becomes his servant and slave, and considers anyone as a dispenser of reward and punishment in his own right, will never have his Din or conduct accepted by God because:

> They were not enjoined anything but that they should serve God, making submission exclusively His, turning away [from all false gods] (al-Bayyinah 98: 5).

God has not created human beings to serve anyone except Himself. It is, therefore, incumbent on them to turn away from all false gods and reserve their submission, or their true Din, for Allah alone. They should single-mindedly devote themselves to His service and consider themselves as being accountable only to Him:

> What! Do they seek a Din other than God's, whereas unto Him surrenders whatever is in the heavens and on earth, willingly or unwillingly, and unto Him all must return? (Āl 'Imrān 3: 83).

How can we human beings incline to be servants and to submit to someone other than God, when all other things on earth and in the heavens are slaves and obedient servants of God alone, accounting for their deeds to no other authority than God? Does man want to adopt a deviant way for himself, some kind of independent and autonomous existence, in defiance of the entire universe?

> He it is Who has sent forth His Messenger with the Guidance and the way of Truth, so that he makes it prevail over all ways [religions], however much Mushriks [who take gods besides God] may dislike it (al-Tawbah 9: 33).

Allah has sent His Messenger with the true Din for the purpose of ending the sovereignty of all false gods and granting us immense freedom so that we live as servants of none but the Lord of the universe, no matter how much the idolaters and polytheists may dislike or oppose such a course.

> And fight them, until there is no rebellion [against God] and all submission is to God alone (al-Anfāl 8: 39).

The lesson is clear: we must fight until the sovereignty of all beings other than Allah is brought to an end, until only the law of God rules in the world, until the sovereignty of God alone is acknowledged, until we serve only Him.

Thus these three meanings of Din stand out:

To acknowledge God as Lord, Master and Ruler.

To obey and serve only Him.

To be accountable to Him, to fear only His punishment and to covet only His reward.

Din also includes obedience to God's Messengers. For the commandments of God have been given to human beings through His Books and His Messengers.

> Children of Adam! If there should come to you Messengers from among you, who convey My revelations unto you, then whosoever refrains from evil and lives rightly – no fear shall be on them, and neither shall they sorrow (al-A'rāf 7: 35).

No individual receives Allah's commandments directly. Hence, whoever acknowledges Allah as Ruler can be accepted as obedient to Him only when he becomes obedient to His Messengers and lives by the guidance received through them.

Din consists of these fundamental principles.

Meaning of Shari'ah

We turn now to the Shari'ah. The meaning of the Shari'ah is 'way' and 'path'. You enter Din when you accept God as your Sovereign, accept to live in service to Him, accept that the Messenger holds authority on His behalf, and accept that the Book has been sent by Him. The ways in which you then have to serve God and the path you have to travel along in order to obey Him is called the Shari'ah.

This 'way' or 'path', too, has been given by God through His Messenger. It is he who teaches you how to worship the Master, how to make your bodies and hearts clean, what is righteousness and piety, how to discharge rights, how to undertake transactions and dealings with our fellow-beings, indeed how to lead our entire lives.

Nature of Differences

The key difference between Din and shari'ah is this: while Din always was, has been, and still is one and the same, many Shari'ahs were revealed. Some were subsequently cancelled or changed, but without changing the Din. The Din of Nūḥ was the same as that of Ibrāhīm, Mūsā, 'Īsā, Shu'ayb, Hūd, Ṣāliḥ and Muhammad, peace be on them, but their Shari'ahs varied from each other to some extent. The prescribed ways of performing the Prayer and observing the Fast were different. Injunctions about Halal (permissible) and Haram (forbidden), rules of cleanliness and codes of marriage, divorce and inheritance also differed. In spite of this, all were Muslims – the followers of Nūḥ, Irānim, 'Īsā or Mūsā, and we too, are all Muslims. Because Din is one and the same for all. This shows that Din is unaffected by differences in the regulations and laws of the Shari'ah. Din remains the same though precise details of following it differ.

An example will illustrate the difference between Din and Shari'ah. Suppose a master has many servants. If some of them do not acknowledge him as their master nor consider his orders worthy of obedience, they cannot be considered servants at all. But those who acknowledge him as their master, consider it their duty to obey him, clearly belong to the category of servants. The duties they perform and the way they serve him may be different, but they still remain his true servants.

If the master has shown one servant one way to serve him and a different way to another, no one has any right to claim that he alone is a rightful servant and that others are not. Similarly, if one servant understands his master's will in one way and another servant in another way, and both try to do his will as understood by them, then both are equally good servants. Quite possibly one may err in understanding the meaning of a particular directive, but as long as he does not refuse to obey it, no one has a right to brand him as disobedient, or excommunicate him.

Understand clearly this difference between Din and Shari'ah. Before the Prophet, blessings and peace be on him, Allah sent various Shari'ahs through various prophets. One mode of service was ordained through one prophet and another through another prophet. Those who served the Master in these differing ways were all Muslims. Then, when the Prophet came, blessings and peace be on him, the Master declared: Now We abrogate all the previous codes. From now on whoever wants to serve Us must follow the code which We are giving through Our last Messenger.

From then on, no servant has the right to serve according to the previous codes. If he does not accept the new code and continues to follow the old, he is in fact obeying his own dictates, not those of the Master. Such a person can no longer be legitimately called a servant; he becomes, in religious language, an Unbeliever.

Juristic Differences Between Muslims

The first part of the example applies to those who claim to follow the earlier prophets. The second part applies to the followers of the Prophet Muhammad, blessings and peace be on him.

Anyone who believes that the Shari'ah given by him has been sent down by Allah, and therefore must be followed, is a Muslim. One person may understand the injunctions of the Shari'ah in one way and another person in another way, and both may follow them according to their particular understanding. However widely they may differ, both will be able to call themselves servants. For both will be acting in the consciousness that they are doing their Master's bidding.

In such a case, what right has one servant to say that he alone is the genuine servant while the other is not? The most he can argue is that he has understood the correct meaning of his Master's order while the other has not. But this does not give him the authority to expel the latter from the fold of servants (that is, call him an Unbeliever). Anyone who does display such temerity assumes, as it were, the status of the Master. He would seem to be saying, 'Just as it is compulsory for you to obey the Master's order, so also it is compulsory for you to accept my way of understanding. If you fail to do that, I shall, with my own power, dismiss you from the Master's service.'

For this very reason the Prophet, blessings and peace be on him, said: 'Whosoever unjustly brands a Muslim an Unbeliever, his verdict will rebound on him' (*Bukhārī, Muslim*). For, God has made the submission to *His* guidance *the* test of whether or not one is a Muslim. A person who insists upon such submission to his own interpretation and judgement and assumes such powers of dismissal for himself, irrespective of whether God Himself dismisses someone or not, is in fact saying that God alone is not God but that he himself is also a small god. Anyone who makes such a presumptuous assertion runs the danger of becoming an Unbeliever, irrespective of whether or not the other Muslim has in fact acted as an Unbeliever.

Brothers! I hope you now fully understand the important difference between Din and Shari'ah and also comprehend the fact that differences in the modes of serving God do not mean deviation from Din. Of course, a person who follows a particular course must genuinely know and believe that God and the Messenger have actually enjoined him to do what he is doing, and in support of his actions, he should produce authentic evidence from the Book of God or the Sunnah of His Messenger.

Ignoring the Nature of Differences

Consider, now, what great harm is being caused to Muslims by not observing this difference between Din and Shari'ah.

There are several ways of performing Prayers among Muslims. We may rest our hands on our chests, or we may place them on our navels. We may recite Surah al-Fātiḥah while praying behind the Imam, or we may not. We may utter *Amin* loudly, or quietly. Each of us will be following his respective method in full consciousness of the fact that it was followed by the Prophet, blessings and peace be on him, and that we have the evidence to support this claim. Each of us is therefore equally a follower of the Prophet.

But some people take these issues of detail in Shari'ah as fundamental issues of Din itself. They have therefore established their own separate congregations and their own mosques. They have abused each other, forcibly driven their opponents from mosques, fought legal battles and split the Prophet's Ummah into various sects. When even this was not enough to satisfy them, they started, on the slightest of pretexts, labelling each other an Unbeliever, sinner and heretic. They are not happy unless they impose their understanding on everyone else.

The different schools (*madhāhib*) of Ḥanafī, Shāfi'ī, Ahl-Ḥadīth and so on which you see among Muslims all acknowledge the Qur'ān and Hadith as their final authority and derive injunctions from them according to their own understanding. It may be that one school's understanding is correct and another's is incorrect. I myself am a follower of one of these schools and argue with those who are opposed to it in order to explain to them what is correct in my view and prove wrong what I consider to be wrong.

But it is one thing for somebody's understanding to be wrong and it is quite another to expel him from Islam. Every Muslim has the right to follow the Shari'ah according to his understanding. If ten Muslims follow ten different methods, all of them are surely Muslims as long as they believe that they must submit to the law of God. They constitute one Ummah and there is no reason for them to form separate sects. Only those who do not understand this point split the Ummah into different factions for trivial reasons, set apart their congregations and mosques, prevent inter-marriages and social relations and organize their groups as if each one is an Ummah by itself.

Sectarianism

It is impossible to overestimate the harm caused by Muslims by this sectarianism. On the face of it Muslims are one Ummah. In India alone today there are about eighty million of them. If such a big community were really united and worked together to make Allah's guidance supreme, who in the world would have the courage to oppose it? But sectarianism has led this Ummah to be split into hundreds of factions, their hearts sundered from each other. They are incapable of uniting even at times of the gravest crisis. A Muslim belonging to one faction is often more prejudiced against a Muslim belonging to another faction than against a Christian or a Jew. At times, members of one Muslim faction have gone to the extent of siding with unbelievers to humiliate a member of another Muslim faction.

You should not therefore be surprised to see Muslims living in servitude to others. This is what they have earned by their actions. Upon them has descended that punishment which Allah has warned them of:

... [He will] divide you in sects and make you taste the violence of one another (al-An'ām 6: 65).

Dissension, cutting each other's throat, subjugation to tyranny and oppression, all these are forms of God's punishments visited upon Muslims of today throughout the world.

This punishment is very evident in the Punjab today. Here sectarian strife is very Widespread. Consequently, in spite of your numerical majority, you are powerless. If you want to further your well-being, you must demolish these sectarian barriers, live as brothers one unto another and become one united Ummah. There is no basis whatever in God's Shari'ah to make Shī'ah, Sunnī, Ḥanafī, Ahl-Ḥadīth, Deobandī, Barelvī and so on into separate Ummahs. These Ummahs are the product of ignorance. Allah made us only one Ummah: the Ummah Muslimah.

12

True Meaning of 'Ibadah

Brothers in Islam! There is an important word which we Muslims use a lot but understand little. This word is *'Ibādah.* It is very important that we understand its true meaning and significance.

The sole purpose of our creation, the end of our lives, Allah says, is to worship and serve Him alone.

> And I have not created *jinn* and mankind except to worship and serve Me (al-Dhāriyāt 51: 56).

This establishes beyond doubt that you must be fully aware of the meaning of 'Ibadah. Otherwise you will not be able to fulfil the purpose for which you have been created. And anything which does not fulfil its purpose is a failure. If a doctor cannot cure his patient, he may be considered to have failed in his work. If a farmer cannot raise a good crop, he may be held to have failed in his job. Similarly, if you have not been able to fulfil the purpose of your lives, 'Ibadah, you must be judged failures. Listen, therefore, carefully and understand the meaning of 'Ibadah, and constantly remember it, too. On this depends the success or failure of your lives.

Meaning of 'Ibadah

What, then, is worship or 'Ibadah?

The Arabic word *'ibadah* is derived from the same root as the word *'abd,* which means servant and slave. Thus, 'Ibadah means to perform the duties of a servant as does a slave or bondsman. A person is a slave of somebody only if he lives his whole life rendering service and obedience to him and behaves as one should behave to his master. But a person who is supposedly a servant and is being paid for his work but who does not render his master service and obedience as a slave ought, is guilty of disloyalty and rebellion.

How should a slave behave toward s his master?

The *first* duty of a slave is to take only his master as his lord. He should be totally faithful to him alone who sustains, nourishes and protects him and give his loyalty to no one else.

The *second* duty of a slave is to be always obedient to his master, to carry out all his orders meticulously and to refrain from following his own desires or opinions or following anybody else contrary to his master's wishes. A slave is a slave, every moment and in all circumstances. He has no right to choose to obey a particular order and disobey another, or to say he will be a slave when it suits him and ignore his duties for the rest of the time.

The *third* duty of a slave is to revere and adore his master. To express his reverence, he should follow the ways laid down by him. If he is constant and firm in his faithfulness and obedience, he must present himself at whatever time his master calls him for audience.

These are the qualities which together constitute 'Ibadah: *first,* loyalty to one's master; *second,* obedience to him; and, *third,* reverence and adoration for him.

What Allah requires – when He says 'I have not created *jinn* and mankind except to serve and worship Me' – is that we should be loyal, above all, to Him alone and to no one else; we should follow, against everything else, His commandments only; and we should honour and revere Him alone by kneeling and prostrating ourselves. Everywhere in the Qur'ān the word 'Ibadah is used in this sense. This is also the substance of the teachings of our Prophet, and of all the prophets sent by God before him, peace be upon them. Each came with the same message, 'Worship and serve none except Him' (Yūsuf 12: 40): there is only one Sovereign to whom you must be faithful, and that Sovereign is Allah; there is one law which you must obey, and that is the law of Allah; there is only one Being you should worship, and that Being is Allah.

Misunderstanding 'Ibadah

Now look at the following situations.

What would you say about a servant who, instead of performing the duties required of him by his master, just stands in front of him with folded hands and keeps on chanting his name? His master orders him to go and discharge his obligations to his fellow human beings, but he stays where he is. Again and again he bows to his master, salutes him and remains standing up with folded hands. His master instructs him to go and fight against evil to eliminate it, but he does not budge an inch; instead he keeps on prostrating himself before him. His master commands him to cut off the hand of a thief, but the servant, still standing there, recites scores of times in an extremely melodious voice: 'Cut off the hand of the thief, cut off the hand of the thief', without ever trying to establish that order under which the hand of a thief may be cut off.

Would you say that this man was really serving his master? And what would be your verdict if you had servants and one behaved in this fashion? Yet how often you regard as devout worshippers so-called servants of God who behave exactly like this! What, for example, about the man who reads from dawn to dusk the Divine injunctions in the Qur'ān, but never stirs himself to carry them out, chanting instead the name of God on a thousand-bead rosary, praying uninterruptedly and reciting the Qur'ān in a beautiful voice? When you see him doing all this you exclaim: 'What a devout and pious person he is!' You are misled because you do not understand the true meaning of 'Ibadah.

Here is another servant. This one is busy day and night carrying out duties given to him by people other than his master, while he constantly flouts the commands of his real master and tries to hide this by always being present at the appointed hours of audience and losing no chance to sing his praises. If any of you had such a servant, what would you do with him? Would you not throw back his greeting in his face? If he called you 'Master' and 'Lord', would you not retort: 'You are an impertinent liar and a cheat, you take wages from me but work for others. You pretend to call me master but actually serve everybody except me'. This is a matter of simple common sense which we can all easily understand.

But how astonishing that you think the Prayers, Fasting, chanting on rosary-beads, recital of the Qur'ān, the Pilgrimage and Almsgiving of those people are in fact acts of worship, who day and night violate or ignore the laws of God and follow the orders of the unbelievers. Here, again, you are misled because you are unaware of the true meaning of 'Ibadah.

Now look at yet another servant. His uniform is perfectly tailored and always smart, just as desired by his master. He presents himself before his master showing the utmost honour and reverence. Whenever he is given an order, he bows his head and says, 'With all my heart I will obey', as if no one could be more faithful. He is always to the forefront in praising his master. Yet, at the same time, this man is serving the rebels and enemies of his master, participating in the conspiracies they hatch against him and co-operating with them in their efforts to belittle his name. In the darkness of night he commits burglary in his master's house, but in the morning presents himself with folded hands before him like the most faithful of servants.

What would you say about such a servant? Clearly, your verdict would be: he is a hypocrite, a rebel, and disloyal. But what do you call those so-called servants of God who behave just like this? You call them Shaikhs, Mawlanas, Pirs, and so on. You consider them pious and godly men. This is because you have been misled by external trappings such as full beards, dresses above their ankles, prostration marks on their foreheads, their long sessions of the Prayers and their big rosaries of beads. Again, your error has arisen because you have not grasped the meaning of 'Ibadah and religiosity.

Too often you think that just facing the Qiblah with folded hands, bowing with your hands resting on your knees, prostrating yourselves with your face on the ground and uttering a few ritual words is in itself 'Ibadah. You think that just to be hungry and thirsty from morning till evening every day from the first of Ramadan till the appearance of the Shawwal moon is 'Ibadah. You think that a mere verbal recital of some parts or Surahs of the Qur'ān is 'Ibadah. You think that a visit to Makka and circumambulation of the Ka'ba is 'Ibadah. In short, you think 'Ibadah consists of merely performing certain outward worship rituals and ceremonies, and whenever you notice anybody doing these actions, and no more, you think that they have done their duty, they are true worshippers performing 'Ibadah of God, they have thus fulfilled the purport of the verse, 'I have not created *jinn* and mankind except to serve and worship Me.'

'Ibadah, Lifelong Service

But in reality the 'Ibadah for which God has created you and which He has enjoined upon you is something quite different. It is this: you must follow at every step in your lives the law of God and refuse to obey all laws which conflict with His law. Everything you do must accord with the guidance given by God. Only then will your entire lives turn into lives of worship.

In such a life, everything is 'Ibadah: whether you sleep or are awake, whether you eat or drink, whether you work or rest, whether you are silent or talk, are all acts of worship. So much so that in going to your wives and kissing your children, too, you serve God. All these actions which are usually considered secular and worldly become religious, provided that during their performance you observe the limits laid down by God and remain conscious every moment and at every step of what is approved by God (Halal) and what is forbidden by Him (Haram), what is a duty and what must be avoided, which actions please God and which displease Him.

For instance, easy opportunities to earn money in a forbidden way may occur during your life. If you resist this temptation and, in obedience to God, confine yourselves to earning money in approved ways only, then your work is itself worship. And you deserve rewards. And the earnings you bring home for yourselves, your wives, your children and other have-nots will be blessed by Allah. Indeed whatever you do and whatever time you spend in doing His will and in pleasing Him, you worship Him: when you remove from the road a stone or other obstacle which might hurt people; when you nurse an ill person or guide a blind man or help a person in distress; when you avoid lying, gossipping about people behind their backs, making sarcastic remarks and slandering; when you refrain from hurting people; when you talk truthfully and justly.

Real worship of God, therefore, is to follow the way laid down by God and lead lives according to His commandments from childhood to death. There can be no fixed time for this worship; it must be performed all the time. Nor does it have one particular form; in everything you say and do, you must serve God. Since you cannot say: 'I am a servant of God at such a time and I am not a servant of God at such a time', you cannot say that such and such a time is earmarked for God's service and the remaining time is not. If you truly honour and adore, love and fear God, all your actions will be motivated by these feelings and they will *all* constitute worship.

Brothers! You may now ask: 'What then is the position of prescribed worship rituals like the Prayer (Salah), Almsgiving (Zakah), Fasting (Sawm), Pilgrimage (Hajj) and so on?'

These acts of worship, which Allah has enjoined upon us, in reality prepare us for that greater overall 'Ibadah that we have to perform throughout our lives. They are *the* means which turn our lives into lives of worship. Prayer reminds you five times a day that you are slaves of Allah and that Him alone you must serve. Fasting prepares you, for an entire month once every year, for this very service. Almsgiving repeatedly brings home to you the truth that the money you have earned is a gift of God. Do not just spend it on physical pleasures or even solely on material needs; you must render what is due to your Master. Pilgrimage engraves on your hearts such a love and awareness of the majesty of God that once they take root, they remain with you all your lives.

If, by performing all these acts of worship, you grasp their true inner significance and your entire lives are transformed into an unceasing act of worship, then undoubtedly your Prayer is real prayer, your Fast is real fast, your Almsgiving is real charity and your Pilgrimage is real pilgrimage. But if you do not, no purpose is possibly served by merely bowing, kneeling and prostrating yourselves (*ruku* and *sujud*), by spending days in hunger and thirst, by going through the formalities of the Pilgrimage and by setting aside money for the Almsgiving. These worship rituals are like a human body: it is a living human being so long as it has a soul and moves about and does work; but if it is soulless, it is no more than a corpse. A corpse has hands and feet, eyes and nose, but you bury it under the earth because it is devoid of soul. So are worship rites if they are devoid of meaning, if they do not generate love and fear of God, loyalty and obedience to Him.

We should try to find out how each act of ritual worship prepares us for a life spent totally in worship; what a great and wonderful difference each can make to our lives if we perform them in full understanding of their meaning and purpose.

PART III
Salah

13

Meaning and Blessings of the Prayer

Brothers in Islam! The basic and most important act of worship among those which Allah has taught us to perform is Salah, or the Prayer. It prepares us to worship Him in our entire lives – the purpose for which He has created us.

Consider carefully why it is so important, what is its true meaning and significance.

Remembering God

The Prayer is an act of worship. We should, therefore, first recollect what worship means.

Worship means revering, serving and obeying God in our whole lives. Being born as God's servants, we cannot give up serving Him at any time or under any circumstances and still remain His servant as God wanted us to be when He created us. Just as you cannot say that you are creatures of God for a particular time only, so you cannot say that you will spend only a certain amount of time in worshipping Him and be free to spend the rest as you please. You are born to worship Him. Your whole lives should therefore be spent in 'Ibadah, you should not neglect it for a single moment.

It is precisely for this reason that worship does not require giving up the day-to-day world and sitting in a corner chanting

God's name. Worship means that whatever you do in the world should be in accordance with God's guidance. Whether you sleep, are awake, eat, drink or work – in fact, whatever activity you do – you worship Allah if these are done in obedience to Him.

When you are at home with your wives and children, brothers and sisters and relatives, behave towards them exactly as God has laid down. When you talk to your friends and amuse yourselves, remain conscious that you are servants of God. When you go out to work and have dealings with other people, keep in view God's commandments about what behaviour is proper and legitimate and what is not.

When in the dark of night you feel you can commit a sin which nobody in the world can see, then is the time to remember that God is seeing you and it is He, and not your fellow humans, who deserves to be feared. When you find yourselves in a place where you can commit a crime without fear of the police or any witnesses, then again it is time to remember that God sees everything and refrain from doing anything for transient gain which would displease Him. And when following the path of truth and honesty causes you material loss or otherwise puts you at a disadvantage, accept this ungrudgingly in the knowledge that you are pleasing Allah by obeying Him and that your gain from Him will far outweigh any temporary, earthly loss.

Abandoning the world and sitting in secluded places counting rosary beads is, therefore, not real worship at all. Worship is to be engaged in everyday affairs and yet follow the way of God. What does remembering God (*dhikr*) mean? It does not mean merely the continual chanting of 'Allah, Allah!'. The real remembrance of God consists in recalling to mind the name and will of Allah when you are caught up in day-to-day worldly activities. Being engaged in pursuits which could tend to make you forget God and yet not forgetting Him is in fact remembering Him. In this life, where opportunities abound for disobeying God and where temptations of huge profits lurk, you must unfailingly remember God and remain steadfast in following His law. This is the true remembrance of God. This is the kind of remembrance the Qur'ān refers to thus:

> Then, when the Prayer is finished, disperse on earth and seek God's bounty; but remember God often, so that you may attain success (al-Jumu'ah 62: 10).

Blessings of the Prayer

Keep in mind this comprehensive meaning of 'Ibadah and see how the Prayer helps us realize the qualities which are necessary to live in such 'Ibadah, what blessings it confers upon us.

Constant Reminder

It is necessary, *first*, for us to be *constantly* aware that we are servants of God, that every moment of our lives must be dedicated to adoring and obeying Him.

To cultivate and keep alive this awareness is not an easy task, because there is a Satan within you whose voice constantly tells you: 'Follow me and great benefits await you.' Similarly, there are multitudes of Satans outside you who, in various guises, keep on telling you: 'Follow us, otherwise you will be in trouble.' The spell cast by these Satans and their urgings cannot be overcome unless you are reminded continually that you are slaves to none but God.

This is what the Prayer does. When you get up in the morning, the Prayer reminds you of this even before you start your day. When you are busy in your work during the day, it again reminds you of this fact three times. And when you are about to go to bed, you are reminded once again. This is the first blessing of the Prayer. And this is why the Prayer is described as 'Remembrance' in the Qur'ān [al-'Ankabūt 29: 45]. Its true meaning and purpose lie in remembering God.

Sense of Duty

Second, since at every step in your lives you should obey God, it is imperative that you know what is your duty and you cultivate the habit of performing it promptly. If you do not even know what your duty is, how can you ever please God and obey His orders? And, one who understands his duty but, despite his knowledge, due to indiscipline, does not care to perform it, can never be expected to remain prepared and willing to come forward and obey God, every hour of every day, as he must.

Those who have served in the army or police know how they were made to understand and carry out their duties. A bugle is blown several times during the day and night and parades are held at short notice. The purpose of this is to train people to respond and carry out orders. This routine also quickly distinguishes those who are incapable or too lazy to do so. In like manner, the Prayer summons you five times a day. On hearing it, Allah's soldiers must quickly gather from all sides and prove that they are prepared to obey His call. Any Muslims who do not respond when they hear the Adhan show that either they do not understand the importance and meaning of their duty to God or, if they do understand it, they are so useless that they are unfit to remain in the army of Allah.

It was for this very reason that the Prophet, blessings and peace be on him, said that he felt like going and setting fire to the houses of those who did not stir after hearing the Adhan (*Bukhārī, Muslim*). And this is why, in one Hadith, performance of the Prayer is described as a mark distinguishing Islam from Disbelief (*Muslim*).

During the times of the Prophet and his Companions nobody was considered a Muslim unless he joined the congregational Prayer – so much so that even the hypocrites felt compelled to come. They were rebuked not for abandoning the Prayer, but for the half-hearted way in which they used to perform it: 'And when they stand up to pray, they stand up reluctantly, only to be

seen and praised by men, and not remembering God but a little'
(al-Nisā' 4: 42).

You can hardly be considered true Muslims, this shows, if
you do not perform the Prayer. For Islam is not a mere matter
of doctrinal faith; it is a way of life to be lived in practice. Islam
means surrendering to God and fighting against Disbelief and
evil every minute of your lives. Its essential message is: always
remain prepared to obey God at a moment's notice.

The Prayer, five times a day, tests again and again whether
you are so prepared. Those who claim to be Muslims are tested
to see whether they can put their claim into practice. If they
cannot, their faith is of little value to Islam. For only they find
the Prayer hard and unwelcome whose hearts are devoid of
reverence to God and who are not ready to live in submission
to Him. 'And it [the Prayer], indeed, is hard save for the humble
who know they shall meet their Lord' (al- Baqarah 2: 45). That
they find the Prayer too difficult to perform is itself proof enough
that they have no faith in God, no certainty about meeting Him,
and are unwilling or unprepared to serve and obey Him.

The sense of duty to God and being ever-prepared to obey
Him is the second blessing that the Prayer confers upon you.

God-consciousness

Third, consciousness of God – being in His presence, His
love and His fear, strength to avoid whatever may displease
Him – needs to be kept alive constantly in our hearts. You
cannot practise Islam unless you believe that God is seeing
you all the time and everywhere, that God is aware of all your
actions, that God sees you even in darkness, and that God is
with you even when you are alone. It is possible to hide from
the world but not from God, to escape from the punishments of
the world, but not from His punishments. It is this awareness,
this feeling, this belief, which restrains man from disobeying
God and which motivates him to observe all the limits Allah has
laid down for his life. Without this awareness you cannot live

like a true Muslim lives. Allah has enjoined upon you praying five times a day precisely to help strengthen this awareness in the hearts of the faithful. He has Himself thus described this blessing: 'Surely the Prayer restrains from all that is shameful and wrong' (al-'Ankabūt 29: 45).

This awareness becomes deeply embedded in you through the Prayer. For instance, you may perform the Prayer only when you are clean and have done the ablution (*wuḍū'*). But who is to know if you have not washed, or if your clothes are unclean, or if you are just pretending to have done *wuḍū'*? No one. But you never do such a thing because you are sure that your actions will not be hidden from God. Similarly, no one will know if you do not in fact recite at all those parts of the Prayer which are supposed to be said in a low voice. But you do not 'cheat' in this way. Why? Because you believe that God hears everything; He is closer to you than your jugular vein. And, you perform the Prayer even when you are alone – although there would be nobody to know that you had not performed it – because you fully realize that it is impossible to hide any crime from Him.

That is how the Prayer evokes and sustains in the heart of man fear of God and the belief that he lives in His presence. How can you worship and serve God and remain loyal to Him throughout the twenty-four hours of the day and night unless this fear and this awareness are revived continuously in your hearts? Devoid of this feeling, how can you embrace goodness and avoid evil in your daily lives for the sake of God alone?

Making you ever-conscious of God is the third blessing of the Prayer.

Knowledge of God's Law

Fourth, to worship God you must know what His law is; without knowing it you clearly cannot follow it. Prayer is the instrument through which this knowledge is fostered. The parts of the Qur'ān that are recited in the Prayer are intended to teach you the law of God. The Friday congregation and the sermon (*khuṭubah*) are also designed to provide you with opportunities to learn Islamic teachings. It is your own fault if you do not take the trouble to find out the meaning of what you are reading in the Prayer. It is no use complaining that you do not understand if you have not bothered to try. On the other hand, it is unfortunate that Friday sermons are delivered in a manner which does little to impart the knowledge of Islam.

Collective Life

It is necessary, *fifth*, that no Muslim should be left alone and on his own in the tumult of life, while worshipping God. Muslims should come together to form strong communities to help each other in their life mission: serving God, obeying Him, observing His law and promulgating it in the world.

Those who are faithful to God and those who reject Him are always arrayed against each other; the struggle between 'surrender' and 'rebellion' is never-ending. The rebels break the laws of God and enforce in their place satanic laws. Individually, Muslims cannot effectively resist this process, and it is therefore necessary for the true servants of God to join forces. The Prayer is central to the establishment of this collective strength. Congregational Prayer five times a day, the Friday congregation, the congregation of two 'Id festivals – all these together make you like a strong wall and create in you that singleness of purpose, cohesiveness and real unity, which are necessary to make you helpers of each other in the cause of Allah in your day-to-day lives.

That the Prayer generates and consolidates the social cohesiveness in the Ummah is its fifth blessing.

14

What We Say in the Prayer

Brothers in Islam! The Prayer prepares us for 'Ibadah, for serving and obeying God. Even if you do not understand the full purport of the words you recite, it helps keep alive in your hearts the fear of God and the awareness that He is with you everywhere and He is watching over you; it helps remind you, too, that one day you, along with all mankind, will have to appear before God to give an account of your lives. The Prayer keeps ever-fresh the consciousness that you are the slaves of God, and of God only, and that it is only to God that obedience and worship are due.

It goes without saying that this faith is all the deeper when you fully appreciate the meaning of the words you are reciting in the Prayer. Then, the power of Prayer is capable of reshaping your entire lives – in thoughts, in words and in deeds.

It is therefore important to know the meaning of what you say in your Prayers.

Adhan and its Effects

First take the *Adhān*, by which you are summoned five times a day in the following words:

Allāhu akbar, Allāhu akbar

Allah is the Greatest, Allah is the Greatest.

Ashhadu an lā ilāha illa 'llāh

I bear witness that there is no god but Allah.

Ashhadu anna Muhammadu 'r-rasūlu 'llāh

I bear witness that Muhammad is the Messenger of Allah.

Ḥayya 'ala 'ṣ-ṣalāh

Come to the Prayer.

Ḥayya 'ala 'l-falāḥ

Come to the well-being.

Allāhu akbar, Allāhu akbar

Allah is the Greatest, Allah is the Greatest.

Lā ilāha ilia 'llāh

There is no god but Allah.

How powerful the Call and how beautiful the words! And how they constantly and powerfully remind us of how bogus are the claims to greatness made by other beings. On earth and in the heavens there is only one Being who is worthy of worship. In His worship alone lies our well-being in this world and in the Hereafter. Who can fail to be moved on hearing this voice? How can anyone who has faith in his heart hear so powerful a call without wanting to rush and bow his head before his Master?

Wuḍū': Ablution

On hearing the call of Adhan you get up, go and wash yourselves. What does this show? It makes you realize that having an audience with the Lord of all the worlds is very different from everything else you do. Unless you are clean, your clothes are clean, you have performed *wuḍū'*, you are not worthy of entering His presence. Then, in the course of *wuḍū'*, while washing your limbs, you constantly remember Allah. After finishing it you recite the prayer taught by the Messenger of Allah, blessings and peace be on him. Thus not only your limbs but your hearts are washed clean. Look at the words of this prayer:

> *Ashhadu an lā ilāha illa 'llāh waḥdahū lā sharīka lah,*
> *wa ashhadu anna Muhammadan 'abduhū wa rasūluh*

I bear witness that there is no god but Allah; He alone is God, none is His partner. I bear witness that Muhammad is God's slave and Messenger.

> *Allāhumma 'j'alnī mina 't-tawwābīna wa 'j'alnī mina*
> *'l-mutaṭahhirīn*

O God! Make me among those who repent and keep themselves pure.

Niyyah: Intention

After this, you stand up for Salah. Your faces are directed towards the Qiblah. The first words you utter are:

> *Allāhu akbar*

Allah is the Greatest.

Proclaiming His sovereignty over everything, you raise your hands to your ears as if you have renounced the world and whatever is in it. You, then, fold your hands; now you are standing reverently before your Lord. Next you make the following submissions.

Tasbīḥ: Glorification

You glorify and praise Allah thus:

Subḥānaka 'llāhumma wa biḥamdika wa tabāraka 'smuka wa ta'ālā jadduka wā lā ilāha ghayruk

Glory be to Thee, O God, and all the praise that is Thine. Blessed is Thy name and exalted is Thy majesty. There is no god but Thee.

Ta'awwudh: Seeking Refuge

You now seek His protection:

A 'ūdhu bi 'llāhi mina 'sh-shayṭani 'r-rajim

I seek refuge in God from Satan, the rejected.

Bismillah: In His Name

You then seek His blessings and help by invoking His name:

Bismi 'llāhi 'r-Raḥmāni 'r-Raḥīm

I begin in the name of God who is Most-merciful, the Mercy-giving.

Ḥamd: Praise and Thanks

You praise Him," thank Him, and seek from Him the guidance for your lives. This is what we do in Surah al-Fātiḥah, the opening Surah in the Qur'ān:

Al-ḥamdu li 'llahi Rabbi 'l-'ālamīn

Praise be to God, Lord of the worlds.

Ar-Raḥmāni 'r-Raḥīm

The Most-merciful, the Mercy-giving.

Maliki yawmi 'd-dīn

Master of the Day of Judgement.

Iyyāka na'budu wa iyyāka nasta'īn

Thee alone do we worship and from Thee alone we seek help.

Ihdina'ṣ-ṣirāṭa 'l-mustaqīm

Direct us on the straight path.

Ṣirāṭa 'l-ladhīna an'amta 'alayhim

The path of those whom Thou hast favoured.

Ghayri 'l-maghdūbi 'alayhim wa la 'ḍ-ḍāllīn

Not those who earn Thy anger nor those who go astray.

Āmīn!

O God! Let it be so. O Lord! Grant this our prayer.

The Qur'ān Reading

Then you recite some parts of the Qur'ān, each of which is full of wisdom and beauty. There are instructions, admonitions and lessons as well as directions to guide you on the same straight path for which you have just prayed in Surah al-Fātiḥah. Let us look at the meanings of some of those which you often recite in your Prayers.

Surah al-'Aṣr (103)

Wa 'l-'aṣr, inna 'l-insāna la fī khusr

157

By the fleeing time! Surely man is in [a state of] loss.

Illa 'l-ladhīna āmanū wa 'amilu 's-ṣāliḥāt

Except those who believe and do good works.

Wa tawāṣaw bi 'l-ḥaqqi wa tawāṣaw bi 's-ṣabr

And enjoin upon one another to keep to Truth and enjoin upon one another to be steadfast.

This Surah teaches us that the only way for man to be saved from loss, failure and destruction is to attain to faith and do good works. Additionally, the faithful must form a group wherein they strive together and help each other in remaining steadfast in the cause of Truth.

Surah al-Mā 'ūn (107)

Ara'ayta 'l-ladhī yukadhdhibu bi 'd-dīn

Have you seen him who gives the lie to judgement.

Fa dhālika 'l-ladhī yadu"u 'l-yatīm

That is he who pushes away the orphan.

Wa lā yaḥuḍḍu 'alā ṭa'ami 'l-miskīn

And urges not to feed the needy.

Fa waylul li 'l-muṣallīna 'l-ladhīna hum 'an ṣalātihim sāhun, alladhīna hum yura'ūna wa yamna'ūna 'l-mā'ūn

Woe, then, unto those praying ones who are unmindful of their Prayer, those who want to be seen, and refuse [even] small kindnesses.

This Surah teaches us that without faith in the Hereafter, which is the basis of Islam, we can never walk on the path of God and fulfil our duties towards our fellow human beings.

Also, a faith which does not lead to responsible and kindly sharing with others is no real faith.

Surah al-Humazah (104)

> *Waylul li kulli humuzati-ni l-lumazah*
>
> Woe unto every slanderer, fault-finder!
>
> *A 'l-ladhī jama'a malan wa 'addadah*
>
> to him who amasses wealth and counts it over
>
> *Yaḥsabu anna mālahū akhladah*
>
> thinking that his wealth will make him live forever!
>
> *Kallā la yunbadhanna fi 'l-ḥuṭamah*
>
> Nay, but he shall surely be thrown into the Crusher;
>
> *Wa mā adrāka ma 'l-ḥuṭamah*
>
> And what could convey to you what the Crusher is?
>
> *Naru 'llahi 'l-muqadatu 'l-latī taṭṭali'u 'ala 'l-af'idah*
>
> The kindled fire of God, which roars over the hearts
>
> *Innahā 'alayhim muṣadatun, fī 'amadin mumaddadah*
>
> Surely, it closes in upon them in endless columns.

This Surah, again, instructs us in important social attitudes. It castigates those who engage in slandering others, spreading false reports. Love of worldly wealth is what leads us to treat others with contempt. But that wealth we will have to leave behind, only to see it again as a fire raging in our hearts.

In short, whichever Surahs or Ayahs of the Qur'ān you recite in the Prayer they impart some kind of instruction or guidance and point out to you those commandments of God which you should follow.

Rukū': Bowing Down

After reciting these instructions you say *Allāhu akbar* and perform *rukū'*. Bending down before your Master with your hands resting on your knees, you repeat (either three or five or seven times):

Subḥāna Rabbiya 'l-'azīm

Glory be to my Lord, the Magnificent

Then you stand up straight and say:

Sami'a 'llahu li man ḥamidah

Allah listens to him who praises Him.

Sujūd: Prostration

Then, again saying *Allāhu akbar*, you prostrate yourselves with forehead on the ground, and repeatedly utter:

Subḥāna Rabbiya 'l-a'lā

Glory to my Lord, the Most High.

At-taḥiyyāt: Salutation

Then you raise your heads, saying *Allāhu akbar*, sit reverently and say:

At-taḥiyyātu li 'llāhi wa 'ṣ-ṣalawātu wa 'ṭ-ṭayyibāt

To God belong all greetings of praise, all prayers, all good deeds.

As-salāmu 'alayka ayyuha 'n-nabiyyu wa raḥmatu 'llāhi wa barakātuh

Peace be on you, O Prophet, and mercy of God and His blessing.

As-salamu 'alaynā wa 'alā 'ibādi 'llāhi 'ṣ-ṣāliḥīn

Peace be on us and on all true servants of God.

Ashhadu an lā ilāha ilia 'llāh wa ashhadu anna Muhammadan 'abduhū wa rasūluh

I bear witness that there is no god but Allah and I bear witness that Muhammad is His servant and His Messenger.

While giving this testimony you raise your first finger: this symbolizes the renewal of your pledge and commitment to the life of witness that you are required to live. While uttering it you must give special attention and emphasis to it.

Ṣalāt 'ala 'n-nabiy: Blessings Upon the Prophet

After this you call down blessings upon the Prophet Muhammad, blessings and peace be on him:

Allāhumma ṣalli 'alā Muhammadin wa 'alā āli Muhammadin kamā ṣallayta 'alā Ibrāhīma wa 'alā āli Ibrāhīm, innaka ḥamīdun majīd. Allāhumma bārik 'alā Muhammadin wa 'alā āli Muhammadin kamā bārakta 'alā Ibrāhīma wa 'alā āli Ibrāhīm, innaka ḥamidun majīd

O God! Have mercy on Muhammad and his people just as Thou blessed Ibrāhīm and his people. Indeed Thou art adorned with the best qualities and art sublime. O God! Bless Muhammad and his people just as You blessed

161

Ibrāhīm and his people. Most certainly Thou art adorned with the best qualities and art sublime.

Seeking Protection

The whole Salah is an act of prayer, but towards the end you make a special prayer seeking His protection from all kinds of evils that might afflict you.

Allāhumma innī a'ūdhu bika min 'adhābi jahannam, wa a'udhu bika min 'adhābi 'l qabr, wa a'udhu bika min fitnati 'l-masīḥi 'd-dajjāl, wa a'ūdhu bika min fitnati 'l-maḥyā wa 'l-mamāt, wa a'ūdhu bika min 'l-ma'thimi wa 'l-maghrim

O God! I seek Your protection from punishment in Hell, and I seek Your protection from punishment in the grave, and I seek Your protection from the mischief of *al-masīḥi ˗'d-dajjāl*, and I seek Your protection from the trials of life and death, and I seek Your protection from sins and from indebtedness.

Salām: Greetings

After reciting the above *Du'ā'*, the Prayer is complete. Now you have to return from the audience with your Master. How do you do this? The first thing you do on your return is to turn your heads to the right and to the left and pray for the safety and blessings of all those present and everything in the world:

As-salāmu 'alaykum wa raḥmatu 'llāh

Peace be on you and the mercy of God.

This symbolizes good tidings that you have brought for the world on your return from the presence before God.

The above is the Salah which you offer at dawn before you start work. At noon you present yourselves again. In the afternoon you offer the same Salah again and repeat it immediately after sunset. Finally, before going to bed, you present yourselves for the last time before your Master.

Du'ā' Qunūt

The concluding part of this Salah consists of *witr*. In the last *rak'ah* of the day, which turns all the *rak'ahs* you have prayed into an odd number, you make an important and comprehensive covenant with your Master. This is called *Du'ā' qunūt*. The meaning of *qunūt* is affirmation of humility, subservience and service before God. Listen carefully to the words with which you make your pledge:

Allāhumma innā nasta'īnuka wa nastaghfiruka wa nu'minu bika wa natawakkalu 'alayka wa nuthnī 'alayka 'l-khayr kullahū wa nashkuruka wa la nakfuruka wa nakhla'u wa natruku man yafjuruk

O God! We seek help from Thee; we ask Thee for guidance; we seek Thine forgiveness; we have faith in Thee; we put our trust in Thee; we give all good praises to Thee; we thank Thee, and do not commit ungratefulness; we abandon and leave everyone who disobeys Thee.

Allāhumma iyyāka na'budu wa laka nuṣallī wa nasjudu wa ilayka nas'ā wa naḥfid, wa narjū raḥmataka wa nakhshā 'adhābaka inna 'adhābaka bi 'l-kuffāri mulḥiq

O God! Thee only do we worship. For Thee alone we perform the Prayer and before Thee alone prostrate ourselves. All our endeavours and strivings are directed towards Thee, all our goals are centred on Thee. We hope to receive Thy mercy and fear Thy punishment.

Certainly Thy dire punishment will befall only those who are disbelievers.

Character-building

Brothers! The call of the Adhan summons you five times a day to the presence of the Lord of the universe; five times a day you put everything aside to rush to Him; before every Prayer you purify your bodies and souls with wudu'; and you are fully aware of the meaning of the things you are saying during the Prayer. In such circumstances is it not inevitable that the fear of God will arise in your hearts, that you will feel ashamed to break God's commandments, that your sins will weigh heavily on your consciences? How, then, when you return to your work after the Prayer, can you justify telling lies, acting dishonestly, usurping others' rights, taking or giving bribes, paying or levying interest, and committing indecent or illegal acts? And how, after doing any of these things, can you possibly go back to God at the next Prayer and seriously reaffirm your obedience to Him? Seriously say, thirty-six times a day, 'Thee alone we worship, Thee alone we ask for help', and afterwards ask favours of others in worship?

Properly understood and performed, Salah must improve your morals and, where necessary, fundamentally change your lives. This is why Allah emphasizes: 'Surely Prayer restrains [man] from all that is shameful and wrong'. If it does *not*, the reason lies in you, not in the Prayer. It is not the fault of soap and water that coal is black.

Perhaps one great obstacle to Prayer doing its purifying work is that you may not fully understand or give serious attention to the words you recite in Arabic. A little extra effort in learning by heart these recitations in our own language may bring you rich reward.

15

Blessings of the Congregational Prayer

Brothers in Islam! That the Prayer as such has extraordinary power to make us attain to greater and greater heights of obedience and worship is quite obvious. Consider now how much more enriched it becomes, how greatly its efficacy increases in transforming us, when the Prayer is performed in congregation. Indeed in this one single act of Prayer God has given us His choicest gift.

But, first, recollect what worship is and how the Prayer prepares us for it. Worship means making yourselves slaves of God, living in submission to His will, and remaining always ready to obey Him. The qualities that enable you to attain to this state of worship are all developed by the Prayer. These are: consciousness of being a slave to God; faith in God, in His Messenger and in His Book; belief in the life to come; fear of God; awareness that God knows everything and is always close to you; strength of will and preparedness to obey Him; and knowledge of His commandments.

Private Worship of God

Further reflection will show you that an individual, however perfect he may be, cannot worship God as is His due unless other servants of God join him. You cannot obey all the injunctions of God until all those people with whom you have to live day by day, and with whom you have to deal continually, become your partners in this worship. Man is not alone in this world: his whole life is bound in a thousand and one relationships with his family members, business associates, friends, neighbours and acquaintances. Worship equally encompasses all these relationships just as it grasps his inner self. If all these people unite in living by the will of God, all of them can succeed in becoming His faithful servants. But if they are, collectively, bent on disobedience or if they do not support each other in following the commands of God, then will it not be virtually impossible for a lone individual to submit his whole life to the law of God?

Careful reading of the Qur'ān shows that God does not desire that simply you, as lone individuals, should become loyal and obedient to Him. This is not enough. You should strive to bring the whole world under God, to spread His word, and implement His laws. Wherever the rule of Satan prevails, you must try to root it out. Let God alone, and no one else, be the Sovereign in man's life.

This enormous duty entrusted by Allah cannot be performed by one Muslim alone; nor can hundreds of thousands of Muslims, if they remain individuals, be effective against the forces of the servants of Satan. You must, therefore, work together, single-mindedly, but not singly, to fulfil your noble mission.

This entails not merely that you become united, but that you become one, knit together. Your mutual relations should be established on a harmonious basis, without strife and discord. You should obey your leaders and fully understand the limitation of such obedience: where to obey and where to disobey.

See how the congregational Prayer develops all these necessary qualities.

Assembling on One Call

First, as the Adhan summons you to the Prayer, you put everything aside and go to the mosque. The mobilization of Muslims from all sides on hearing this call and their gathering at one centre creates in them a sense of discipline as is found in an 'army'. The sound of a 'bugle' tells 'soldiers' that their 'commander' is calling them; their immediate thought is to obey the call and assemble at a previously agreed place. And so they do. The army adopts such a system to ingrain in every soldier the habit of obedience, both at individual and group levels, and to weld them into a cohesive team. Thus if they ever face armed combat it will be as a unit with identical objectives. If soldiers, however good they may be individually at fighting, however well trained and brave, fight with each fighting his own battle, a platoon of fifty soldiers of the enemy can defeat one thousand such brave soldiers by picking them off individually.

For exactly the same reason, you are required to assemble for the Prayer five times a day on hearing the call of the Adhan, leaving behind everything. But, the resemblance ends here. Beyond this, you, as Muslims, are the army of God and the duty of this army is much harder and radically different than that of any other army in the world. For other armies, wars are fought on one front at a time, and for selfish ends. But the army of God has to wage perpetual war, and that too, against the forces of Satan, within their selves and in the world at large. Gathering five times a day at the sound of the Divine 'bugle' is a sign of its constant readiness for this continuing battle. In view of the gigantic task they face, this strict discipline should look easy.

Purposeful Assembly

Gathering in the mosque, then, itself yields many benefits: here you meet each other, come to recognize each other, and come to know each other. And what makes you come close to one another? You come together as slaves of God, followers of one

Prophet, believers in one Book, with a single objective in life, both inside and outside the mosque. Such acquaintance, such unity, and such attachment automatically leaven and quicken in you the feeling that you are all one community, soldiers of the same army, brothers unto each other. Your interests, your aims, your losses and gains, are the same; and your lives are bound in with one another.

Fellowship

Again, you see and meet each other not like enemies or strangers, but like friends and brothers. As such, when you notice that one brother is in ragged clothes, another seems unhappy, another does not have enough to eat, while others are disabled, crippled or blind, then inevitably compassion is aroused in your hearts. Those of you who are well-off will help the poor and needy; the afflicted will find the courage to approach the rich; you will visit those who, for some reason, cannot get to the mosque; and if one of our brothers dies you will also join in his funeral prayer and share the grief of the bereaved family. All these things strengthen the spirit of mutual affection and make you mutual helpers.

The Sacred Purpose

Think further: you have gathered at a sacred place for a sacred purpose. This is not an assembly of thieves, drunkards, gamblers, or exploiters, but a gathering of slaves of Allah for the purpose of worshipping Allah in Allah's house. In such a setting, a sincere person would, automatically, feel ashamed of his sins. But his shame would be overwhelming and he would particularly want to repent if any of those who were affected by his sin or who witnessed it were gathered with him. Indeed, the blessings of congregational Prayer will multiply manifold if you also know how to counsel each other and help each other in correcting yourselves, with sympathy, love and understanding.

Individual deficiences will then easily be removed and the whole community will quickly grow together in virtue and piety.

Brotherhood

This is how merely getting together to pray benefits you. But there are many more blessings in the way the congregational Prayers are performed.

You stand in a row shoulder to shoulder with each other. No one is higher or lower in status than his neighbour. In the Divine court, in the presence of God, you all belong to one class, you all have the same status. Nobody feels polluted if a fellow-worshipper's hand or body touches him. We are all equally pure because we are all human beings. We are all slaves of one God and believers in one Din.

All ethnic and linguistic prejudices are also* destroyed. Although there are differences among Muslims of family, tribe and country – someone is Sayyid, someone is Pathan, someone is Rajput, someone is Jat, someone belongs to one country and someone to another, some speak one language and some another – yet all stand in one row, worshipping the One God. This signifies that you all are one people, belong to one nation. Divisions on family, tribal or national lines have no basis whatever. What binds you together is that you all serve and worship God. When you are one in the Prayer, why should you be divided about other things?

Uniformity in Movements

Again, when you stand shoulder to shoulder with each other, you look like an army presenting itself for service before its monarch. By standing in a line and by making movements in unison, a remarkable spirit of unity develops in your minds. You are made to do this practice, to become one in the service of God, in such a manner that all of you raise your hands together and move your feet together as if you are not ten, twenty, one hundred or one thousand people, but have become one person.

Uniformity in Prayers

What do you do after thus standing together in one line? With one voice you submit to your Master:

Iyyāka na'budu wa iyyāka nasta'īn

Thee alone do *we* worship; Thee alone do *we* ask for help.

Ihdina 's-sirāta 'l-mustaqīm

Guide us to the straight path.

Also:

Rabbanā laka 'l ḥamd

Our God! All praise is for Thee only.

And:

As-salāmu 'alaynā wa 'alā 'ibādi 'llāhi 's-sālihīn

Peace be on us and on all true servants of God.

Then, as you finish the Prayer, you pray thus for peace, mercy and grace upon each other:

As-salāmu 'alaykum wa raḥmatu 'allāh

Peace be on you *all*, and the mercy of God.

This means that all of us wish each other well. Everyone unites to pray to one Master for the well-being of all. None of us is alone and by himself. None of us asks for everything for himself only. Everybody's wish is that God's benevolence be bestowed on all, that all be granted the ability to walk on the one straight path and that all share together the blessings of God. In this way the Prayer unites your hearts, creates harmony in your thoughts and develops among you a relationship of well-wishing towards each other.

Leadership

Now remember that we never offer the congregational Prayer without an Imam who leads the congregation. Even when two men pray together, one of them will be Imam and the other follower. Once the congregation (Jamā'ah) has been formed, it is strictly prohibited to perform the Prayer outside it. If you do, your Prayer will be invalid. Latecomers must join the congregation behind the same Imam.

All these teachings are not meant for the Prayer only. In fact, they impart a very important lesson: if you want to live as Muslims, live as you pray: united and organized. You cannot be an organized community at all unless you have an Imam. Once you are organized, to secede from it means that your lives have ceased to be the lives of Muslims.

Nature and Qualities of Leadership

A Muslim's entire life is a life of prayer; the entire earth, for him, is a 'mosque' where only one God is to be worshipped. The relation between the Imam and his followers within the congregational Prayer has therefore been designed to teach us important lessons about leadership: how you should relate to your leaders outside the mosque, what their duties and their rights are; how you should obey them, and in what matters; what you should do if they make mistakes; to what extent you are obliged to follow them when they go wrong; on what occasions you have the right and duty to point out their errors; when you can demand that they correct their mistakes; and, at what juncture you can remove them from leadership. How to fashion your organized and communal living is something you can learn about five times a day in any small mosque.

Consider only a few obvious and important principles regarding an Imam and the guidance they provide us in our macro-life.

Piety and Virtue

One: An Imam must be the best in character, piety and righteousness. He must have greater knowledge of Islam, especially of the Qur'ān, than others. He should be of mature years. The Prophet, blessings and peace be on him, has also explained which of these qualities is more important than the other. This tells you, too, which attributes you should keep in view when choosing a leader for a community or state.

Majority Representation

Two: An Imam should be liked and respected by the majority of the congregation; none should lead the Prayer against their wishes. Here again is an important principle for electing a leader.

Sympathy and Compassion

Three: An Imam should lead the congregation in Prayer in such a way that no trouble is caused even to the old in the congregation. He should not make lengthy recitations nor make long *rukū'* and *sujūd*, which may suit only the young, strong and healthy and those with plenty of leisure time. He should take note also of those who are old, sick and weak and those who are busy in their work. The Prophet, blessings and peace be on him, set an example of such kindness and compassion and love: if he heard children crying while he was leading the congregation in Prayer, he used to shorten it so that their mothers, if they were behind him, could leave quickly (*Bukhārī, Muslim*).

Vacating Office

Four: If an Imam meets with an accident while leading the Prayer, he must immediately hand over his office to one of the men behind. This means that it is obligatory on a nation's leader too to resign when he feels unable to carry out his functions. In this there is no shame, nor should selfishness prevent him from doing so.

Obedience to Leaders

Five: The actions of an Imam should be strictly followed. To make a move before he moves is strictly prohibited, so much so that, according to one Hadith, a person who bends or prostrates himself before the Imam does will be raised after death as an ass (*Bukhārī, Muslim*). Here citizens of a nation have been given a lesson on how they should obey those who govern them.

Criticizing and Correcting Mistakes

Six: An Imam may make a mistake in Salah. For example, he may rise when he should sit, or sit when he should rise. Such errors must be pointed out to him with the phrase, *'Subḥānallāh'* (Glory be to Allah). To say *Subḥānallāh* when the Imam commits a mistake means: Allah alone is pure, holy and above error; as you are a human being it is not surprising that you have made a mistake, but correct yourself. Thus warned, it is incumbent on the Imam to correct his mistake without any hesitation or discomfort, without any feeling of loss of prestige.

If, after this notice of correction, the Imam feels confident that what he did was right he can continue as he thinks fit, and in such an eventuality the duty of the congregation is to follow him in spite of knowing that he is wrong. After finishing the Salah the followers have the right to try to convince the Imam of his mistake and to demand from him that he conduct the Salah afresh.

No Obedience in Sin

Seven: This procedure is limited to situations which involve minor mistakes. But if the Imam, contrary to the Prophet's Sunnah, changes the method of the Salah, or knowingly recites the Qur'ān incorrectly in the Salah, or, while conducting it, indulges in acts of Disbelief or Shirk, or commits a clear sin, it is incumbent on the members of the *Jamā 'ah* immediately to break away from the congregation and discontinue the Salah.

In all the above seven points concerning the congregational Prayer, striking parallels can be drawn between the relationship of an Imam and his followers and a head of state and the citizens of that state.

16

Has the Prayer Lost its Power?

Brothers in Islam! Undoubtedly you often ask yourselves: Why is it that the Prayer, good and beneficial as it is, seems to make no difference to our lives? Why does it neither improve our morals, nor transform us into a force dedicated to Allah? Why do we continue to live disgraced and subjugated?

The usual answer will be that you are not offering the Prayer regularly or in the manner prescribed by Allah and the Messenger. Such an answer may not satisfy you. I shall therefore try to explain the matter in some detail.

Parable of the Clock

Look at the clock fixed to the wall: there are lots of small parts in it, joined to each other. When you wind it, all the parts start working and, as these parts move, the result appears on the clock face outside it which you observe. Both hands move to denote each second and each minute. The purpose of the clock is to indicate correct time. All those parts which are necessary for this purpose have been fitted together and the winding system has been made so that each of them moves as required. Only when all the parts have been assembled correctly and the clock wound up properly will it begin fulfilling the purpose for which it is made.

If you do not wind it, it will not show the time. If you wind it but not according to the prescribed method, it will stop or, even if it works, it will not give the correct time. If you remove some of the parts and then wind it, nothing will happen. If you replace some of the parts with those of a sewing machine and then wind it, it will neither indicate the time nor sew the cloth. If you keep all the parts inside the case but disconnect them, then no part will move even after winding it up. The presence of all the parts will not serve the purpose for which the clock is made because you will have disrupted their arrangement as well as their connection.

In all these situations, both the existence of the clock and the act of winding it become useless, although an observer from a distance cannot say that it is not a clock or that you are not winding it. He will surely consider that it is a clock and will expect it to be useful as a clock. Similarly, when from a distance he observes you winding it, he will take it as a genuine effort on your part to do the job, hoping to notice the result which comes from winding the clock. But how can this expectation be fulfilled when what looks like a clock from a distance has in reality lost its 'existence'?

Aim of Muslim Ummah

Imagine Islam like this clock. Just as the purpose of the clock is to indicate the correct time, so the aim of Islam is that you should live in this world, as the vicegerents of God, as witnesses of God unto mankind and as standard-bearers of truth. You must yourselves follow the commandments of God and bring all other people under Him:

> You are indeed the best community brought forth for mankind: you enjoin the doing of right and forbid the doing of wrong, and you believe in God (Āl 'Imrān 3:110).

> And thus We have made you a just community, that you might be witnesses unto mankind (al-Baqarah 2: 143).

God has promised those of you who believe and do righteous deeds that He will surely make you to accede to power on earth (al-Nūr 24: 55).

And fight them, until there is no rebellion [against God], and all submission is to God alone (al-Anfāl 8: 39).

Wholeness of Islamic Teachings

To fulfil this purpose, various parts as were required, like those of the clock, have been brought together in Islam. Beliefs and principles of morality; rules for day-to-day conduct; the rights of God, of His slaves, of one's own self, of everything in the world which you encounter; rules for earning and spending money; laws of war and peace; principles of government and limits of obedience to it – all these are parts of Islam. As in a clock, they are linked to each other in such a way that as soon as the winding is done, every part starts moving and, with the movement of all these parts, the desired result is obtained. Rule of God's law in the world, domination of Islam, start manifesting just as, with the movement of the parts of the clock in front of you, the time appears on its face.

In order to fasten together different parts of the clock, screws and small pieces of metal have been used. Similarly, to join all the parts of Islam together, there is an arrangement called the *Jamā 'ah* or organization. Muslims should organize themselves, and have leaders equipped with proper knowledge and endowed with *taqwā*; the brains should help them and the limbs should obey them, as they all strive to live under God.

When all the parts have been brought together and properly assembled, regular winding is necessary to set them in motion and to continue their movement: Salah which is offered five times a day provides that winding, creating the energy which sets an Islamic life in motion. Cleaning this clock is also necessary: fasting observed for thirty days a year cleanses hearts and morals. Lubrication, too, is required: Zakah is like the oil which is applied to its parts once a year. Then it is also necessary to overhaul it periodically: Hajj is that overhauling which should be performed at least once in a lifetime. And the more often it is done, the better.

Abusing the Clock

The processes of winding, cleaning, lubricating and overhauling are of use only when all the parts are present in the frame, when they are linked in the order designed by the clock-maker, and when all are so trained that immediately on winding they start moving and begin showing results.

Alas, today the situation has become very different. For a start, the very *Jamā'ah,* the organizational structure, which was supposed to link the parts of the clock together has ceased to exist. The result is that all the fittings have come apart, each has gone its own way. Everybody does whatever takes his fancy. There is nobody to question anything. Everyone is autonomous. If someone wants to follow the Islamic code, he can; if he does not want to, he need not.

Since even this so-called freedom has not satisfied you, you have pulled out many parts of the clock and in their place put anything and everything: a spare part from a sewing machine, perhaps, or from a factory or from the engine of a car. You call yourselves Muslims, yet you render loyal service to Disbelief, yet you take interest, you insure your lives, you file false law suits, your daughters, sisters and wives are forsaking Islamic manners and your children are being given secular materialistic educations. Some have become disciples of Gandhi; others are following Lenin. Which un-Islamic gadget is there that you have not fixed into the frame of the clock of Islam?

Despite this, you expect the clock to work when you wind it! And you suppose that cleaning, lubricating and overhauling it will also be of use. With a little reflection, however, you should see that in the condition to which you have reduced the clock you can wind it, lubricate it, and overhaul it, for the whole of your lives without any effect. Nothing will happen until you remove the parts brought in from other appliances, replace them with the original parts, and restore the original priorities. Then, and only then, will the winding and so forth produce any results.

Why Worship Rites Are Ineffective

This state of affairs is the real reason why your Salah, Sawm, Zakah and Hajj make no impact upon your lives. First, there are so few among you who perform these acts of worship. Due to the dissolution of Islamic *Jamā'ah* everybody has become autonomous. Whether you fulfil your obligations or not, there is nobody to care. Nor do those who do apparently carry out their obligations do so in a proper manner. They are not constant in attending the congregational Prayer. People are selected to lead the Prayers in the mosques simply because they are fit for no other work: people who exist on the free bread doled out to mosques, who are uneducated, who lack moral calibre. How can congregations led by them turn you into the leaders of mankind? Similar is the situation regarding your Fasting, Almsgiving and Pilgrimages.

Despite all these facts, you may argue, there are nonetheless many Muslims who do discharge their religious duties conscientiously. Why does that make no difference? But, as I have said, when the parts of the clock have become unhinged and numerous foreign bodies have been inserted in it, it makes no difference if you wind it or not, clean it or not, lubricate it or not. From a distance it does look like a clock. An outside observer may say: This is Islam and you are Muslims. But what he cannot see is how badly its inside machinery has been tampered with.

Our Deplorable Condition

Brothers! You understand why it is so that you pray and fast and yet remain trampled under the heel of cruel tyrants. But, should I tell you something even more distressing? Although most of you no doubt regret this situation but, I would say, 999 people out of 1000 are not prepared to change their situation. They have no urge in their hearts to assemble the clock of Islam again properly. They are afraid that any such reconstruction would mean that their own favourite imported parts would be thrown out, and this they are not prepared to accept. They are afraid that any tightening of various parts would mean that they will have to discipline themselves, and this they are not willing to undertake.

Instead, they prefer that the clock remains a piece of decoration on the wall for people to be shown and told how wonderful Islam is, what miracles it can perform. Those who are supposed to love this clock more than others would like to wind it repeatedly and zealously and to clean it most laboriously; but they want to do nothing to reset its parts properly or tighten them, nor will they seek to get rid of the extraneous parts.

I wish I could endorse your attitudes and behaviour, but I cannot say anything which I believe is wrong. I assure you that if, in addition to praying five times a day, you were to offer *Tahajjud* (pre-dawn), *Ishrāq* (post-sunset) and *Chāsht* (mid-morning) Prayers, read the Qur'ān for hours every day, and observe, over and above Ramadan, extra fasts for five and a half months in the remaining eleven months, you would still achieve nothing. What is needed is to restore the original parts to the clock and fix them firmly. Then even the little necessary winding will make it work smoothly; and the minimal amount of required cleaning and lubrication will be needed.

Wa mā 'alaynā illa 'l-balāgh

There is no responsibility on us except conveying the truth.

PART IV
Sawm

17

Meaning and Blessings of the Fasting

Brothers in Islam! The second act of worship that Allah enjoins upon you is *Ṣawm* or the Fasting. It means abstaining from dawn to sunset from eating, drinking and sex. Like the Prayer, this act of worship has been part of the Shari'ahs given by all the Prophets. Their followers fasted as we do. However, the rules, the number of days, and the periods prescribed for fasting have varied from one Shari'ah to another. Today, although fasting remains a part of most religions in some form or other, people have often changed its original form by accretions of their own.

> O Believers! Fasting is ordained for you, even as it was ordained for those before you (al-Baqarah 2: 183).

Why has this particular act of worship been practised in all eras?

Life of Worship

Islam aims to transform the whole life of man into a life of worship. He is born a slave; and to serve his Creator is his very nature. Not for a single moment should he live without worshipping, that is surrendering to Him in thoughts and deeds. He must remain conscious of what he ought to do to earn the pleasure of God and what he ought to avoid. He should, then, walk on the path leading to Allah's pleasure, eschew that leading to His displeasure just as he would avoid the embers of a fire. Only when our entire lives have become modelled on this pattern can we be considered to have worshipped our Master as is His due and as having fulfilled the purport of 'I have not created *jinn* and men except to worship Me'.

Rituals Lead to a Life of Worship

The real purpose of ritual acts of worship – Salah, Zakah, Sawm and Hajj – is to help us come to that life of total worship. Never think that you can acquit yourselves of what you owe to Allah only if you bow and prostrate yourselves five times a day, suffer hunger and thirst from dawn to sunset for thirty days in Ramadan and, if wealthy, give the Alms and perform the Pilgrimage once in a lifetime. Doing all this does not release you from bondage to Him, nor make you free to do whatever you like. Rather, one of the underlying purposes of enjoining these rituals upon you is to develop you so that you can transform your whole lives into the 'Ibadah of God.

How does the Fasting prepare us for this lifelong act of worship?

How Does Fasting Develop Us?

Exclusively Private Worship

All acts of worship include some outward physical movement, but not the Fasting. In the Prayer you stand, sit, bow down and prostrate yourselves; all these acts are visible to everybody. In Hajj you undertake a long journey and travel with thousands of people. Zakah, too, is known to at least two persons, the giver and the receiver. None of these acts can remain concealed; if you perform them, other people will come to know about it.

But the Fasting is a form of 'Ibadah which is entirely private. The All-knowing God alone knows that His servant is fasting. You are required to take food before dawn (Suḥūr) and abstain from eating and drinking anything till the time to break the Fast (Iftār). But, if you secretly eat and drink in between, nobody except God will know about it.

Sure Sign of Faith

The private nature of the Fasting ensures that you have strong faith in God as the One who knows everything. Only if your faith is true and strong, you will not dream of eating or drinking secretly: even in the hottest summer, when your throats dry up with thirst, you will not drink a drop of water; even when you feel faint with hunger, when life itself seems to be ebbing, you will not eat anything. To do all this, see what firm conviction must you have in that nothing whatsoever can ever be concealed from your God! How strong must be His fear in your hearts. You will keep your Fast for about 360 hours for one full month only because of your profound belief in the reward and punishment of the Hereafter. Had you the slightest doubt in that you have to meet your Maker, you would not complete such a fast. With doubts in hearts, no such resolves can be fulfilled.

Month-long Training

In this way does Allah put to the test a Muslim's faith for a full month every year. To the extent you emerge successful from this trial, your faith becomes firmer and deeper. The Fasting is both a trial and a training. If you deposit anything on trust with somebody, you are, as it were, testing his integrity. If he does not abuse your trust, he not only passes his test, but, at the same time, also develops greater strength to bear the burden of greater trusts in future. Similarly, Allah puts your faith to severe test continuously for one month, many long hours a day.

If you emerge triumphant from this test, more strength develops in you to refrain from other sins. This is what the Qur'ān says:

> O believers! Fasting is ordained for you, even as it was ordained for those before you, that you might attain to God-consciousness (al-Baqarah 2: 183).

Practising Obedience

The Fasting has another characteristic. It makes us obey the injunctions of the Shari'ah with sustained intensity for prolonged periods of time. Salah lasts only a few minutes at a time. Zakah is paid only once a year. Although the time spent on Hajj is long, it may come only once in a lifetime, and for many not at all. In the school of the Fasting, on the other hand, you are trained to obey the Shari'ah of the Prophet Muhammad, blessings and peace be on him, for one full month, every year, day and night.

You have to get up early before dawn for *Suḥr*, stop all eating and drinking precisely at a certain time, do certain activities and abstain from certain activities during the day, break your Fast (*Ifṭār*) in the evening at exactly a certain time. Then, for a few moments only you relax, before you hurry for long late evening prayers (*Tarāwīḥ*).

Every year, for one full month from dawn to sunset and from sunset to dawn, you, like a soldier in an army, continuously live a disciplined life, following certain rules all the time. You are then sent back to continue your normal duties for eleven months so that the training you have received for one month may be reflected in your conduct, and if any deficiency is found it may be made up the next year.

Communal Fasting

Training of such profound nature cannot be imparted to each individual separately. Like how an army is trained, everyone has to act at the same time at the sound of the bugle so that they may develop the team spirit, learn to act in unison, and assist each other in their task of development. Whatever one person lacks may be made up by another, whatever deficiency remains in him may be compensated by yet another.

The month of Ramadan is earmarked for *all* Muslims to fast together, to ensure similar results. This measure turns individual 'Ibadah into collective 'Ibadah. Just as the number one, when multiplied by thousands, becomes a formidable number, so the moral and spiritual benefits accruing from the Fasting by one person alone are increased a millionfold if a million people fast together.

The month of Ramadan suffuses the whole environment with a spirit of righteousness, virtue and piety. As flowers blossom in spring, so does *taqwā* in Ramadan. Everyone tries extra hard to avoid sin and, if they lapse, they know they can count on the help of their many other brothers who are fasting with them. The desire automatically arises in every heart to do good works, to feed the poor, to clothe the naked, to help those in distress, to participate in any good work being done anywhere, and to prevent evil. Just as plants have their season of flowering, so Ramadan is the time of year for the growth and flourishing of good and righteousness.

For this reason the Prophet, blessings and peace be on him, said:

> Every good deed of a man is granted manifold increase, ten to seven hundred times. But says Allah: Fasting is an exception; it is exclusively for Me, and I reward for it as much as I wish (*Bukhārī, Muslim*).

All good deeds grow, this shows, in proportion to both the intention of the doer as well as their results, but that there is a limit to their growth. The Fasting, however, has no such limit. In Ramadan, in the season for the flourishing of good and piety, not one but millions of people jointly water this garden of virtue. The more you sincerely perform good deeds in this month and the greater you avail yourselves of its blessings, the more will you radiate their benefits to our other brothers. The more you sustain the impact of the Fasting on your life during the subsequent eleven months, the more will our garden flourish, and flourish without limit. Should its growth become inhibited, the fault must lie with you.

Where Are the Results?

You are now probably saying to yourselves: We do observe the Fasting and perform the Prayers but the promised results are nowhere to be seen. One reason for this situation I have explained earlier. After snapping the vital links between various parts of Islam and injecting into it many new things, you cannot expect the same results as from the whole.

A second reason is that the way you look at the 'Ibadah has changed. You believe that mere abstention from food and drink, from morning till evening, amounts to 'Ibadah; once you do all these things you have worshipped Allah. Ninety-nine per cent or even more among you are unmindful of the real spirit of 'Ibadah which should permeate all your actions. That is why the acts of 'Ibadah do not produce their full benefit. For everything in Islam depends on intention and understanding.

18

True Spirit of the Fasting

Spirit and Form

Brothers in Islam! Essentially every work which we do has two components. The first is its purpose and spirit; the second, the particular form which is chosen to achieve that purpose. Take the case of food. Your main purpose in eating is to stay alive and maintain your strength. The method of achieving this object is that you take a piece of food, put it in your mouth, chew it and swallow it. This method is adopted since it is the most effective and appropriate one to achieve your purpose. But everyone knows that the main thing is the purpose for which food is taken and not the form the act of eating takes.

What would you say if someone tried to eat a piece of sawdust or cinder or mud? You would say that he was mad or ill. Why? Because he clearly would not have understood the real purpose of eating and would have erroneously believed that chewing and swallowing constituted eating. Likewise, you would also call someone mad who thrust his fingers down his throat to vomit up the food he had just eaten and then complained that the benefits said to accrue from taking food were not being realized. Rather, on the contrary, he was daily getting thinner.

This person blames food for a situation that is due to his own stupidity. Although outward actions are certainly necessary, because without them the bread cannot reach the stomach, the purpose of eating cannot be achieved by merely fulfilling these outward actions.

The Outward Replaces the Real

Perhaps you can now understand why our 'Ibadah has become ineffectual and empty. The greatest mistake of all is to take the acts of the Prayer and Fasting and their outward shape as the real 'Ibadah. If you do so, you are just like the person who thinks that merely performing four acts – taking a piece of food, putting it in the mouth, chewing it, and swallowing it – make up the process of eating. Such a person imagines that whoever does these four things has eaten the food. He, then, expects that he should receive the benefits of eating irrespective of whether he pushed down into his stomach mud and stone, or vomited up the bread soon after eating it.

Otherwise, how can you explain, that a man who is fasting, and is thus engaged in the 'Ibadah of God from morning till evening, in the midst of that 'Ibadah, tells a lie or slanders someone? Why does he quarrel on the slightest pretext and abuse those he is quarrelling with? How dare he encroach on other people's rights? Why does he make money illegally and give money to others illicitly? And how can he claim, having done all these things, that he has still performed the 'Ibadah of Allah? Does this not resemble the actions of that person who eats cinders and mud and thinks that by merely completing the four requirements of eating he has actually done the job of eating?

How, too, can we claim to have worshipped Allah for many long hours throughout Ramadan when the impact of this whole exercise in spiritual and moral upliftment vanishes on the first day of the next month? During the 'Id days we do all that Hindus do in their festivals, so much so that in some places we even turn to adultery, drinking and gambling. And have seen some degenerates who fast during the day and drink alcohol and commit adultery at night. Most Muslims, thank God, have not fallen so low. But how many of us still retain any trace of piety and virtue by the second day of 'Id?

Wrong View of Worship

The reason most of you behave as you do is that the very meaning and purport of 'Ibadah has become distorted in your minds. You think that mere abstention from eating and drinking throughout the day is the Fasting. You therefore are very particular to observe the minutest details about it. You fear God to the extent that you avoid even the slightest violation of these rules; but you do not appreciate that merely being hungry and thirsty is not the purpose but only the form.

This form has been prescribed to create in you such fear of God and love, such strength of will and character, that, even against your desire, you avoid seemingly profitable things which in fact displease Allah and do those things which possibly entail risks and losses but definitely please God. This strength can be developed only when you understand the purpose of the Fasting and desire to put to use the training you have undergone of curbing your physical desires for the fear and love of God only.

But what happens as soon as Ramadan is over? You throw to the winds all that you gain from the Fasting, just as a man who has eaten food vomits it up by thrusting his fingers down his throat. Just as physical strength cannot be obtained from bread until it is digested, transformed into blood, which spreads through every vein, so spiritual strength cannot be obtained from the Fasting until the person who keeps fast is conscious of its purpose and allows it to permeate his heart and mind and dominate his thoughts, motives and deeds.

Fasting as a Way to Piety

This is why Allah, after ordaining the Fasting, has said that Fasting is made obligatory on you, 'so that you *may* attain to God-consciousness', *la'allakum tattaqūn*.

Note that there is no guarantee that you will definitely become God-conscious and righteous. Only someone who recognizes the purpose of the Fasting and strives to achieve it will receive its blessings; someone who does not, cannot hope to gain anything from it.

Conditions of True Fasting

The Prophet, blessings and peace be on him, has in various ways pointed out the real spirit of fasting and has explained that to go hungry and thirsty while ignoring the spirit carries no value in the sight of God.

Abstention From Falsehood

Once, he said:

> If one does not give up speaking falsehood and acting by it, God does not require him to give up eating and drinking (*Bukhārī*).

On another occasion, he said:

> Many are the people who fast but who gain nothing from their fast except hunger and thirst; and many are those who stand praying all night but gain nothing except sleeplessness (*Dārimī*).

The lessons are clear and unequivocal: merely being hungry and thirsty is not by itself worship, but a means for performing real worship. Real worship means desisting from violating the law of God out of this fear and this love of God, pursuing activities that please Him, and refraining from the indiscriminate satisfaction of physical desires. If you fast while ignoring this essence of the Fasting, you are simply causing unnecessary inconvenience to your stomachs.

Faith and Self-scrutiny

The Prophet, blessings and peace be on him, draws attention to another aim of fasting thus:

> Whoever observes the Fast, believing and counting, has all his past sins forgiven (*Bukhāri, Muslim*).

Believing means that faith in God should remain alive in the consciousness of a Muslim. Counting means that you should seek only Allah's pleasure, constantly watching over your thoughts and actions to make sure you are doing nothing contrary to His pleasure, and trusting and expecting the rewards promised by Allah and the Messenger. Observing these two principles brings the rich reward of all your past sins being forgiven. The reason is obvious: even if you were once disobedient, you will have now turned, fully repentant, to your Master – and 'a penitent is like one who has, as it were, never committed a sin at all', as said the Prophet, blessings and peace be on him (*Ibn Mājah*).

Shield Against Sins

On another occasion, the Prophet, blessings and peace be on him, said:

> The Fast is like a shield [for protection from Satan's attack]. Therefore when one observes the Fast he should [use this shield and] abstain from quarrelling. If anybody abuses him or quarrels with him, he should simply say: Brother, I am fasting [do not expect me to indulge in similar conduct] (*Bukhāri, Muslim*).

Hunger for Goodness

The Prophet, blessings and peace be on him, once directed that a man, while fasting, ought to do more good works than usual and ardently desire to perform acts of kindness. Compassion and sympathy for his brothers should intensify in his heart because, being himself in the throes of hunger and thirst, he will all the more be able to realize the misery of other servants of God who are destitute.

In Ramadan, whoever provides food to a person who is fasting to break that Fast will earn forgiveness for his sins, deliverance from the Fire and as much reward as the one who is fasting, without any reduction in the recompense of the latter (*Baihaqī*).

Abdullah Ibn 'Abbas tells that the Prophet, blessings and peace be on him, used to become unusually kind and generous during Ramadan. No beggar in that period went empty-handed from his door, and as many slaves as possible were set free (*Baihaqī*).

PART V
Zakah

19

Fundamental Importance of Zakah

Brothers in Islam! After the Prayer, Zakah or the Almsgiving is the most important pillar of Islam. The Qur'ān makes the importance of Zakah abundantly clear, although in popular imagination the Fasting is ranked after the Prayer, because it is usually so listed. On these two great pillars rests the edifice of Islam. If they are demolished Islam can hardly survive.

Meaning of Zakah

Primarily the word *zakah* means purity and cleanliness. Islam uses this very word for the act of setting aside a portion of your wealth for the needy and poor. This is very significant. For it means that it is by 'giving' to others that your wealth is purified. And, along with it, your own self (*nafs*) too. If anyone does not give to the poor and needy what is their due, his wealth remains impure. And that person's inner self, too, is impure. His heart is too narrow; it is filled with ingratitude. He is too selfish. He almost worships wealth. While God has been kind and generous to give him wealth in excess of his requirements, it pains him to render what is His due. How can we expect such a person ever to do some good with the sole motive of pleasing God, or make any sacrifice for the sake of Islam and his faith?

Zakah, a Test

By enjoining upon us to pay Zakah, Allah has put every one of us to the test. Only if you willingly take out what you must for the sake of God from that wealth which exceeds your requirements, and help with it the poor and needy, you are worthy in the sight of Allah and deserve to be counted among the faithful. If you do not sacrifice even this little you are totally unfit to be valued by Allah and accepted as a truly faithful servant. You are then like a rotten limb which is better cut off to stop it decomposing the whole body. After the death of the Prophet, blessings and peace be on him, some tribes refused to give Zakah; Abū Bakr declared war on them, as if they had disowned Islam and turned Unbelievers, even though they performed the Prayer and professed faith in Allah and the Messenger. For, they were like a rotten limb. Islam is an integral whole of which the Almsgiving is an essential part; without the Almsgiving, even Salah, Sawm and Iman lose their credibility.

Early Practice

Study the Qur'ān and you will find that from the earliest times the Prayer and the Almsgiving were laid down upon the followers of all the prophets. Speaking about the Prophet Ibrāhīm, his progeny and followers, it is said:

> And We made them leaders [of men] who would guide by Our command, and We instructed them to do good deeds, and to perform the Prayer, and to give the Alms, and Us alone did they serve (al-Anbiyā' 21: 73).

About the Prophet Ismā'īl it is said:

> He used to enjoin upon his people the performing of the Prayer and the Almsgiving and he found favour with his Lord (Maryam 19: 55).

The Prophet Mūsā once prayed thus for his people:

My Lord! Bestow upon us good, in this world, as also in the world to come.

Do you know what Allah said in reply?

With My punishment do I smite whom I will; but My mercy embraces everything, and I shall ordain it for those who are God-conscious and give the Alms and who believe in Our messages (al-A'rāf 7: 156).

Since the Prophet Mūsā's followers were obsessed with worldly gains then, as so many among us are today, even a prophet as distinguished as Mūsā was plainly told that the mercy he had asked for would be granted to only those who observed the Almsgiving; those who did not would be deprived of it, and punished.

Similarly, even after the Prophet Mūsā died, the Israelites were repeatedly admonished about their niggardly and stingy behaviour. Time and again covenants were taken from them to worship none save Allah and to be steadfast in Salah and Zakah (al-Baqarah 2: 85) till ultimately clear warning was given:

And said God: I surely shall be with you! If you perform the Prayer, give the Alms, and believe in My Messengers and support them, and lend to God a good loan, surely I will efface your bad deeds (al-Mā'idah 5: 12).

Before the Prophet Muhammad, blessings and peace be on him, the last prophet was 'Īsā. He, too, was ordained by Allah to perform the Prayer and give the Alms:

He has blessed me, wherever I may be; and He has enjoined upon me the Prayer and the Alms so long as I live (Maryam 19: 31).

Thus from the earliest times Islam has always been founded on these two acts of worship: the Prayer and the Almsgiving. People who believed in God were never exempted from them.

Categorical Imperative

What important position do these two acts of worship occupy in the Shari'ah of the Prophet Muhammad, blessings and peace be on him? Open the Qur'ān and see what you read in the very beginning.

> This is the Book of God, there is no doubt in it. It is a guide for the God-conscious who believe in the Unseen and perform the Prayer and spend of that We have provided them. . . . It is they who follow the guidance from their Lord, and it is they who are successful (al-Baqarah 2: 2–3).

That is to say, those who have no faith and do not adhere to the Prayer and the Almsgiving will neither receive guidance nor achieve success in life. A little later, in the same Surah, we again read:

> Perform the Prayer, and give the Alms, and bow with those who bow (al-Baqarah 2: 43).

Look at some of the many more similar Ayahs which stress performing the Prayer and the Almsgiving.

> It is not true piety that you turn your faces to the East and the West. But truly pious is he who believes in God, and the Last Day, and the angels, and the Book, and the prophets; and gives his wealth, for love of Him, to kinsmen, and to orphans, and the needy, and the wayfarer, and the beggars, and to set human beings free from bondage; and performs the Prayer and gives the Alms. And they who keep their promises whenever they

promise, and are patient in misfortune and hardship and time of peril. It is they who have proved themselves true, and they are the God-conscious (al-Baqarah 2: 177).

Further we read:

Indeed, your true friend is only God, and His Messenger, and the believers who perform the Prayer and give the Alms and bow them down. For, whoso makes God his Friend, and His Messenger, and the believers, it is they, the party of God, who shall triumph! (al-Mā'idah 5: 55–6).

The Sign of Faith

Great are the truths expounded here. *First,* that only those can be taken as true believers who perform the Prayers and give the Alms. Those who disregard these two fundamental teachings are not true in their profession of faith. *Second,* that Allah, the Messenger and the believers form one separate entity – they are like one party – and it is the duty of a true believer to join this party, superseding and severing all other ties of loyalty. If a Muslim is loyal to a person, or his ally, who is outside this party, whether father, brother, son, neighbour, countryman or anyone else, and maintains with him a relationship of love and mutual support, he should not expect Allah to love and help him. *Finally,* that believers can gain ascendancy on earth only when they become one – in their love and loyalty, friendship and fidelity – with Allah, His Messenger and other believers.

Foundation of the Ummah

Let us read the Qur'ān further where Allah commands Muslims to wage war against those who rebel against God and take gods beside Him:

Yet if they turn [to God] from disbelief and polytheism, and perform the Prayer and give the Alms, they become your brothers in faith (al-Tawbah 9: 11).

What should make Muslims accept those rebels against God as their brothers in faith, as members of the Ummah? Merely turning aside from rebellion and polytheism is not enough. They should also perform the Prayer, as well as give the Alms, as a sign of true repentance and conversion. Only then war against them is to be ceased and they become brothers in faith.

A little further, again we read:

And the believers, the men and the women, are friends one of the other: they enjoin the doing of right and forbid the doing of wrong, and they perform the Prayer, and they give the Alms and they obey God and His Messenger. It is they upon whom God will have mercy (al-Tawbah 9: 71).

Listen carefully: only those can become Muslims, brothers united with one another, who declare their faith, and then perform the Prayer and give the Alms. These three elements – Iman, Salah and Zakah – constitute the basis to bring the community of believers into existence. Only in such a community should loyalty, friendship and mutual support supersede all other loyalties and ties. Those who refuse to accept or who put aside these three principles in fact fall outside this community, though they may be Muslim in name. To give them love and loyalty is to violate the law of Allah and disrupt the party of Allah. How then can those who accept such behaviour expect to be in the ascendancy?

Conditions for God's Help

Still further we read:

And God will most certainly help him who helps Him. Surely God is All-strong, All-mighty. Those who, if

We give them power in the land, perform the Prayer and give the Alms and enjoin the right and forbid the wrong. Unto God belongs the outcome of all affairs (al-Ḥajj 22: 40–1).

Here, Muslims have been served with the same notice as was served on the Israelites. They were told: 'I shall be with you so long as you perform the Prayer, give the Alms and support My Messengers in their mission. The moment you give up this work I shall withdraw My support from you.' Similarly, to the Muslims Allah says: 'If after gaining power on earth you perform the Prayer, give the Alms, make the good to grow and eliminate the evil, only then I will be your helper – and who can subdue him whom I support. But if you turn away from the Almsgiving and, after acquiring power on earth, promote evil instead of good, curb good instead of evil, make your own word prevail instead of Mine, and consider collecting taxes and building palatial houses as the sole purpose of your rule on earth, then, listen: My support will not be with you; Satan alone will be your supporter.'

Warning to Muslims

Shall we not heed this warning?

The Israelites took their warning as an empty threat, and they paid the consequences. They are still scattered across the earth and, although their coffers are brimming with wealth, their money is of no use to them.* By adopting the evil system of interest instead of Zakah, and by turning away from Salah, they have invoked Allah's curse.

---

*In 1938, Jews, despite their grip over world finances, were soon going to face enormous tortures in Germany.

We Muslims have been given the very warnings by God as He had given to the Israelites. And what has our conduct been? We, too, have neglected Salah and Zakah. We forsook our duty to use our power in spreading good and eliminating evil. And the consequences have been no different. We have been dislodged from power. We have become the victims of tyrants throughout the world. We are weak and live in servitude wherever we are found. Yet despite such clear warnings, and such manifest consequences, some Muslims propose the creation of economies based on interest and other man-made ideologies like capitalism and socialism. If ever they did implement their proposals, the disgrace and ignominy would overtake Muslims and they would suffer as the Israelites have suffered.

Fate of Zakah Defaulters

What immense blessings does Zakah have? That, brothers, I shall explain later, but let me emphasize how the very fact of our being Muslims depends on paying Zakah. Many Muslims think, and some of their Ulema, too, assure them, that they remain true Muslims even though they may not perform the Prayer and give the Alms. But the Qur'ān clearly rejects such an idea. It states beyond doubt that the affirmation of the Kalimah Tayyibah has no weight unless accompanied by the performance of the Prayer and the giving of the Alms. Abū Bakr, the first Caliph, as I have stated above, had no hesitation in taking up arms against Muslims who believed in God and the Messenger and performed Salah, but refused to give Zakah. Some of the Prophet's Companions, initially, had some confusion whether war could be waged against them, but not Abū Bakr, who categorically stated:

> By God! If these people withhold the Alms they used to give during the time of the Prophet, Allah's blessings and peace be on him, even if it be a piece of rope by which a camel is tied, I shall raise my sword against them (*Abū Dā'ūd*).

His arguments convinced all the Companions and they unitedly accepted that Jihad must be waged against those who refuse to give the Alms. In the Qur'ān, too, it is stated that refusal to give the Alms is the mark of idolators who deny the Hereafter:

> And woe unto the idolators who give not the Alms and who deny the life to come (Fuṣṣilat 41: 6–7).

20

Meaning of Zakah

Brothers in Islam! It is abundantly clear that Zakah, the Almsgiving, is no less important than performing Salah, the Prayer. Indeed those who refuse to pay Zakah fall outside the pale of Islam; against them even Jihad may be waged as did the Companions. But why is Zakah so crucially important? What is its true meaning? To these questions I shall address myself now.

Becoming God's Friends

Let us first look at another important question: How can one come near to God and be His friend? What makes one worthy of being included in His party? Only some among you may be so naive as to befriend a person without considering whether he is really fit to be a friend or not. Those who do so are likely to be deceived in their friendship and face disappointments because of it. But if you are wise and prudent, you always choose your friends carefully after ascertaining whether they are true and loyal friends or not.

Allah is the Wisest and most Prudent of all. Will He ever make anybody His friend, or include him in His party, or accord him a place of honour in His sight, without first testing and trying him? Obviously not. Of all the millions of people on earth, by no means everyone is fit to deserve a place in God's party, be made His vicegerent, or accorded a place near Him in the eternal life. He must see if the person concerned meets the

LET US BE MUSLIMS

necessary criteria. Not because Allah is unaware, but because, through this process of testing and trial, anyone who is true in his faith is shaped and uplifted to become worthy of God's highest rewards and honours.

What, then, are these criteria and the tests?

Wisdom and Understanding

First of all Allah tests your wisdom and understanding. You should possess the proper understanding. You should be able to conclude from all the evidence around you that none but Allah alone is your Creator and Lord; no one but He can sustain you, hear your prayers and help you. You should be able to recognize the revelation and message which has come from Him. You should also be able to distinguish between a true prophet and a false claimant to prophethood and between their morals, dealings, teachings and achievements. You should also be able to discern true guidance from the false.

Only if you pass this test, will Allah include you in His party. If not, you will be left to your own devices.

Moral Strength

Then comes the second examination: here your moral strength is tested.

To show that you have the necessary moral strength you must demonstrate that, after having recognized and accepted truth and righteousness, you have the will to live by them and renounce the ways of falsehood and evil. You must further prove that you are no more slaves to your own physical desires, nor do you blindly follow the practices and customs of your ancestors and families, the values and norms of your cultures and societies. Neither should you knowingly accept anything contrary to God's guidance, nor reject anything it tells you.

If you fail this examination you are refused admission into Allah's party, for He picks only those whose definition is:

So whosoever rejects false gods and believes in God has indeed taken hold of the most firm handle which shall never break (al-Baqarah 2: 256).

Obedience and Dutifulness

Once you pass this examination you appear in a third examination. This time your obedience and sense of duty are put to the test. Here, you are told: Whenever We call you, you must come. Give up the warmth and comfort of your sleep, but come and present yourself before Us. Interrupt your work, but come you must to Our work. On Our command remain hungry and thirsty from morning till evening and abstain from gratifying your physical desires. Give up your pleasures, forgo your profits, sacrifice your interests, but discharge your duty. Whether hot or cold, easy or difficult, in all circumstances, rush when summoned to duty, disregarding every difficulty, surmounting every obstacle.

God's summons must be answered, no matter whatever the odds, whatever the temptations, however long and hard the road. If you fail this examination you are not worthy of God's trust. If you pass it, however, you will have shown that you can be expected to obey all laws which have been given you by God in all circumstances, whether they appear to your advantage or disadvantage.

Sacrificing Wealth

Even now, you cannot be reckoned entirely worthy of employment in the service of God. One more test remains: that you are not narrow-hearted and niggardly. That you are not like those who make big claims of love and friendship but when required to part with their wealth for the sake of the so-called friend, they fall back and begin to make excuses. That you are not like those Hindus who worship a cow, but when it tries to eat some of their food, they hit it and push it away.

While anyone with a little common sense would not befriend such a selfish and mean money-worshipper, a large-hearted person would not like even to sit next to such a despicable creature. So how can the Most-generous God, the Most High and Exalted, who showers His treasures incessantly and lavishly on His creatures, admit you to His friendship? Are you not then guilty of refusing to spend the very money in the cause of God, which He gave you in the first place? And how can that God who is All-wise trust such a person for His party whose friendship is confined to mere verbal jugglery?

If you fail this fourth examination you are told unequivocally: 'Go away. There is no room for you in Allah's party. You cannot discharge that great responsibility which is entrusted to a vicegerent of God. For in this party only those are included who sacrifice their love of life, wealth, children, family, country, everything for the love of God.'

> Never shall you attain piety unless you spend [in the way of God] out of what you love (Āl 'Imrān 3: 92).

Requirements for Admittance to God's Friendship

To be admitted into the party of Allah, you must therefore possess some fundamental qualities, with respect to your wealth.

Large-heartedness

First: The niggardly and stingy have no place in God's party; only the large-hearted who give willingly and abundantly in His way deserve to be admitted.

> And whoso is saved from the avarice of his inner self, it is they who are successful (al-Ḥashr 59: 9).

Magnanimity

Second: You must be magnanimous, by a greatness of heart that rises above every feeling pertaining to your selves, above resentment against any injury or insult. If somebody causes you harm or grief, you must still not, for the sake of Allah, refuse him food and clothing nor should you hesitate to help him when he is in trouble:

> Let not those of you who possess bounty and plenty among you swear not to give to the kinsmen and the poor, and those who have emigrated in the way of God. Let them pardon and forgive and show indulgence. Yearn you not that God should forgive you? God is All-forgiving, the Mercy-giving* (al-Nūr 24: 22).

Selflessness

Third: You must be selfless, seeking no reward, placing no burden.

> They give food, for love of Him, to the needy and the orphan and the prisoner, [saying]: we feed you only for the sake of God. We desire no reward from you, nor thanks (al-Dahr 76: 8–9).

Purity of Heart

Fourth: You must have such purity of heart that you give away, in the cause of Allah, only your most treasured possessions, realizing full well that they are God's and not yours:

> O believers! Spend out of the good things you have earned, and of that We bring forth for you from the earth. And intend not to spend the bad thereof (al-Baqarah 2: 267).

---

*This verse was revealed when a relative of Abū Bakr took part in an accusation against his daughter, 'Ā'ishah, and Abu Bakr stopped helping him financially. When this verse was revealed Abū Bakr sought Allah's forgiveness and again began helping the man who had caused him so much mental agony.

Giving in Adversity

Fifth: Even when in poverty and adversity, you should not hesitate to deny yourselves your basic needs to find money to spend in Allah's cause and in helping His creatures.

> Vie with one another, hastening to forgiveness from your Lord, and towards a Paradise as wide as are the heavens and earth, prepared for the God-conscious who spend both in prosperity and in adversity (Āl 'Imrān 3: 133).

Giving in Affluence

Sixth: In affluence and prosperity, too, you must not forget God. While living in luxury and comfort you must remember Him and spend your wealth in His way.

> O believers! Let not your possessions neither your children divert you from God's remembrance; who so does so, it is they who are the losers (al-Munāfiqūn 63:9).

Giving For Allah Alone

Seventh: Your faith must be strong that whatever is spent in the cause of Allah is never wasted, that God will give you better and abundant rewards for it, both in this world and in the Hereafter. You should therefore spend your money for one motive alone: to earn the pleasure of Allah. Whether people know about your generosity or not, whether someone has thanked you or not, should not matter at all.

> Whatever good you spend, it is for your own good. And spend not but only for seeking God's countenance. Thus whatever good you spend shall be recompensed in full and you will not be wronged (al-Baqarah 2: 272).

These seven qualities are essential if you aspire to belong to Allah's party; without them you cannot claim to be His friends. They constitute not only a test of your morals but a more severe and revealing test of your Iman. When called upon to give your wealth for the sole purpose of earning God's pleasure, if you avoid spending, regard such spending as a fine imposed on you, make excuses to wriggle out of it, or, when you do spend, try to lessen your pain by stressing your benevolence upon the recipients, then indeed your faith in God and in the Hereafter is not true. The same is true if you think that whatever you spend in the cause of God is wasted; if luxury, comfort, enjoyment and fame are all dearer to you than God and His pleasure; if you think that all that matters is confined to the present life which only is real; if you believe that money should be spent only for self- glorification. The Qur'ān clearly states that all these things in a person make his spending unacceptable in the sight of Allah. He claims to possess Iman, but in fact he is a hypocrite. Note what the Qur'ān says:

Stressing Benevolence

O believers! Void not your charitable deeds by stressing your own benevolence and by hurting [the recipients], like the one who spends his wealth only to show off to people and believes not in God and the Last Day (al-Baqarah 2: 264).

Amassing Wealth

They who hoard up treasures of gold and silver and spend them not in the way of God, unto them give the good tidings of a painful punishment (al-Tawbah 9: 34).

Making Excuses

Those who believe in God and the Last Day ask no leave of you, lest they may strive with their wealth and their lives. God knows the God-conscious. Only those ask leave of you who believe not in God and the Last Day, and whose hearts are filled with doubt, so that in their doubt they waver (al-Tawbah 9: 44–5).

Spending Reluctantly and Resentfully

And nothing prevents that their spendings be accepted from them, but that they believe not in God and His Messenger, and perform not the Prayer save reluctantly and spend not without resenting (al-Tawbah 9: 54).

The hypocrites, the men and the women, are as one another. They enjoin the doing of wrong and forbid the doing of right, and they keep their hands shut [from spending in the way of God]. They have forgotten God, so He has forgotten them. The hypocrites, it is they who are the iniquitous (al-Tawbah 9: 67).

Considering Spending a Fine

Some of the Bedouins [hypocrites] take what they spend [in the way of God] for a fine (al-Tawbah 9: 98).

Niggardliness

There you are! You are called upon to spend in the way of God yet some among you are niggardly. Whoso is niggardly is niggardly only to his own soul. God is the All-sufficient; you are the needy ones. If you turn away [from spending in the way of God], He will substitute another people instead of you, then they will not be the likes of you (Muḥammad 47: 38).

The Real Test

This, brothers, is the real meaning and import of Zakah which sustains the edifice of Islam. Do not consider it a tax like the tax levied by governments. It is the basis and essence of Islam and its very life-blood. It tests your faith and strengthens it. Just as one progresses from one examination to another until he graduates on passing his final examination, so are there several examinations to test your willingness to sacrifice your wealth. Even then this is not the final test. A much harder test is that of sacrificing life, to which I shall come later. That is the final component of the examination which determines your membership in the party of Allah.

Some people today say that Muslims have been told enough how to spend money and to squander wealth and that, in their present state of poverty, they ought to be taught how to earn and amass money. These people are unable to understand that giving in the way of Allah, which arouses their displeasure, is the very spirit of Islam. What has plunged Muslims into their present ignominy is the lack of this spirit, not an abundance of it. This spirit was not the cause of their decline, but they declined because this spirit had evaporated.

21

Zakah,
a Social Institution

Allah's Unique Beneficence

Brothers in Islam! *Infāq fi sabīli 'llāh* (spending in the way
of God) is the phrase frequently used in the Qur'ān to denote
Zakah, and other acts of charity (*ṣadaqāt*). Very often Allah
invites us to 'give Him a loan', that is whatever we spend in
His cause He will treat as a loan which He will return with huge
growth in our original investment.

What does this mean? Does it mean, for example, that the
Lord of all the worlds is (God forbid) your dependant? That
He needs to borrow from us? That He needs to beg from us?
How can such a thing be! Is it not by His largesse alone that
our lives are sustained? Does not our food and everything else
we possess, rich and poor alike, all come from Him as a gift?
Beggars, millionaires and multimillionaires: we are all His
dependants. So how can He need to ask us for a loan?

The answer lies not in terms of God's *needs*, for He has
none, but in His love and unbounded generosity towards you.
When He 'asks' for a loan what He purports to say is this:
This expenditure is made in My cause and I accept it as My
obligation to repay it. The needy of your communities have no
way of repaying you, so I will do it on their behalf. When you

help your poor relatives, the obligation to repay is not on them but on Me; I will recompense you for this favour. Whatever you give to orphans, widows, the disabled and the homeless, will be entered against My account. If your borrowers are unable to pay you back, do not threaten them with prison, do not make them sell off their possessions, do not make their wives and children homeless by evicting them, your debt is not owed by them but by Me. If they return the capital I will pay interest on it, and if they cannot do even this, I will pay you both capital and interest. Indeed every time you spend something for your social welfare, for the good and betterment of your fellow beings, I shall consider it as a 'favour' to Me – even though you yourselves will benefit. Every single penny of it I shall return to you along with huge, unimaginable profits.

Imagine how generously the Most-merciful, the King of kings treats you. Although all that you possess is a gift from Him and belongs to Him alone, and although whatever you spend you spend on your own families, relatives, communities, or on your collective well-being, and not on Him, He nevertheless says: You have given it to Me; I will return it to you.

Allah is indeed great: the Lord of the worlds alone could exhibit such sublime generosity; no human being can even conceive of approaching it.

Man's Selfishness

Why has Allah chosen to speak in such a manner? Why does He arouse in us the spirit of charity and generosity through such logic? The more you reflect on this the more you will become convinced of the power and purity of Islamic teaching. Your hearts will grow in the faith that such matchless sublimity could emanate from none but God.

Man by his very nature is capable of doing wrong and acting without reason. His perceptions are limited; he is narrowminded; he finds it difficult to embrace lofty ideals. He is selfish, and his vision of human interest, too, does not embrace any wider context. By nature he is imbued with impatience and love of what is immediately at hand. 'Man is created out of haste' (al-Anbiyā' 21: 37). If he does not see any immediate results and benefits in something, he thinks that it has no value, nor does he consider it worth doing. He is unable to see his actions in a wider or long-term context or to judge the benefits which may accrue to him from them.

This inherent weakness of looking to selfish interests and that, too, in a very narrow perspective, leads him to be constantly on the look-out for quick, specific and personal gain from what he does. He says, for example: I am the owner and sole beneficiary of whatever I have earned or whatever I have inherited, and nobody has a share in it. It should therefore be spent on fulfilling my needs and desires, on providing me comfort, physical pleasures and luxuries. If spent otherwise, it should at least bring me fame and honour: some title, some high office, some devotion, some admiration and applause. There is no point in parting with my money if it does not achieve these things.

Why should I take on the responsibility of helping an orphan? His father should have made provision for him. And why should I bother about the problems a widow may have? Her husband ought to have thought earlier about what would happen to her if he died. What has it got to do with me if a traveller is in trouble? He should never have left home without having made all the necessary arrangements. People in trouble should help themselves; Allah has given them hands and feet the same as me. And if I *do* give anyone some money, I must give it as a loan, on which I shall expect to receive interest. Otherwise my money is not working for me. I could have better used it to build a new house or buy a new car or for investment purposes. If the borrower is going to benefit why should not I as well?

What Selfishness Leads To

A rich man with such a selfish attitude is like a snake guarding treasure. If he spends anything, he will only spend or lend for personal aggrandizement or to make more money. He will, in fact, fleece a poor man by taking back from him more than he has given him. If he gives anything to a destitute person, he will stress upon him his favours and will insult and humiliate him to destroy his self-respect. If he has to take part in some social work, his first concern will be to examine how much will his personal benefit from it be. And if he can see no personal gain, his support will not be forthcoming.

What are the consequences of this selfish disposition? It is fatal not only for community life, but ultimately for that person himself. When selfishness prevails, wealth concentrates in a few hands and the poor become poorer. The rich, on the strength of the money they already have, continue to draw more money into their coffers, while the poor find life harder and harder.

A poverty-stricken society breeds various evils. General health declines and people become less resistant to illness. Productivity dwindles. Unemployment rises. Ignorance increases. Morals deteriorate. People turn to crime to fulfil their basic needs. And, ultimately, they loot and plunder. Widespread unrest and rioting break out. The rich are murdered and their houses burnt and ransacked. Wholesale destruction follows and society collapses.

Individual and Collective Welfare

You can now see how the well-being of *every* individual is inextricably linked with that of the society at large. If you help your neighbours with the wealth you possess, then that wealth will circulate and come back to you bringing many more benefits. But if you keep it selfishly to yourselves or spend it only for your own personal benefit, it will ultimately dwindle and lose its value.

For example, if you bring up an orphan and give him an education which enables him to become an earning member of the community, you will have contributed to the overall wealth of the community, and, as members of it yourselves, you will also share in the increased prosperity your action has generated, even though you may not be able to put it on your balance sheet. But if you say, 'Why should we help him, his father should have left something for him', then he will never be able to contribute anything to the wealth of the community. In fact, he may well become a professional criminal and burgle your own houses. By refusing to help make this person a useful member of society, you would have harmed not only him but yourselves too.

If you look around, you will see that people who spend money selflessly for the good of the community tend to flourish: the wealth that is created returns with countless extra benefits to the pockets from which it came. And people who keep their money to themselves through selfishness and avarice, apparently increasing their wealth by lending at interest, or by indulging in exploitation, are in reality, in the long term, ensuring their own destruction. This is the law which Allah has described thus:

> God deprives interest of all blessings, but charitable deeds He blesses to increase with interest (al-Baqarah 2: 276).

> And whatever you give on interest, so that it may increase through people's wealth, increases not with God; whereas what you give in Alms, seeking God's countenance, it is they who shall receive recompense manifold (al-Rūm 30: 39).

Man's selfishness and ignorance all too often prevent him grasping this reality and acting on it. Being a slave of material things, he sees only the money which jingles in his pocket and the savings which continue to grow in his bank account. Spending money makes sense to him only if he can see an immediate and direct return from it. He attaches no value to the benefits which will accrue to him by helping the society in which he lives. He is unable to comprehend how the wealth given away for the sake of God alone grows manifold. He is unable to unravel the knot of his ignorance.

That is how we have arrived at the position we find ourselves in today. On the one hand is the world of capitalists which continues to grow through interest and exorbitant profiteering, which brings in its wake far more problems than can be solved by the apparent continuing growth in wealth. And on the other hand, groups have emerged, their hearts aflame with jealousy, who are bent upon not only emptying the coffers of capitalists but, with it, also destroying the whole basis of human culture and civilization.

What is the Solution?

The only solution to this problem is that given by that Allwise God who has guided us through the Qur'ān. Faith in Allah and faith in the Last Day constitute the keys to changing this situation. If you have faith in Allah and believe that He is the real Lord of all the treasures on earth and in the heavens, that sovereignty over human affairs rests in Him only, and that He will reward or punish you all in the Hereafter according to your deeds, down to the minutest atom, you did on earth – if you believe all these things, putting your trust in God rather than your own inclinations, will and strength to spend your wealth will inevitably follow. You will spend as and when directed by God, disregarding the question of profit and loss which you will leave entirely to Him. Whatever you spend in this way will be in fact a present to God Himself and God will surely know it and acknowledge it – whether men recognize it or not – either in the Hereafter or both in this world and the next.

22

General Principles of Spending

Brothers in Islam! There is one significant characteristic of the God-given Law (Shari'ah). First, certain general instructions and teachings are laid down in respect of any particular virtue or good deed. These help people mould and shape their lives and attitudes. These general teachings are then translated into specific injunctions, which are easy to observe.

Remembrance of God

For example, take the remembrance of Allah. It is an act of virtue, in fact the greatest virtue, and the basis of all good deeds. On one level, there is a general directive to remember Allah at every moment and in every circumstance of life.

> Remember God, standing and sitting and lying down (al-Nisā' 4: 103).

> And remember God often, that you may be successful (al-Anfāl 8: 45).

> Surely in the creation of the heavens and earth, and in the alternation of night and day, there are signs for those who possess understanding, who remember God, standing

and sitting and lying down, and reflect upon the creation of the heavens and the earth. Our Lord, Thou hast not created this without meaning and purpose. Glory be to Thee (Āl 'Imrān 3: 190–1).

And obey not him whose heart We have made neglectful of Our remembrance, who follows his own desires, and whose every affair exceeds all bounds (al-Kahf 18: 28).

These, and many other Ayahs, direct us to always remember Allah, for remembering Him keeps our affairs in proper order and keeps us on the right path. Whenever we forget Him we are liable to become easy prey to the temptations of evil and go astray.

Specific directives show us *how* to obey the general directives. Thus, the remembrance of Allah has been translated into the specific act of Prayer and performing some Prayers five times a day has been made obligatory. But making Allah's remembrance obligatory for a few minutes at a time in no way implies that we should remember Him only during these fixed periods and forget Him for the rest of the time. It means that during those periods we ought to be *exclusively* engaged in the remembrance of Allah. And at other times, for example while busy in our work, the awareness of Allah should continue to be present in our minds.

Spending in the Way of Allah

Spending in the way of Allah is a similar case in point. On the one hand, general directives have been given: Refrain from avarice and selfishness as they are the root of evil and mother of vices. Model your morals on the attributes of Allah who is all the time bountifully showering His beneficence on His countless creations although no one has any right or claim upon Him. Spend whatever you can in the way of Allah. Save as much as you can from your requirements and fulfil the wants of other needy servants of Allah. Never flinch from sacrificing life and money to serve Allah and make Islam dominant. If you love Allah, sacrifice your love of wealth for the love of Him.

Specific injunctions arise from these general directives. If you possess wealth over a certain amount, called *Niṣāb*, it is incumbent on you to spend at least a certain minimum proportion of it in the cause of Allah; and similarly, a certain amount of the produce of your land must be offered to Him. Just as the making of some Prayers obligatory does not mean that God should be forgotten for the rest of the time, so the fixing of a certain ceiling (*Niṣāb*) which makes spending in the cause of Allah obligatory, does not mean that only those who possess that much wealth should spend something or those who possess less should spend nothing. Nor does it mean that the rich should give only the minimum prescribed Alms and refuse to help the needy or donate for Jihad after they have met their basic obligations. Zakah only means that at least the minimum amount must be given, but over and above that minimum, as much as possible should be spent in the way of Allah.

Essential Prerequisite to Guidance

Before explaining to you the general Quranic teachings about spending in the way of God, let us see why we are required to spend in His way and what main benefits we should derive. The Qur'ān always explains the reason for any injunctions that it gives so that those who are required to obey do so in full understanding of its real meaning and import.

As you open the Qur'ān the first Ayah you come across is this:

This is the Book of God, there is no doubt in it. It is a guide for the God-conscious who believe in the Unseen, perform the Prayer and spend of what We have provided them (al-Baqarah 2: 2–3).

A fundamentally important principle has been stated here. In order to be guided on the right path in the present life, three essential conditions are necessary: faith in the Unseen;* performing the Prayer, and spending in the cause of God those gifts which He has given you. At other places Allah says:

Never shall you attain true piety unless you spend [in the way of God] out of what you love (Āl 'Imrān 3: 92).

Satan threatens you with poverty and bids you unto shameless things [like being niggardly] (al-Baqarah 2: 268).

Spend in God's cause and throw not yourselves, by your own hands, into destruction (al-Baqarah 2: 195).

And whoso is saved from avarice in his self, it is they who are the successful (al-Taghābun 64: 16).

Thus, we are told, there are two ways we can lead our lives. One is the way of God; virtue and goodness, well-being and success, all are ensured herein. To walk on this path, you must generously help your brothers and support Jihad out of whatever resources God in His bounty and wisdom has given you. The other is the Satanic way: apparently full of benefits, but in reality it leads to ruin. The hallmark of this way of life is worshipping money and amassing wealth at the expense of all other considerations.

Let me now put before you the general, basic principles that have been laid down for spending in the way of Allah.

Spend Only to Please Allah

First: Spend solely to please Allah and seek only His approval. Neither to put the recipient under obligation nor to

---

*Unseen here means realities which are beyond human perception like God, Hereafter, revelation (*wahy*), etc. etc.

earn a name for yourselves or win approval and acclaim should be your aim.

> Spend not but only for seeking God's countenance (al-Baqarah 2: 272).

Do Not Stress Your Benevolence

Second: Never stress upon the needy what a great and generous benefactor you have been in helping, feeding or clothing them; nor expect them to acknowledge it; nor treat them with contempt or humiliate them or injure their feelings in any way.

> Those who spend their wealth for the sake of God, and then follow not up their spending with stressing their own benevolence and hurting, their reward is with their Lord and no fear shall be on them, neither shall they sorrow. A kind word, and [seeking] forgiveness, are better than a charitable deed followed by hurting (al-Baqarah 2: 262–3).

> O believers! Void not your charitable deeds by stressing your own benevolence and hurting, like the one who spends his wealth only to show off to people and believes not in God and the Last Day. For his parable is that of a smooth rock on which is [a little] earth – and then a rainstorm smites it, leaving it hard and bare (al-Baqarah 2: 264).

Give Only Good Things

Third: In the way of Allah give only those things which are good and have been rightfully earned. Do not sort out shoddy things for this purpose. Why should those who dig out torn and old clothes to give to a poor man or who set aside the worst possible food to dole out to a beggar not expect the same kind of reward from God?

> O believers! Spend out of the good things you have earned, and out of that which We bring forth for you from the earth and intend not to spend the bad thereof, which you would never accept yourselves, except that you avert your eyes from it (al-Baqarah 2: 267).

Give Unobtrusively and Secretly

Fourth: Give in as secret a manner as possible so that your act of charity does not run the risk of being tainted with hypocrisy and ostentation. Although there is no harm in giving openly, it is far better to do so discreetly.

> If you do a deed of charity openly, it is well; but if you hide it and give it to the poor, that is even better for you, and it will acquit you of your evil deeds (al-Baqarah 2: 271).

Guard Against Misuse

Fifth: Do not give money in excess of their actual needs to people who lack understanding, in case they are tempted by it to fall into bad habits. Allah wants everyone, even the most sinful, to have food and clothing; but in no circumstances should money be given for evil purposes or for alcohol, drugs or gambling.

> Do not give to fools your wealth which God has made a support for you, but provide them out of it and clothe them (al-Nisā' 4: 5).

Do Not Harass Debtors

Sixth: If a loan is given to a poor man, do not harass him to return the loan, and give him enough time so that he can repay it without great hardship. If he cannot pay it back and you are wealthy enough to do without it, then better write it off.

And if [the debtor] is in difficulties, let him have respite till things are easier; and that you remit [the debt] by way of charity would be better for you, did you but know (al-Baqarah 2: 280).

Take Due Care of Family

Seventh: You should not exceed certain limits in spending. Allah does not desire that you keep your wives and children hungry because you have given away all you have. In fact, what He has laid down is that you spend first on yourselves and your families whatever you need to lead simple but adequate lives, and to give away what is left over in Allah's cause.

They ask you what they should spend. Say: Whatever you can spare (al-Baqarah 2: 219).

Those [servants of the Most-merciful] who, when they spend, are neither wasteful nor niggardly, but between those two is a just mean (al-Furqān 25: 67).

And keep not your hand shackled to your neck nor outspread it altogether, lest you find yourself blamed or even destitute (al-Isrā' 17: 29).

Give to the Deserving

Eighth: And, finally, take note of the categories of persons as given by Allah, who deserve your help.

And give the kinsman his right, and the needy, and the traveller (al-Isrā' 17: 26).

[True piety is] to give wealth, for love of Him, unto kinsmen, and ophans, the needy, the traveller, and the beggars, and for freeing necks from bondage (al-Baqarah 2: 177).

And do good unto parents, and the near kinsmen, and un to orphans, and unto the needy, and unto the neighbour who is of kin, and unto the neighbour who is a stranger, and unto the companion by your side, and unto the traveller and unto that your right hand owns (al-Nisā' 4:36).

And they give food unto the needy and the orphan and the prisoner, for the love of Him, [saying]: We feed you only to seek God's countenance; we desire no reward from you, nor thanks, for we fear from our Lord a distressful, fateful day (al-Dahr 76: 8, 10).

And in their wealth there is a right for beggars and the have-nots (al-Dhāriyāt 51: 19).

[What you spend is] for the poor who are wholly confined to God's cause, and are unable to go about the earth [to earn their livelihood]. The ignorant man supposes them to be rich because of their abstinence [from begging], but you shall recognize them by their mark – they do not beg of men with importunity. And whatever good you spend, surely God knows it all (al-Baqarah 2: 273).

23

Specific Injunctions of Zakah

Brothers in Islam! We turn now from the general directions concerning spending in the way of God to the specific injunctions about Zakah, as an obligatory act of worship.

Produce of the Earth

In the Qur'ān, you will find three injunctions regarding Zakah. The following two Ayahs relate to the produce of the earth:

> O believers! Spend out of the good things which you have earned and out of that which We bring forth for you from the earth (al-Baqarah 2: 267).

> Eat of their fruits when it comes to fruition and give their due on the harvest day (al-An'ām 6: 141).

According to the Ḥanafī jurists, to Allah is due a share of every produce of the earth except self-growing things such as wood and grass. Other Hadith specify that Allah's due is one-twentieth of irrigated crops and one-tenth of the rain-fed crops. This due becomes payable as soon as the harvest is in.

On Wealth and Financial Assets

The third Ayah relates to Zakah on cash, gold, silver, trade goods and other similar wealth.

> And those who hoard up treasures of gold and silver and spend it not in the way of God – unto them give the good tidings of a painful punishment, on the day when that [hoarded wealth] shall be heated in the fire of Hell and their foreheads and their sides and their backs will be branded therewith: Here is what you had hoarded up for yourselves. Taste, then, your hoarded treasures (al-Tawbah 9: 34–5).

Further, we read:

> The Alms are [meant] only for the poor and needy, and those who administer them, and those whose hearts are to be reconciled, and for freeing the necks from bondage, and for the overburdened debtors, and in the way of God, and for the traveller: so ordains God; and God is All-knowing, and All-wise (al-Tawbah 9: 60).

And, again:

> Take of their wealth the Alms, so that you may cleanse them thereby and purify and develop them (al-Tawbah 9: 103).

The wealth, as you know, which is saved and made to grow but is not spent in the way of Allah, becomes impure. The only way to purify it is to take out of it Allah's due and give it to His servants.

It is narrated that when severe warning came against the hoarders of gold and silver, Muslims became worried because they thought it meant they had to spend all the money they had. 'Umar conveyed their anxieties to the Prophet, blessings and peace be on him, and requested him to clarify the situation. He said:

Allah has made it obligatory to pay Zakah for this very reason that your remaining wealth may become pure for you (*Abū Dā'ūd*).

Abū Sa'īd al-Khudrī also narrates that the Prophet, blessings and peace be on him, told him: Once you take Zakah out of your wealth, then what was due upon you has been paid off.

The above injunctions are about the Zakah on produce from the earth and gold and silver, but, according to the Sunnah, Zakah is also due on merchandise, camels, cows and goats. '*Niṣāb*' or scale (amount on which Zakah becomes payable) of some kinds of wealth is as below:

Silver:	200 dirhams or 52½ tolas (595 grams)
Gold:	7½ tolas (85 grams)
Merchandise:	Equal to the price of 52½ tolas of silver (595grams).*
Camel:	5 camels
Goat:	40 goats
Cow:	30 cows

Jewellery

If gold and silver are in the form of jewellery, even then, according to 'Umar and Abdullah Ibn Mas'ūd, Zakah is payable on them. Abū Ḥanīfah has accepted this view. Once the Prophet, blessings and peace be on him, seeing two women wearing golden bracelets, asked them: 'Do you give Zakah?' One of them said 'No'. He said, 'Would you like that on the Day of

---

*Whoever remains in possession of the above amounts or quantities must pay Zakah on them. For wealth, the rate is 2½ per cent. According to the Ḥanafī school, Zakah is payable on gold and silver if their quantities, together, are equal to the *niṣāb*.

Judgement you are made to wear, in their place, bracelets of fire?' (*Tirmidhī*).

Umm Salamah tells that she once asked the Prophet, blessings and peace be on him, if her golden anklets would also be regarded as 'hoarded treasure'. He replied: 'If the gold in it equals the *niṣāb* and Zakah has been given on it, then it is not a 'hoarded treasure' (*Abū Dā'ūd*).

Zakah, thus, must be paid on gold and silver, even if they are in the shape of ornaments, just as on cash. According to some jurists, however, Zakah need not be given on jewels and precious stones.

Who Are Entitled to Receive Zakah

Eight categories of people, according to the Qur'ān, are entitled to receive Zakah.

Fuqarā: the poor

Fuqarā' are those who do have some money but not sufficient to meet their essential needs. They live under great hardship and difficulties but do not beg from anybody. *Fuqarā'* have been so defined by Zuhrī, Abū Ḥanīfah, Abdullah Ibn 'Abbās, Ḥasan Baṣrī and many other eminent jurists.

Masākīn: the destitute and needy

Masākīn are totally destitute, they have nothing to meet their needs with. 'Umar also includes among them those who are fit to work but are unemployed.

'Amilīna 'alayhā: who administer Zakah

People who are appointed by an Islamic government to collect Zakah will be paid their salaries from Zakah funds.

Mu'allafatu 'l-qulūb: who need to be reconciled

These are the people who require to be given money to seek their support for Islam or to prevent them from opposition. Muslim converts are also included in this category. Those of them who may lose their jobs or homes upon becoming Muslims deserve every help, but even wealthy converts may be given Zakah to reconcile them by showing at first hand the caring nature of Islam. After the battle of Ḥunayn, the Prophet, blessings and peace be on him, gave so much of the booty to Muslim converts that some Anṣār complained about it. He replied: 'These people have just entered Islam after giving up Disbelief, and I want to please their hearts.' On this basis, Zuhrī has defined mu'allafatu 'l-qulūb thus: 'Any Christian or Jew or non-Muslim who has entered Islam, though he may be a wealthy man.'*

Fī 'r-riqāb: freeing from bondage

A slave who wants to free himself from slavery should be given Zakah so that he can pay the necessary money to his master. Today, as slavery no longer exists, this category can be extended, in my opinion, to other such people like those who have been imprisoned for their inability to pay fines imposed upon them, they can be helped with Zakah money to secure their release.

Al-ghārimīn: overburdened debtors

People who are so overburdened with debt that they cannot pay it on their own. But Zakah should not be given to debtors whose wealth exceeds their debts. It can be given to people whose debts are so large that, after paying them off, their remaining

---

*This was not the occasion to discuss the juridicial controversies arising from this issue. We have discussed them in *Tafhimul Qur'ān,* Vol. 2, under the commentary on Surah al-Tawbah.

wealth falls below the minimum amount on which Zakah is leviable. Some Jurists have said that it is undesirable to give Zakah to people who have fallen into debt due to extravagant habits, because the expectation of continuing help from Zakah will encourage them to continue their extravagance.

Fī-sabīli 'llāh: in the way of Allah

This is a general term used for all good deeds. But, in particular, it means giving help to a struggle for making Islam supreme on earth. The Prophet, blessings and peace be on him, once said that it was not normally permissible for a wealthy person to take Zakah but if such a person required help for the sake of Jihad, he should be given it.

Ibnu 's-sabīl: travellers

A traveller may have any amount of wealth in his home, but if he is in need of money while travelling, he may be given Zakah.

Other Important Principles

The eight categories of people described above are all, in principle, entitled to Zakah. There are, however, some other rules about entitlement within these categories.

1. All schools of law are agreed that parents and children cannot give Zakah to each other, nor can husbands and wives. A distant relative is beyond doubt entitled to it, in fact more entitled than others, though Auzā'ī says: Do not go about searching your own relatives after taking out Zakah.

2. Only Muslims are entitled to receive Zakah. The definition of Zakah, as given in Hadith is:

> It will be taken from the wealthy among you and distributed to the poor *among you* (*Bukhārī, Muslim*).

Non-Muslims, however, have a share in all other general charities, or social security payments, where it is wrong to discriminate against them.

3. Abū Ḥanīfah, Abū Yūsuf and Muhammad say that the Zakah raised in a locality should be spent on the poor inhabitants of the same locality. It is not proper to send Zakah from one locality to another unless no one there is entitled to receive it or some calamity such as flood or famine necessitates urgent despatch. But this does not mean that sending Zakah from one place to another is prohibited.

4. Some early scholars think that Zakah should not be accepted by a person who has enough provision for two meals. Others set varying minimum qualifying amounts. It is important to remember here that law is one thing and desirable conduct another. An example of desirable conduct was given by the Prophet, blessings and peace be on him, when he said that if a person who had enough for morning and evening meals asked for charity, he would 'collect fire [in the Hereafter] for himself' (*Muslim*). He is also reported as saying: 'I would like a person to cut wood from a tree and feed himself from its proceed instead of going about begging' (*Bukhārī*).Another Hadith states that a person who has got something to eat or is strong enough to earn his livelihood must not accept Zakah (*Tirmidhī*).

But this is a lesson in sublime conduct. The minimum legal requirements for being eligible to receive Zakah are found in other Hadith. For instance:

> The Prophet, blessings and peace be on him, said: Zakah is the right of anyone who asks for it, though he may have come to you on horseback (*Abū Dā'ūd*).

> On another occasion two persons called on him and asked for Zakah. He looked at them and said: If you want to take it I shall give it you. But in this wealth there is no share for the rich and for the able-bodied who can earn (*Abū Dā'ūd*).

Once, a person asked him: I have ten coins with me. Am poor? He replied: Yes.

What is clear is that whoever possesses money below the amount, *niṣāb,* which makes him liable to pay Zakah, is eligible to receive it. It is a different matter that the right to take Zakah really belongs to those who are in dire need of it.

Need For Collective System

I want to draw your attention to one further important aspect of Zakah which Muslims today tend to overlook. In Islam all obligatory acts of worship are carried out on a collective basis. It does not approve of unreined individualism. If you are far from the mosque, you may perform the Prayer alone. But the Shari'ah demands that it should be offered in congregation whenever possible. Similarly, if there is no alternative, it is permissible to take out Zakah and distribute it on an individual basis. But efforts should always be made to collectivize the giving of Zakah in order that its distribution be conducted systematically. That is why the Prophet, blessings and peace be on him, and not every Muslim individually, was instructed by Allah to collect Zakah from Muslims and distribute it.

> Take of their wealth the Alms so that you may cleanse them thereby and purify and develop them (al-Tawbah 9: 103).

Similarly, the fixing of a share in Zakah for its collection and distribution costs clearly indicates that the correct method is for the head of the Muslim Ummah to receive it regularly and distribute it systematically. That is why the Prophet, blessings and peace be on him, said: I have been commanded to collect Zakah from the rich among you and distribute it to the poor among you.

He himself, and the Caliphs, may Allah be pleased with them, arranged so that all Zakah was collected by the officials of the Islamic government and distributed from the centre. Where there is no arrangement to collect Zakah and distribute it in this manner, you should individually take out your Zakah and spend it under the heads laid down in the Shari'ah. But it is incumbent on all Muslims to work to establish a collective system for this purpose, because without it the benefits accruing from making Zakah obligatory remain incomplete.

PART VI
Hajj

24

Origin and Significance of Hajj

Brothers in Islam! Hajj, or the Pilgrimage, is the last among those acts of worship which Islam enjoins upon you. Like the Prayer, Fasting and Almsgiving, it moulds your life and prepares you so that you may live in surrender to Allah.

The word Hajj means to make a resolve to visit a holy place: visiting the Ka'ba in Makka is therefore called Hajj.

How did it begin? The origin of Hajj is rooted in the Prophet Ibrāhīm's life, peace be on him. That story is very instructive, and illustrative, too, of the true meaning and significance of Hajj. That story you must know to fully understand the benefits Hajj can bring to you.

Life and Mission of the Prophet Ibrāhīm

Which Muslim, Christian or Jew does not know the name of Ibrāhīm (peace be on him)! Two-thirds of mankind revere him as their leader. The Prophets Mūsā, 'Īsā and Muhammad, peace be on them, are all his descendants. It is the lamp of guidance lit by him that has for long illuminated the whole world.

Ibrāhīm's Times

Ibrāhīm was born in what is now Iraq, over four thousand years ago. At that time the people had forgotten the One God. No one recognized Him as the Master, no one lived in surrender and obedience to Him. The people among whom Ibrāhīm was born, while the most advanced in the world in art and science, industry and agriculture, were also the most steeped in ignorance and error. One simple thing they, despite their technological advance, could not understand: anything which has itself been created cannot be worthy of worship. Idolatry was the norm. Superstitions like astrology, idol-worship, divination, witchcraft and use of talismen and amulets were widespread.

A priest class controlled the temples, supervised worship rites and rituals, conducted marriage and funeral ceremonies, and claimed to be oracles, able to disclose the unknown, foretell the future, and determine Divine wishes. And the people, in general, believed that they indeed had such powers, that they had access to their deities, that they could intercede with them on their behalf or invoke their wrath to fall upon them. For them the priests were the lords of their fate.

The kings were in collusion with the priests, the two sides working together to keep the people under their servitude. They gave full backing to the priests, and the priests made the people believe that the king of the day, as well as being the owner of his country and complete master of his subjects, was also a god among other gods. His word was the supreme law; his power over their lives and properties was absolute. Indeed, worship rites were performed for and before the king so that the belief in his godhood came to be entrenched in the minds of his subjects.

In times like this, the Prophet Ibrāhīm was born into a family of privileged priests. His forefathers were high priests and it was quite natural that he should follow in their footsteps. He received the same education and training; the same gifts and offerings were awaiting him. Many adherents were eagerly waiting for the moment when they could bow their heads before him with folded hands. The ancestral seat of priestly power could be his for the taking.

In this dismal darkness, where not a single soul existed who knew or believed in the Truth, it would not ordinarily have been possible for a man like Ibrāhīm to find its light, nor break away from the life of comfort and power mapped out for him by his family.

Commitment to the Truth

But the Prophet Ibrāhīm was no ordinary man; he was made of different stuff. On reaching maturity he began to reflect thus: How can the sun, moon or stars, which are rotating as if by order like slaves, and these stone idols, which are made by man himself; and these kings, who are human beings like ourselves, be gods? What is there in these powerless objects, which cannot move of their own volition, which have no power to help themselves and have no control over their own lives and deaths, that man should worship them, seek fulfilment of his wants from them, fear their powers and submit in obedience to them? Among all the objects on earth and in the heavens, there is not a single one which itself is not subject to some higher power and which does not fade away into oblivion at some time or other.

When none of them is my creator, when neither my life nor death is in the hands of any of them, when none of them possesses the key to my means of sustenance or the fulfilment of my needs, why should I accept them as lords, surrender to them, and obey them? Only that Being can be my Lord who created all things, on whom depends everything and in whose hands are the lives and deaths of all people.

These thoughts led the Prophet Ibrāhīm to the decision that he would never worship the deities which his people worshipped, and he openly declared before them:

O my people, I am quit of all those you take as gods beside God. I have turned my face unto Him who brought into being the heavens and the earth, having turned away from all false gods; and I am not of those who take gods beside God (al-An'ām 6: 79–80).

Tribulations and Calamities

No sooner had he made this declaration than tribulations and calamities of the greatest magnitude descended on him. His father threatened him with expulsion from the family home. His community warned him that no one among them would give him refuge. And the government officials insisted on his case being brought before the King. But Ibrāhīm, lonely and forsaken by his relatives and friends, stood firm as a rock in the cause of Truth. He told his father respectfully: The knowledge I have has not been vouchsafed to you. As such, instead of my following you, you should follow me [Maryam 19: 41–5]. In answer to the threats of his community he broke their idols with his own hands to prove how powerless they were [al-Anbiyā' 21: 57–70]. In the court of the King, he boldly declared: You are not my Lord. My Lord is He in whose hands are your life and death as well as mine, and within the bounds of whose law even the movements of the sun are circumscribed [al-Baqarah 2: 258].

The royal court decided that Ibrāhīm should be burnt alive and he willingly came forward to suffer this horrible punishment for the sake of his unshakeable faith in the One God. After Allah with His supreme power saved him from this fate, he abandoned his home, his relations, his community and his country. He set out with his wife, Sarah, and a nephew, Lūṭ, to wander from one land to another.

To this man the undisputed religious leadership of his people had been available. Yet he gave up wealth and power and preferred the life of a homeless and destitute wanderer rather than have to mislead people into the continuing worship of false gods. He chose to live for the purpose of summoning people to their true God, even though he would be driven from place to place.

Migration

After leaving his home, the Prophet Ibrāhīm wandered in Egypt, Palestine and Arabia. God, alone, knows what sufferings he went through on his journeyings. He had no money or possessions nor did he have time to earn his livelihood. His sole vocation, day and night, was to bring people to the worship of the One God. If a man of such ideas could not be tolerated by his own father and his own community, how was he going to be any more successful elsewhere? Where would he be welcomed? Everywhere the same temple priests and kings claiming godhood held sway; everywhere the same confused and ignorant common men lived, who were completely hoodwinked by them.

How could, then, Ibrāhīm live peacefully in such an environment? For, not only was he himself not ready to accept the godhood of anybody except God, but he was also committed to proclaiming to the people that none except Allah was their Master and Lord and that, therefore, they should ignore the authority of their leaders and demi-gods and submit only to that One Being.

Thus condemned to a nomadic existence, wandering through Palestine, Egypt and the vast deserts of Arabia, he passed his whole adult life.

Raising a New Generation

During the last period of his life, when he was eighty-six and had despaired of offspring, Allah gave him a child, Ismā'īl. But even then, this loyal servant of Allah did not think that, having himself wrecked his own home life, he should at least prepare his children to earn their living. No. His only concern was that the mission on which he had spent his whole life should be carried on after his death. It was for this purpose that he had prayed to Allah to grant him children [al-Baqarah 2: 128]. And when Allah granted his request, his only thought was to educate and train them to continue his mission.

The life of this perfect man was the life of a true and genuine *muslim*. In early adulthood, when he had found God, God asked him: '*aslim*', that is, enter Islam, surrender yourself totally to Me, be solely Mine. In reply, he gave the pledge: '*aslamtu li-rabbi 'l-ālamīn*', that is, I have entered Islam, I belong to the Lord of the worlds, I have entrusted myself wholly to Him, I am ever-ready to obey (al-Baqarah 2: 13).

To this pledge Ibrāhīm remained true throughout his life. He gave up, for the sake of the Lord of the worlds, his ancestral religion together with its beliefs and rituals and renounced all the material benefits he could have derived from it. He braved the danger of fire, suffered homelessness, wandered from country to country, but spent every moment of his life in obedience to the Lord and in propagating His Dīn.

The Greatest of Trials

But even after all these tribulations, there was still one trial left to determine whether Ibrāhīm's love for his Lord was supreme above all else. Before the birth of his second son, he was asked to sacrifice what was then his only child to God [al-Ṣāffāt 37: 99–111]. When Allah had shown that Ibrāhīm was prepared to slaughter his son for His sake with his own hands, He said: 'You have fully vindicated your claim to be a totally true Muslim. Now you deserve to be made the leader of the whole world.' This act of investiture has been described in the Qur'ān thus:

And when his Lord tested Ibrāhīm with [His] commands, and he fulfilled them all, He said, Behold, I make you a leader of mankind. Said he [Ibrāhīm]: And of my offspring [will they too be leaders]? He said: My covenant shall not reach the evil-doers (al-Baqarah 2: 124).

The Universal Islamic Movement

In this manner Ibrāhīm became a pioneer of the universal Islamic movement and set about establishing permanent missions in different regions. In this task he was aided by his nephew, Lūṭ, his eldest son, Ismā' īl who, on learning that the Lord of the worlds wanted the sacrifice of his life, had himself willingly placed his neck under the knife, and his younger son, Isḥāq.

Lūṭ in Sodom

Ibrāhīm settled his nephew, Lūṭ, in Sodom, which was infamous for its moral depravity. Ibrāhīm's objective was to reform the people and also to influence the far-flung area around; traders travelling between Iran, Iraq and Eqypt used to pass through the region, and it was therefore an ideal place from which to spread God's message.

Isḥāq in Palestine

The younger son, Isḥāq, was settled in Palestine. This region, situated between Syria and Egypt, and being on the coast, was also a good centre for spreading Ibrāhīm's message. From this region the Islamic movement reached Egypt through Isḥāq's son, Ya'qūb (whose name was also Israel), and through his grandson, Yūsuf, peace be on all of them.

The elder son, Ismā' īl, was assigned his headquarters at Makka in the Hijaz and Ibrāhīm himself stayed with him for a long time to propagate the teaching of Islam throughout Arabia.

Construction of the Ka'ba

It was in Makka that Ibrāhīm and his son built the Holy Ka'ba, the centre of the Islamic movement, on a site chosen by Allah Himself. This building was not intended for worship only, as mosques are; its purpose was to act as the centre for spreading the universal movement of Islam, a world-wide gathering point for believers in the One God to assemble to worship Allah in congregation and go back to their respective countries carrying with them the message of Islam. This was the assembly which was named Hajj. Exactly how this centre was constructed, with what hopes and prayers both father and son raised its walls, and how Hajj was initiated are described thus in the Qur'ān:

> The first House ever set up for mankind was indeed that at Bakkah, a blessed place, and a guidance unto all beings; wherein are clear signs – the place whereon Ibrāhīm stood; and whosoever enters it finds peace (Āl 'Imrān 3: 96–7).

> Have they not seen that We have made the sanctuary immune [from violence], while men are being carried away by force all around them (al-'Ankabūt 29: 67).

Peace always reigned in and around the Ka'ba, when all around it were rampant plunder, murder, devastation, conflict, and warfare – such was its sanctity that even the Bedouins who respected no law, if they detected in its precincts the murderer of even their father, did not dare to touch him.

Prayers of Ibrāhīm

Look at Ibrāhīm's prayers to find out what the real purpose and significance of Hajj is:

> And when We made the House a place of visitation for mankind, and a sanctuary: take, then, the place whereon

Ibrāhīm stood for place of prayer. And We commanded Ibrāhīm and Ismāʿīl, 'Purify My House for those who will walk around it, and those who will abide therein in worship, and those who will bow down and prostrate themselves.' And when Ibrāhīm prayed: My Lord! Make this a land secure and provide its people fruits, such of them as believe in God and the Last Day . . .

And when Ibrāhīm was raising the foundations of the House, and Ismāʿīl, [they prayed]: Our Lord! Accept Thou this from us. Thou, Thou alone, art the Allhearing, the All-knowing. Our Lord! And make us surrender ourselves unto Thee, and out of our offspring make people surrender themselves unto Thee; and show us our rites of worship, and turn toward us; surely Thou alone turnest, and art the Mercy-giving. Our Lord! Do Thou send to them a Messenger, from among them, who shall convey unto them Thy revelations, and teach them the Book and the Wisdom, and purify and develop them. Thou alone art the All-mighty, the All-wise! (al-Baqarah 2: 125–9).

And when Ibrāhīm prayed, My Lord! Make this land secure, and keep me and my sons away from worshipping idols. My Lord! They have led astray many people. Hence whoso follows me truly belongs to me; and whoso disobeys me – surely Thou art All-forgiving, Mercy-giving. Our Lord! I have settled some of my offspring in a valley where are no arable lands, near Thy sanctified House, our Lord, so that they may perform the Prayer, and Thou make peoples' hearts to incline towards them, and provide them fruits so that they may be thankful (Ibrāhīm 14: 35–7).

And when We assigned unto Ibrāhīm the place of the House, [We said]: You shall not take any god beside Me, and purify My House for those who will walk around it and those who will stand, and those who will bow down and prostrate themselves. And proclaim unto mankind the Pilgrimage; and they will come unto you on foot and on every lean mount, they will come from every deep ravine, so that they may witness things that are of benefit to them, and mention God's name during the days appointed over such heads of cattle He has provided them. Eat, then, thereof, and feed therewith the unfortunate poor (al-Ḥajj 22: 26–8).

Brothers in Islam! This is the story of the beginning of that Hajj which is the fifth pillar of Islam. You now understand that Makka was the headquarters for the mission of the first Prophet appointed to propagate the message of Islam. The Ka'ba was the focal point from where this preaching was spread across the world, and the worship rites of Hajj were introduced so that all those who chose to live in surrender to God alone should belong to one centre where they could assemble every year, and go around it again and again. Their lives of faith were to be like the wheel tied to and revolving around its axle.

25

Restoration of True Hajj

Brothers in Islam! Hajj, or the Pilgrimage, was instituted by the Prophet Ibrāhīm to serve as the focal meeting place for all believers in the One God. Thus he made Makka the centre of the world-wide Islamic movement and installed his elder son, the Prophet Ismāʿīl, there to continue his mission.

Idol Worship Among Ibrāhīm's Descendants

Only God knows exactly how long Ismāʿīl's children stayed on the right path. But within a few centuries of the death of Ibrāhīm and Ismāʿīl people had abandoned their teachings and had gradually gone astray like all other people around them. Hundreds of idols were installed in the sacred Kaʿba, which had been built as a centre for the worship of the One God. Ironically enough, idols were made of Ibrāhīm and Ismāʿīl too, whose whole lives had been spent eradicating idol-worship. The descendants of Ibrāhīm, who had repudiated all idols, began to worship idols like *Lāt, Manāt, Hubal, Nasr, Yaghūth, ʿUzzā, Asāf, Nāʾilah* and many more. They also worshipped the sun, moon, Venus, and Saturn. They also worshipped *jinns,* ghosts, angels and the spirits of their dead ancestors. Superstition rose to such a level that if they did not have the family idol with them while away from home, they worshipped any stone they came across on their way. Or, if no stone was available, even a round ball made of clay with a sprinkle of goat's milk over it served as their god. Reverting to the same kind of priesthood which Ibrāhīm had fought so fiercely against in Iraq, they turned the Ka'ba into a sort of temple and installed themselves as priests there. Adopting all the tricks of priests, they began accepting gifts and offerings from pilgrims flocking from the four corners of Arabia. In this way all the work done by Ibrāhīm and Ismā'īl was destroyed and the purpose for which they had introduced the system of Hajj was superseded by different types of objectives.

How Corrupted Hajj Became

A Yearly Carnival

The degree to which Hajj was corrupted in that period of Ignorance can be gauged from the fact that it degenerated into an annual carnival. For many tribes from near and far, Hajj became an important social event. Poets and clowns used it to brag and boast about the bravery, renown, dignity, strength and generosity of their tribes. They even resorted to hurling insults at one another. The chiefs of the tribes vied with each other in flaunting their generosity. They slaughtered camel after camel with the sole purpose of extolling their name, generosity and hospitality. Singing, revelry, drinking, and adultery were part and parcel of the festivities. The thought of God scarcely occurred to anybody.

Perverse Rites

Circumambulation [*ṭawāf*] of the Ka'ba did continue, it is true; but in what form? Men and women walked together around God's House stark naked, saying, 'We go before God just as our mothers gave birth to us.' Worship also continued to be performed in the mosque of Ibrāhīm, but again, in what form? By clapping hands, by whistling and by blowing horns. The name of God was proclaimed, but with what words? They said: Here am I, my Lord, I am present. No one is Thy partner except the one who is Thine. Thou art its master, of whatever it possesses.

They did make sacrifices in the name of God. But the blood of the sacrificial animals was spilt on the walls of the Ka'ba and their flesh thrown at its door in the belief that Allah needs that flesh and blood.

Sacrilege of Sacred Months

Ibrāhīm had declared four months of Hajj as sacred and had directed that no warfare should be waged in these months. These people partially observed this sanctity; but if they wanted to fight during the sacred months, they simply declared Ibrāhīm's ruling null and void for a particular period and added extra 'holy months' the following year.

Self-imposed Restrictions

Even those who were sincere towards religion were led into strange, excessive ways by their ignorance. Some people used to set out for Hajj without any provisions for the journey and lived by begging food. They considered this an act of piety, claiming that they had full trust in God and, while proceeding towards the House of God, had no need of worldly goods. Doing business or working during the Hajj journey were generally considered unlawful. Many people gave up food and water during Hajj, and regarded this abstention as worship. Others stopped speaking while on Hajj, which they called *al-Hajju' 'l-Muṣmit,* the dumb Pilgrimage.

There were countless other customs of this type which I do not want to waste your time describing.

Restoration of Hajj

Fulfilment of Ibrāhīm's Prayer

This situation lasted for about two thousand years. No prophet was born in Arabia during this long period nor did any prophet's genuine teachings reach the people of Arabia. Finally, however, the time arrived for granting Ibrāhīm's prayer which he had made while raising the walls of the Ka'ba:

> Our Lord! Do Thou send to them a Messenger, from among them, who shall convey unto them Thy revelations, and teach them the Book and the Wisdom, and purify and develop them (al-Baqarah 2: 129).

The perfect man who descended from Ibrāhīm was Muhammad Ibn Abdullah, blessings and peace be on him.

Just as Ibrāhīm was born into a family of priests, so was Muhammad, blessings and peace be on him, into a family which had been for centuries priests of the Ka'ba. Just as Ibrāhīm struck a blow with his own hands against the priesthood of his family, so did Muhammad, blessings and peace be on him, finally eradicating it for good. Again, just as Ibrāhīm strove to end the worship of false gods and bring people under submission to the One God, so did the Prophet Muhammad, blessings and peace be on him, revive the same pure Din which had been introduced by Ibrāhīm. After 21 years, when he had completed this work, once again, at God's command, he declared the Ka'ba the centre of all those in the world who surrendered to God alone and issued the same summons to the people to come to it for Hajj as had Ibrāhīm.

> A duty owed to God by all men is the Pilgrimage to the House, if one is able to make his way there. And as for the disbeliever, God is All-sufficient, needing nothing from all the worlds (Āl 'Imrān 3: 97).

Revival of Ibrāhīm's Ways

Along with the renewal of Hajj in its proper form came an end to the customs of the time of Ignorance which had persisted for two thousand years.

End of Idolatry

All the idols in the Ka'ba were smashed. The worship of any and every object other than God was completely eliminated. All fairs and sports were closed down and it was laid down that worship would be carried out only in the manner ordained by God.

> And remember Him as He has guided you, for formerly you had gone astray (al-Baqarah 2: 198).

Prohibition of Indecent Acts

All indecent acts were strictly banned.

> Whoso undertakes the Pilgrimage in those [months] should abstain from lewd speech, from iniquity, and from quarrelling during the Pilgrimage (al-Baqarah 2: 197).

Bragging and Showing Off

Contention among poets, boasting of forefathers' achievements, contests in satire and sycophancy were all stopped.

> And when you have completed your rites, then remember God as you remember your fathers, or yet more intensely (al-Baqarah 2: 200).

End of Ostentatious Generosity

All competitions in so-called generosity which were meant solely for ostentation and fame were banned, and in their place was revived the customs of Ibrāhīm's days of slaughtering animals exclusively in the name of Allah, so that the sacrifice made by the well-to-do people provided poor pilgrims with meat.

> Eat and drink, but be not wasteful. Surely He loves not the wasteful (al-A'rāf 7: 31).

> So mention God's name over them [the animals] when they are lined up; then, when their sides fall [dead], eat of them and feed the beggar and the suppliant (al-Ḥajj 22: 36).

Spattering of Blood and Flesh Banned

The practice of spattering the blood of the sacrificial animals on the walls of the Ka'ba and throwing their flesh at its door was stopped.

> Never does their flesh reach God, and neither their blood, but godliness from you reaches Him (al-Ḥajj 22: 37).

Prohibition of Perverse Rites

Circumambulation in the state of nudity was strictly prohibited:

> Say: 'Who is there to forbid the adornment which God has brought forth for His servants' (al-A'rāf 7: 28).

> Say: 'Never does God enjoin indecent acts' (al-A'rāf 7: 28).

> Children of Adam! Take to your adornment for every act of worship (al-A'rāf 7: 31).

Changing the Months of Hajj Forbidden

Interchanging the months of Hajj so as to make fighting permissible was prohibited:

> Postponing [of a sanctified month] is but an increase in disbelief whereby Unbelievers are led astray. They allow it one year and forbid it another year, to agree with the number of the months which God has sanctified and thus they allow what God has forbidden (al-Tawbah 9: 37).

Hajj Provisions Made Obligatory

People were prohibited from starting out on Hajj without taking adequate provisions. Clarification was made that not taking provisions for a journey in this world did not mean, as was popularly believed, that one was thereby taking provisions for the Hereafter:

> And take provision for yourselves, but the best provision is God-consciousness (al-Baqarah 2: 197).

Permission to Work During Hajj

The popular belief that it was an act of piety not to work for money or earning a livelihood during Hajj was refuted:

> It is no sin for you that you seek bounty from your Lord [by trading] (al-Baqarah 2: 198).

End of Other Customs

The customs of performing Hajj, while remaining silent, hungry and thirsty were also ended.

After abolishing all perverse customs of the pre-Islamic days, Hajj was made a model of piety, fear of God, purity, simplicity and austerity. The pilgrims were ordered to purify themselves spiritually, to give up worldly things, to avoid all sexual desires, even refrain from intercourse with their wives, and to totally refrain from using bad and abusive language.

Fixing Boundaries

Boundaries were defined on all roads leading to the Ka'ba to indicate the points beyond which no pilgrims were allowed to proceed without putting on two seamless garments, the *Iḥrām,* or the robes of poverty, so that the rich and the poor would become equal, distinctions of nationality would disappear, and everyone would arrive at the court of Allah in a state of oneness as humble suppliants.

Ensuring Peace and Security

It was prohibited to kill any animal while wearing *Iḥrām,* let alone a human being. The object was to ensure that peace and security prevailed, aggressiveness was controlled, and spiritually gripped the hearts and minds of the pilgrims. The four months of Hajj were made sacred so that no fighting took place during this period, peace reigned on all the roads leading to the Ka'ba and no pilgrims were molested *en route.*

When the pilgrims reached the Ka'ba, there were no funfairs, no carnivals. Instead, there was remembrance of God at every step. There were Prayers, sacrifices and circumambulation (*ṭawāf*) of the Ka'ba. The only cry that one could hear was that which arose from the heart of the pilgrim:

> Here am I before Thee, O God, doubly at Thy service. Before Thee I am, there is no partner unto Thee, doubly at Thy service here am I. All praise and blessings are Thine, and power. There is no partner unto Thee.

Such selfless and sincere Hajj the Prophet, blessings and peace be on him, has described thus:

> Whosoever performs Hajj solely for the sake of God and, in the course of it, abstains from sensuality and

disobedience, he returns from there as immaculate as a child just born (*Bukhārī, Muslim*).

Importance of Hajj

See, now, how important this Hajj is. Allah says:

A duty owed to God by all men is the Pilgrimage to the House, if he is able to make his way there. And as for the disbeliever, God is All-sufficient, needing nothing from all the worlds (Āl 'Imrān 3: 97).

Here, failure to perform Hajj if you have the means to do so, is described as Disbelief. Its explanation is found in two Hadith of the Prophet, blessings and peace be on him:

Whosoever possesses provisions and conveyance for a journey to the House of God, but, in spite of this, does not perform Hajj, then his dying is like the dying of a Jew or a Christian (*Tirmidhī*).

Whosoever is not prevented from proceeding for Hajj by any clear, dire need that he must fulfil, or by a tyrant ruler, or by a disease which confines him, and yet he fails to perform Hajj and dies in this condition, he may as well choose to die either a Jew or a Christian (*Dārimī*).

Elucidating this Hadith, 'Umar said: I wish to impose *jizyah* (poll tax meant specifically for non-Muslims who were exempt from conscription) on those who do not perform Hajj in spite of possessing the required means. They are not Muslims, they are not Muslims!

From the commandment of Allah and its elucidation by the Prophet, blessings and peace be on him, and his Caliph, you can clearly see that Hajj is not something which may or may not be performed according to personal whim. It is obligatory

LET US BE MUSLIMS

at least once in a lifetime on all Muslims, wherever they live in the world, who can afford to make the journey and who are physically able to. Responsibilities to one's family or business are no grounds for exemption.

Those who, despite the necessary means, put off Hajj year after year on some pretext or other should take care of the state of their Iman. As for those who never bother to think about performing the Hajj at all, but who nonetheless manage to travel all over the world, perhaps even passing within a few hours' journeying time of Makka on their way to Europe – such people are certainly not Muslims. They lie if they call themselves Muslims, and people who consider them Muslims are ignorant of the Qur'ān. At least their hearts are devoid of any feeling of obedience to God and they have no faith in His commandments.

26

Renewal of Self

Brothers in Islam! What are the blessings of Hajj? One may describe them in great detail. But, in the Qur'ān, where Allah instructs Ibrāhīm to invite people to come for Hajj, it is said:

> So that they may witness things that are of benefit to them (al-Ḥajj 22: 28).

Hence, the real blessings of Hajj can only be experienced by those who actually perform it. Imam Abū Ḥanīfah, it is narrated, was unsure which act of worship was more excellent among the various ones laid down by Islam. But once he had performed Hajj, he had no hesitation in declaring that Hajj was the most excellent of all.

Still, I shall now try to give you, briefly, some idea of its blessings.

The Journey

We usually think of journeys as of two kinds: those made for business and those made for pleasure. In both cases, it is to fulfil your worldly desires and benefit yourselves that you leave your homes, separate from families, spend money – all is done for your own sake. No question arises of sacrifice for any higher, sublime purpose.

But the journey that is the Hajj is quite different in nature. This is not meant for any personal end. It is undertaken solely for Allah, and the fulfilment of the duty prescribed by Allah. Nobody can be prepared to undertake this journey until and unless he has love of Allah in his heart as well as fear of Him, and is convinced that Allah wants him to do what he is doing. That you are willing to bear the privations arising from separation from your family, to incur great expenses on a journey that will bring no material rewards and to suffer any loss of business or job, all are signs of certain inner qualities: that you love and fear Allah more than anything, that you have a strong sense of duty to Him, that you are willing to respond to His summons and ready to sacrifice your material comforts in His cause.

Virtue and Piety

You will find that your love of God heightens as you start preparing for your pilgrimage journey, with the sole intention of pleasing Allah. With your heart longing to reach your goal, you become purer in thought and deed. You repent for past sins, seek forgiveness from people whom you might have wronged, and try to render your due to others where necessary so as not to go to God's court burdened with injustices that you may have done to your fellow beings. In general, the inclination for doing good intensifies and abhorrence for doing evil increases.

After leaving home, the closer you get to the House of God, the more intense becomes your desire to do good. You become careful so that you harm nobody, while you try to render whatever service or help you can to others. You avoid abuse, indecency, dishonesty, squabbles and bickerings, because you are proceeding on the path of God. Thus your enure journey constitutes an act of worship. How can, then, you do wrong? This journey, in contrast to every other, is a continuing course through which a Muslim attains a progressive purification of the self.

On this journey, then, you are pilgrims to God.

Iḥrām and its Conditions

When the pilgrim reaches a certain point in his journey on the way to Makka, he must put on *Iḥrām,* the mendicant-like clothes consisting of two unsewn sheets of cloth and a pair of sandals. What does putting on *Iḥrām* symbolize: whatever your position in the world, before God you must come as a beggar and destitute, as in outward appearance so in the depths of your heart. Take off your colourful clothes; put on simple ones. Do not wear socks. Keep your heads bare. Do not use any perfume, nor comb your hair. Do not use any kind of adornment. Stop sexual relations with your wives, refrain even from any gestures which may arouse eagerness for, and be a reminder of, these relations. Do not hunt, and do not help anyone you see hunting.

Adopting such outward postures will influence your inner lives also. You will develop an ascetic attitude. Pride and vanity will disappear. Humility and peace of mind will grow. The impurities that have sullied your souls due to indulgence in worldly pleasures will be removed and a feeling of godliness will dominate both your internal and external selves.

Talbiyyah: the Cry of Response

Soon after putting on *Iḥrām* the pilgrim utters certain words that he must repeat in a loud voice after every Prayer, when climbing a height and descending from it, when meeting other pilgrims and when getting up in the mornings. These words are:

Labbayk, Allāhumma labbayk, labbayk, lā sharīka laka labbayk, inna 'l-ḥamda wa 'n-ni'mata laka wa 'l-mulka lā sharika lak

Here am I before Thee, O God, doubly at Thy service. Before Thee I am, there is no partner unto Thee, doubly at Thy service here am I. All praise and blessings are Thine, and power. There is no partner unto Thee.

This, in fact, is an answer to that general proclamation which Ibrāhīm, as commanded by Allah, made more than four thousand years ago: O slaves of Allah! Come to the House of Allah. Come from every corner of the earth, either on foot or by transport.

Thus, with every cry of *labbayk* the pilgrim answers God's summons; every time he answers His summons he becomes more closely knit with that movement which has been inviting to true and genuine worship of the One God since the time of Ibrāhīm and Ismā 'īl. The distance in time of four and a half thousand years vanishes and it appears as if Ibrāhīm is here calling on behalf of Allah and the pilgrim is answering his call.

At every step, as the pilgrim, thus responding to Ibrāhīm, proceeds further and further, the yearning and longing get more and more intense. At every ascent and descent the voice of Allah's proclaimer rings in his ears and he goes on and on welcoming it with *labbayk*. Every group of pilgrims appears to him like a message-bearer of his Lord; and, like a lover, on getting the message from his beloved, he cries out: 'I am present, I am present.' Every morning is a message from his Friend to which he has but one answer: 'I am at Thy service.'

This recurrent cry of *labbayk* in conjunction with the ascetic dress of *Iḥrām,* the special nature of the journey and the feeling of getting nearer and nearer to the Ka'ba combine to produce in the pilgrim the feeling of being enveloped in Divine love; nothing of any importance any longer resides in his heart except the remembrance of his Friend.

Ṭawāf: Walking Round the House

Thus overwhelmed with the love of God, the pilgrim reaches Makka, and immediately proceeds towards the sacred precincts to which he has been summoned. He kisses the 'threshold' of his Friend's house. Then he goes round and round it, the focus of his faith, the hub of his life. Every round he starts and ends by kissing His 'doorstep', symbolizing a renewal of his pledge of allegiance and loyalty and obedience to his Lord and Master.*

After completing the seven rounds, he goes to the place where lies the stone on which Ibrāhīm stood and called men to the House of God, called the Muqām Ibrāhīm. He then offers two *rak'ahs* of Prayer to thank God.

Sa'ī: Hurrying Between Ṣafā' and Marwah

From Muqām Ibrāhīm he proceeds to climb the hillock of Ṣafā', from where he looks down at the Ka'ba and cries out:

Lā ilāha ill 'allāh wa lā na'budu illā iyyāhu mukhliṣīna lahu 'd-dīna wa law kariha 'l-kāfirūn

There is no god but Allah. We worship none but Him, making exclusive for Him our submission, even though Unbelievers may dislike it.

Then he hurriedly walks between Ṣafā' and the other hillock, Marwah. This act, which is called *Sa'ī*, symbolizes that the pilgrim will be ceaselessly endeavouring to serve his Master and seek His pleasure. In the course of this *Sa'ī*, he may say:

Allāhumma ista'milnī bī sunnati nabiyyika wa tawaffanī 'ala millatihī wa a'idhni min muḍillati 'l-fitan

Grant me to live, O God, the way as was Thy Prophet's way, and to die on his path. Protect me from trials which lead astray.

---

*Some ignorant people object to the kissing of the Black Stone, arguing that it is a kind of idol worship. It is in fact no more than a symbol for kissing the 'doorstep' of the Master. The circumambulation of the Ka'ba starts where the Black Stone is fixed and, during the seven rounds, it is either kissed or touched, or a sign is made towards it at the end of every round. There is not the slightest vestige in this of worshipping it. That the Stone itself is ascribed no powers is demonstrated very well in what 'Umar is reported to have said while kissing it: You are a mere stone. If the Prophet, blessings and peace be on him, had not kissed you, I would have never kissed you.

Or he may say:

Rabbi ghfir warham wa tajāwaz 'ammā ta'lam, innaka anta 'l-a'azzu 'l-akram.

O Lord! Forgive me and have mercy on me and overlook all that Thou knowest I have done wrong. Thou art the Mightiest and the Noblest.

Wuqūf (Stay) at Minā', 'Arafāt and Muzdalifah

On completion of the *Sa 'ī*, the pilgrims become like soldiers in the cause of Allah. Now they have to live a camplike life for five or six days. For one day they will camp at Minā',* and the next day at 'Arafāt† where they will hear their commander's directives, too. Returning from 'Arafāt, they encamp for the night at Muzdalifah‡.

Ramī Jimār: Stoning the Pillars

At daybreak, the pilgrims march back toward Minā' and throw stones at the pillars which mark the place where the army of Abraha, the Christian king of Yemen, known as the *Aṣḥābu 'l-fīl* (the people of elephants), had reached in their effort to demolish the Ka'ba. While throwing each stone, the soldiers in the cause of Allah say:

Allāhu akbar, raghman li 'sh-shayṭani wa ḥizbihī Allahumma taṣdiqan bi kitābika wa ittibā'an li sunnti nabiyyik

---

45* A place 5–6 kilometres to the east of Makka, where the pilgrims stay on the eighth day of Dhu' 1-Hijjah, the twelfth month, and then from the tenth to the twelfth.

†A place 15–17 kilometres further to the east of Makka, where the pilgrims stay on the ninth day of Dhu' 1-Hijjah.

‡ A place where the pilgrims spend the night on their way back to Minā' from 'Arafāt.

God is the Greatest, I throw these stones against Satan
and his party, testifying to the truth of Thy Book, O God,
and following the way of Thy Prophet.

By throwing these stones the pilgrim reaffirms his pledge:
'O God! Like this, I will fight whosoever rises to destroy Your
Din and subdue Your word, and thus I shall strive to make Your
word supreme.

After throwing stones, animals are sacrificed. This sacrifice
demonstrates the intention and resolve of the pilgrim to give his
life in the way of God, whenever required.

After sacrifice, the pilgrims return to the Ka'ba just as a
soldier, having performed his duty, returns triumphantly to
his headquarters. After performing another round of *ṭawāf*
and offering two *rak'ahs* of Prayer, *Iḥrām*, the dress of
consecration, is removed. Whatever was especially prohibited
(Haram) during the period of consecration now again becomes
permissible (Halal) and the pilgrims' lives resume their normal
pattern.

They now come back to Minā' and continue to camp there
for another two or three days. The following day they again
throw stones at the three pillars. These are called *jamarāt* and
serve to remind them of the defeat and destruction of that
elephant army which we have just referred to. It was in the year
of the birth of the Prophet, blessings and peace be on him, that
it invaded Makka at the time of Hajj to demolish the House of
Allah, but which, by the command of Allah, was destroyed by
stones dropped by birds.*

After finally throwing stones at these pillars on the
third day, the pilgrims return to Makka and perform seven

---

*It is often said that this act of flinging stones is done in commemoration of the
incident which happened to Ibrāhīm when he was about to sacrifice Ismā'īl: Satan
tried to tempt him, and he flung stones at him. It is also said that when a lamb was
given to Ibrāhīm to sacrifice in place of Ismā'īl, the lamb ran away and Ibrāhīm threw
stones at it. But in no authentic Hadith have these incidents been narrated from the
Prophet, blessings and peace be on him, as the background of *ramī jimār*.

circumambulations of the centre of their Din. This is called *ṭawaf wadā'* (*ṭawāf* for taking leave) and completing it means the completion of Hajj.

The Impact of Hajj

It is now easy to see that for two to three months,* from the time of deciding and preparing for Hajj to the time of returning home, a tremendous impact is made on the hearts and minds of pilgrims. The process entails sacrifice of time, sacrifice of money, sacrifice of comfort, and sacrifice of many physical desires and pleasures – and all this simply for the sake of Allah, with no worldly or selfish motive.

Together with a life of sustained piety and virtuousness, the constant remembrance of God and the longing and love for Him in the pilgrim leave a mark on his heart which lasts for years. The pilgrim witnesses at every step the imprints left by those who sacrificed everything of theirs in submission and obedience to Allah. They fought against the whole world, suffered hardships and tortures, were condemned to banishment, but ultimately did make the word of God supreme and did subdue the false powers which wanted man to submit to entities other than God.

The lesson in courage and determination, the impetus to strive in the way of God, which a devotee of God can draw from these clear signs and inspiring examples, can hardly be available from any other source. The attachment developed with the focal point of his Din by walking round (*ṭawāf*) the Ka'ba, and the training received to live a Mujahid's life through the rites (*manāsik*) of Hajj (such as running from place to place and repeated departures and halts) are great blessings indeed.

Combined with the Prayer, Fasting and Almsgiving, and looked at as a whole, you will see that Hajj constitutes a preparation for the great task which Islam wants Muslims to

---

*This was the average duration of time required to perform Hajj in 1938, when this address was delivered. In this jet age it may take as few as seven days.

do. This is why it has been made compulsory for all who have the money and the physical fitness for the journey to the Ka'ba. This ensures that, in every age, there are Muslims who have passed through this training.

Hajj, a Collective Worship

The great blessings of spiritual and moral regeneration which Hajj imparts to each person are before you. But you cannot fully appreciate the blessings of Hajj unless you keep in view the fact that Muslims do not perform it individually: hundreds of thousands perform it communally during the time fixed for it. At one stroke Islam achieves not one or two but a thousand purposes.

The advantages of performing the Prayer singly are by no means small, but by making it conditional with congregation and by laying down the rule of *Imamah* (leadership in the Hajj) and by gathering huge congregations for the Friday and 'Id Prayers, its benefits have been increased many times. The observance of the Fasting individually is no doubt a major source of moral and spiritual training, but by prescribing that all Muslims must fast in the month of Ramadan those benefits have been greatly increased. The Almsgiving, too, has many advantages even if dispensed individually, but with the establishment of a centralized *Baytulmāl* (exchequer of the Islamic state) for its collection and disbursement its usefulness is increased beyond measure.

The same is true of Hajj. If everyone were to perform it singly, the effect on individual lives would still be great. But making it a collective act enhances its effectiveness to a point which gives it a new dimension altogether.

27

Renewal of Society

Brothers in Islam! Muslims who should perform Hajj, because they have the means to do so, are not few in number. They are found in thousands in every city and hundreds of thousands in every country. Many of them set out every year to perform the Pilgrimage. Imagine how, in every part of the world where Muslims live, the life of Islam becomes alive as the season of Hajj approaches, and how this sense of lively purpose extends over many months of the year.

From the month of Ramadan till Dhu 'l-Qa'dah, many people from different parts of the world start off for Hajj, while afterwards, from the last part of Dhu 'l-Hijjah till the month of Rabī'u 'l-Thānī, the homeward journey continues. For these six to seven months an incessant religious movement prevails among Muslims throughout the world. Those who go to perform Hajj and return home are no doubt enraptured with devotion to God. But even those who do not go receive some share of the experience by virtue of the emotional farewells and homecoming welcomes they accord to the pilgrims, and listening to their accounts of Hajj.

Growth in God-consciousness

As soon as the intending pilgrim makes up his mind to perform Hajj, fear of God, piety, repentance, seeking forgiveness from God, and desire to do good begin to blossom within him. As

273

he starts saying goodbye to his relatives, friends and associates and settles all of his pending affairs, everyone can notice that he is no longer the same man as before: his heart is now pure and clean because of the newly-kindled spark of love of God. It is easy to imagine the effect of the changed condition of the pilgrim on the people around him. And if every year all over the world hundreds of thousands of pilgrims prepare for Hajj in this manner, the aura cast by their enthusiasm and renewal must improve the moral state of vast numbers of people.

As the pilgrims' caravans pass through various places the hearts of more and more people are warmed by seeing them, meeting them and by hearing from them the cry of *labbayk, labbayk* (I am present before Thee). There must be many whose thoughts will be redirected towards Allah and His House, and the eagerness for Hajj will reawaken their slumbering souls.

And when the pilgrims, enthused with the spirit of Hajj, return from the centre of their Din to their cities and towns and villages in all parts of the world, they are met and welcomed by all those who have stayed at home. Their words and deeds telling the story of the Pilgrimage must rekindle the devotional feelings of those listening to them.

A Season of Reawakening

As such it will not be wrong if we say that just as the month of Ramadan is a season of God-consciousness and piety throughout the Islamic world, so also is the Hajj one of reawakening and rebirth of hearts and societies. The Wise One who has given us the Shari'ah has thus ensured that whatever adverse turn world conditions may take and however bad times may become, they will never succeed in erasing the universal Islamic movement so long as the Ka'ba is there.

For, it has been placed in the body of the Islamic world just like a heart in a man's body. As long as the heart beats, a man cannot die. In exactly the same way this 'heart of the world' draws blood from its far-off veins and circulates the blood back into each and every artery. As long as this throbbing of the heart continues and as long as this process of drawing the blood and circulating it lasts, it will be impossible to end the life of this body of the Muslim Ummah, however run-down diseases may have made it.

Inspiring Spectacle of Unity

Close your eyes and visualize what it must be like to see people from countless communities and countries converging on one 'Centre' through a thousand and one routes – from the east and from the west, from the north and from the south. Their faces are different, their colours are different, their languages are different, but on reaching a frontier near the 'Centre' all exchange the varied clothes they are wearing for a simple uniform of the same design. This single, common uniform of *Ihrām* distinguishes them as the army of one single King. It becomes the insignia of obedience and service to one Being; all are strung in one cord of loyalty and are marching toward one 'Capital' to file past their 'King'.

When these uniformed soldiers move beyond the frontier, the same cry issues forth loudly from their mouths:

Labbayk, Allāhumma labbayk, lā sharī ka laka labbayk

Here am I before Thee, O God, doubly at Thy service, There is no partner unto Thee, here am I.

There languages are different but the words they utter are the same; they have the same meaning.

As the centre approaches, the circle containing the pilgrims contracts. Caravans from different countries continue joining each other. All perform their Prayers together in one and the same manner. All are dressed in similar uniforms, all are led by one Imam (leader), all are moving simultaneously, all are now using the same language, all are rising, sitting, bowing down (*rukū*)and prostrating themselves (*sujūd*) at one signal of *Allāhu akbar,* and all are reciting and listening to one Arabic Qur'ān. In this way the differences of nationality, country and race are obliterated and a universal community of God-worshippers is constituted.

When these caravans pass on, loudly raising with one voice the call of *labbayk, labbayk,* when at every ascent and descent the same words resound, when at the time of meeting of caravans these same voices are raised from both sides, and when at the time of every Prayer and at dawn these exclamations reverberate, a unique atmosphere is created whose exhilarating effect makes a man forget his self and become absorbed in the ecstasy of *labbayk.*

After reaching the Ka'ba comes the act of circumambulation, then the doing of *Sa'ī* by all together between Ṣafā' and Marwah, then the encampment of all at Minā', then the departure of all towards 'Arafāt and the listening to their leader's address, then a night's sojourn by all at Muzdalifah, then the return of all together towards Minā', then the throwing of stones in unison by all at *jamarāt,* then the animal sacrifice performed by all, then the return of all together to the Ka'ba for further circumambulation, and then the offering of Salah by all together around the centre – all this carries within itself an effect which has absolutely no parallel.

Greatest Movement for Peace

This assembling at one centre of people drawn from all nationalities of the world, and that, too, with a remarkable unity of heart and purpose, identity of thought and harmony of feeling, pure sentiments and noble objectives and deeds, is the greatest gift of Islam to the children of Adam. The nations of the world have long been meeting each other, but in what circumstances? On battlefields, cutting each other's throats; or at peace conferences, carving up countries and nations for themselves; or in the League of Nations, indulging in deception and plotting against each other or conspiring against each other. The meeting of common men of all nations, with sincerity and love, with mental and spiritual affinity, with unity in thoughts, deeds and aims – and not only once but always at the same centre every year – is a blessing available to mankind nowhere else but in Islam. Has anyone else devised a better system than this for establishing peace in the world, for removing hostility among nations and for creating in the place of quarrels and bickerings an atmosphere of love, friendship and brotherhood?

Nor do the blessings of Hajj in establishing peace stop here. During the four months fixed for Hajj and 'Umrah (the lesser Pilgrimage performed outside the days of Hajj), every effort must be made to maintain peace on all roads leading to the Ka'ba.

This is the greatest movement of a permanent nature for the establishment of peace in the world. And if the reins of world politics were in the hands of Islam, it would be the Muslims' main concern to ensure that no disturbances took place in the world that would disrupt Hajj and 'Umrah.

Centre of Peace and Equality

Islam has given to the world an inviolable territory, a city of peace till Doomsday. Within the prescribed boundaries around the Ka'ba, called the *Ḥaram*, the hunting and shooting of animals is strictly prohibited, the cutting of grass is not allowed, thorns may not be pruned, nor fallen articles picked up. And, of course, no human being may be harmed.

Islam has given to the world a city where it is forbidden to bring arms, where it is tantamount to 'heresy' to hoard cereals and other articles of common need and sell them at a higher price, and where those doing wrong to others or oppressing them are thus threatened by Allah:

We shall cause them to taste a painful punishment (al-Ḥajj 22: 25).

Islam has given a centre to the world which is defined as:

A place where the resident and the visitor are equal (al-Hajj 22: 25).

This means that the rights of all human beings are equal here. Whoever acknowledges the sovereignty of God and accepts the leadership of Muhammad, blessings and peace be on him, enters the brotherhood of Islam, no matter if he is American or African, Chinese or Indian. If one has become a Muslim, his rights are identical to those of the Makkans themselves.

The position of the whole area of the *Ḥaram* is similar to that of a mosque in that if anyone moves into any part of a mosque that portion belongs to him. Nobody can remove him or ask for rent from him. But, at the same time, he has no right to call it his property, even if he lives there for his whole life. Nor can he sell it or rent it to anybody. When this person leaves his place in the mosque, another person has the same right to occupy it as he had had.

This is exactly the position of the whole of the *Ḥaram* at Makka. The Prophet, blessings and peace be on him, said: Whosoever first comes to this city and settles at a place, that place is his.

'Umar issued an order to the people of his time not to fix doors on the compound around their houses so that whoever wanted to could come and stay in the compound. Some jurists have gone so far as to say that nobody has the right to own houses in Makka or to leave them to their heirs when they die.

Brothers! This is the Hajj about which it was said: 'Undertake it and see how many blessings it has in store for you.' No words are adequate to express all of its advantages; you can only get a glimpse of them from the brief sketch that I have tried to give here.

Our Lack of Appreciation

Now, listen to the voice of my afflicted heart! We, the present-day born Muslims, are like a child born in a diamond mine. He may have diamonds all around, but if he plays with them as if they were stones, these diamonds become as valueless for him as stones. Our attitudes toward Islam are exactly similar, because the treasures which the world is searching for, and is suffering through being deprived of, have all been given to us by virtue of our having been born Muslims.

The *Kalimah Tawḥīd* (the creed of Oneness of God), which shows men the right way to lead their lives, has been drummed into us from our earliest childhoods; those priceless prescriptions of Salah and Sawm, which elevate men from a mere animal existence to the human level, we have inherited, without effort, from our forefathers; that matchless practice of Zakah, which purifies the heart as well as the financial systems of the world, without which people of the world are at loggerheads with each other, is ours as our birthright.

Similarly Hajj has been part of our heritage for hundreds of years. This magnificent way is more effective and powerful than any other ever conceived to propagate our movement throughout the world and keep it alive for all eternity. This universal movement is more powerful than any other to draw out human beings in the name of God and make them into a brotherhood transcending race, colour and nationality.

We are surrounded by treasures, but how do we treat them? We play with them in the same way as that ignorant child who, surrounded by diamonds, regards them as stones. My heart bleeds when I see us frittering away such tremendous wealth and power through ignorance and foolishness.

My dear brothers! You must have heard this couplet of the poet:

If the ass of Jesus goes to Makka,

It remains an ass when it returns.

That is to say, an ass, even one living in the company of a Prophet like Jesus, cannot benefit from a visit to Makka; it would still be as unenlightened as before. Today we have at our disposal gifts like the Prayer, Fasting and Pilgrimage. But these devotional acts are meant to train human beings, not to tame animals. Although the people carry out the external trappings of these precious gifts, their minds have no concept of their inner significance. They have no concern for their outcome. They imitate the actions of their forebears, but it is a stereotyped imitation, devoid of comprehension or spiritual content. How can good results be expected out of such exercises?

Every year thousands of pilgrims go to the centre of Islam and come back after having had the privilege of performing Hajj without that experience having had the slightest effect on them. Nor do they make any impact on those they meet upon their return or live with. Worse, many of them continue to exhibit their bad habits and bad manners; thus the very name of Islam is tarnished by their behaviour. Not only in the eyes of strangers but also among Muslims. Eventually some young Muslims who have not themselves been on Hajj have come to question its value.

Year after year for centuries, hundreds of thousands of the adherents of a powerful movement, Islam, gather at one place, travel along various routes, pass through villages, towns and cities and demonstrate their faith through their words and deeds. How can, one wonders, such an event fail to impress people with the blessings it can bring.

Yet if only Hajj was performed as it was intended it should be, even the blind would see its benefits and the deaf would hear of its advantages! Every year it would change the lives of millions of Muslims, and attract thousands of non-Muslims to Islam!

Deriving Full Bebefit From Hajj

To derive the full benefits from Hajj, what we need at the centre of Islam are such hands that could make it effective, such hearts that could pump pure blood into the body of the Ummah, such minds that could turn the pilgrims into ambassadors of Islam, carrying its message far and wide. At least Makka should have been a living example of Islam.

Alas, this is not the case at present. From the time of the Abbasids till the Ottomans, the kings of every period, in order to serve their political ends, tried to weaken the Arabs. They brought them to the lowest levels of decadence in knowledge, morals and culture. The result was that the land from which emanated the light of Islam, spreading its rays to all corners of the world, reached almost the same state of ignorance in which it was before the advent of Islam. There is little knowledge of Islam or Islamic life. People from far-off places flock to the sacred precincts of the *Ḥaram* with the deepest devotion, only to find ignorance, filth, greed, indecency, love of this world, bad manners and disorganization. The result is that, for many, the experience of Hajj, instead of strengthening their faith, weakens it.

Priestly exploitation which was imposed in the Ka'ba after Ibrāhīm and Ismā'īl, and which was abolished by the Prophet, blessings and peace be on him, has again been revived. The administration and the *Mu'allimīn* (who guide the pilgrims) have again adopted the ways of priests. The House of God has become their property and Hajj a source of business. They consider the pilgrims as their customers. Agents have been appointed in different countries on big salaries to canvas and bring in these customers. Every year a whole army of brokers leaves Makka to seek out and fetch them from all parts of the world. People are induced to perform Hajj by having Quranic verses and Hadith quoted at them. The motive is not to remind them of the duty imposed by Allah but to make money.

It almost looks as if Allah and His Messenger initiated Hajj for the sole purpose of sustaining the *Mu'allimīn* and brokers. Trading in religion, *Mu'allim, Muṭawwif,* their attorneys, keepers of keys to the Ka'ba – all confront a pilgrim at every stage. They and the Government itself are all co-sharers in the Hajj 'industry'. The performance of the rituals of Hajj is conducted on payment and even the door of the Ka'ba is only opened for a fee. How strange that such is the condition of the followers of a religion which abolished all priesthood!

How can the true spirit of worship survive where the work of conducting it has become a source of wage-earning and trade, where sacred places are exploited for personal gain, where Divine commandments are employed to lure people to empty their pockets, where a man is obliged to make payment for every rite he performs, and where Din has become a business commodity?*

In mentioning these facts I do not intend to cast blame on anyone. My purpose is simply to point out what factors have so seriously weakened such a potentially tremendous source of spiritual, moral and social power as Hajj. There should be no misunderstanding in anybody's mind that this state of affairs is due to any deficiency in Islam. The deficiency lies with those who do not follow Islam correctly. The situation is like that of an expert physician whose prescriptions fall into the hands of quacks and thus become useless and possibly positively harmful.

---

*This address was given in 1938. Conditions have now greatly improved and the Saudi Arabian Government is trying to enforce further reforms. Two matters require special attention. Firstly, the two sacred precincts of Makka and Madina must be protected from the onslaughts of Western civilization. Second, the methods and procedures employed by *Mu'allims* should be improved. May God enable the Saudi Government to adopt correct measures in this regard!

PART VII
Jihad

28

Meaning of Jihad

Brothers in Islam! The Prayer, Fasting, Almsgiving, and Pilgrimage are so important that they are described as the pillars of Islam. They are not, however, like the worship rites in other religions. This we must understand clearly. Nor are they meant to please Allah by their mere outward observance. These acts of worship have in fact been ordained to prepare us for a greater purpose and to train us for a greater duty. Now that we have seen in some detail the nature of this training and the mode of this preparation, let us come to the most crucial question: What exactly is that great ultimate purpose?

The Ultimate Objective

Stated simply: the ultimate objective of Islam is to abolish the lordship of man over man and bring him under the rule of the One God. To stake everything you have – including your lives – to achieve this purpose is called Jihad. The Prayer, Fasting, Almsgiving and Pilgrimage, all prepare you for Jihad. But as you have long since forgotten this objective as well as the mission entrusted to you, and because all acts of worship have been reduced to their spiritual contents, this brief statement may be difficult to understand. Explanation is therefore necessary.

Root of All Evil

Corrupt rule is the root of all the evils you find in the world. Governments have access to power and resources; they frame laws; they control administration, they possess the instruments of coercion like the police and army. Evils exist and flourish in the life of society because governments themselves either spread them or condone them. Obviously the power required to make anything prevail lies with governments.

For example, why is adultery being openly indulged in, why is prostitution carried out publicly? Only because adultery is not a crime in the eyes of those who govern. They themselves indulge in it as well as allowing others to do so. If they wanted to stop it, it could not flourish.

Why is interest rampant? Why are the rich sucking the blood of the poor? Because governments themselves acquire wealth through interest and help others to do the same. Big money-lending houses and banks flourish only because of governmental support.

You also notice that moral depravity and permissiveness are increasing. Why? Simply because that is how governments have educated and trained people. If you want to produce a different kind of man, you simply do not possess the resources to provide a different kind of education. And even if you somehow do produce a few people, where will they find jobs? All means of livelihood and employment are controlled by corrupt governments.

Fighting and killing are taking place across the world on an unprecedented scale. Knowledge so assiduously acquired by man is being employed to exterminate man himself. The hard-earned fruits of human civilization are being put to the fire. Precious lives are being destroyed with less thought than would be given to the fate of a potter's vessel of clay. Why is this so? Simply because the most wicked and mischievous among the children of Adam have come to command authority and leadership over the nations of the world. Since they hold the reins of power, the world must go the way they want to take it.* Knowledge, wealth, labour, lives, all are directed towards the goals they have chosen.

Oppression prevails throughout the world. The weak are denied justice. The poor find life a hard burden. Courts have become shops where justice can be bought in return for money. Exorbitant taxes are levied upon people, which are then wasted on high salaries for public officials, on giant buildings, on armaments and on other extravagances. Feudal lords, money-lenders and creditors, religious leaders, dealers in pornography, gambling bosses, drug pushers, manufacturers of alcohol, and pimps are ruining the life, wealth, honour and morality of God's creation and there is nobody to stop them.

Why is all this happening? Simply because governments are corrupt, the hands that hold power are evil. They themselves perpetuate oppression and side with oppressors. The perversion of thinking, the degeneration of morals, the misuse of human capacities and capabilities, the dishonest and exploitive business practices, oppression and injustice, and destruction of God's creation, all result from this: the keys of power are in the wrong hands. So long as power is wielded by wicked and evil hands, human society cannot be set on the right course.

The First Step

Human well-being and happiness, therefore, will only come about by attacking the evil afflicting society at its roots, that is, by getting rid of all powers based on rebellion against the laws of God.

If people are free to commit adultery, no amount of sermons will stop them. But if governments forbid adultery, people will find it easier to give up this evil practice. Similarly, it is not enough to preach sermons against drinking, gambling, usury,

---

*This was the time when the Second World War (1939–45) was about to start.

bribery, pornography and morally corrupting education if the overall environment of the surrounding society encourages or at least condones these things. Power, however, can do much to eradicate them.

Likewise, merely exhortations and good counsels will not help if you want to eradicate exploitation of man by man, prevent misuse of human wealth and talent, stamp out oppression and establish justice, erase corruption, stop bloodshed, give dignity to the down-trodden, restore equality, prosperity and peace to all. What is needed is a demonstration from those in power that corruption, oppression, injustice, exploitation, immorality and godlessness will not be tolerated; and that positive actions will be taken in accordance with God's laws to promote the creation of a just, God-fearing and God-loving society.

So, I say to you: if you really want to root out corruption now so widespread on God's earth, stand up and fight against corrupt rule; take power and use it on God's behalf. It is useless to think you can change things by preaching alone.

Origin of Corrupt Rule

What is the root cause of corrupt rule? What is the most fundamental change that would prevent power from becoming corrupt?

The lordship of man over man is the root cause of all corrupt rule. The only way to reform and change is to accept the sovereignty of God over man. Do not be surprised at hearing such a brief answer to the complex and profound question of the origin of evil in the world today. Search as long as you like for other answers, you will not find any.

Let us ask ourselves a few simple questions. Has the earth we live on been made by God or by some other being? Have the human beings who inhabit the earth been created by God or by somebody else? Have all the countless necessities of our lives been provided by God or by somebody else? If the answer to these questions is God, if the earth, human beings and all the things needed to sustain them have been created by God alone, then obviously the land belongs to God, the wealth belongs to God and the people belong to God.

In such a situation, how can it be right and proper for anyone to establish his rule on God's earth or govern God's subjects by any law except that of God? Do you find it reasonable that the land be owned by one being but another being rules over it, that a property belongs to one person but some other person is treated as its owner, that the subjects belong to one sovereign but another sovereign reigns over them? Such things clearly run contrary to reality, reason and justice. And because of this, wherever and whenever such a situation is found, the results are always disastrous.

Human beings who assume absolute powers to make laws of their own are bound to make mistakes because of their ignorance, and act unjustly and oppressively because of their selfish ends. First, they do not possess sufficient knowledge to frame correct and just' laws for human life; and, second, devoid of fear of God and not seeing themselves accountable to God, they assume absolute powers.

Being in power, they control people's means of livelihood; they are absolute masters of their lives and properties; they subject them to total obedience. Do you think, therefore, that, in such circumstances, they can be trusted to govern according to the tenets of truth and justice? Can you expect them to be proper trustees of public money? Can you hope that they will refrain from usurping people's rights, from collecting illegal wealth, and from subjugating God's creation to their own desires? Is it possible that such people will follow the right path and encourage others to walk along it? Never! Never! Thousands of years of human experience testify to the contrary. Witness those who feel no fear of God today, and are heedless of accountability in the Hereafter. How great despots, oppressors, betrayers of trust, and evildoers have they become after they have acquired power.

God's Lordship Over Man

No man should rule over another man; all men should live under the One God. Thus fundamental change is needed in the framework of all human governments. Those who govern must not become masters but, recognizing God as their only Sovereign, must rule as His deputies and trustees. They must discharge their responsibilities with the consciousness that ultimately they will have to give an account of their trust to that King who knows both the seen and unseen. All laws should be based on the guidance of that God who has knowledge of all realities, who is the source of all wisdom. Nobody has the power to change God's laws or to amend them or to repeal them, otherwise corruption will creep in due to human ignorance, selfishness and desires.

What Islam demands from those who submit to God as the real Sovereign, their only Ruler, and who accept to abide by His laws as brought by His Prophet, blessings and peace be on him, is quite obvious. They should rise to bring their King's land under His law, to disempower those rebels among His subjects who have set themselves up as sovereigns, in order to free His subjects from the burden of slavery to others. The real empowerment of man comes trrough supremecy of the Divine Law.

Merely believing in God as God and in His law as the true law is not enough. As soon as you believe in these two things, a sacred duty devolves upon you: wherever you are, in whichever country you live, you must strive to change the wrong basis of government, and exercise all powers to rule and make laws from those who do not fear God. You must also provide leadership to God's servants and conduct the affairs of their government in accordance with God's laws, remaining fully conscious of living in God's presence and being accountable to Him in the Hereafter. The name of this striving is Jihad.

Temptation of Power

We all know that power can corrupt. Temptations rise within our hearts to behave as gods once we acquire control over the lives and wealth of people. Taking power is less difficult than protecting ourselves from abusing that power when it is taken. The problem is how to stop ourselves turning ourselves into gods rather than being servants of God. For what benefit is it to anyone if we get rid of one Pharaoh and promptly replace him with another? Therefore, before calling upon us to undergo this severe trial of having power, Islam considers it necessary to prepare us for it.

You have no right to start struggling for power until you have cleansed your hearts of all selfishness. You should develop such purity of heart that when you fight you do not fight for personal or national aggrandizement, but solely to secure Allah's pleasure and to improve the lot of His creation. Merely on the basis of reciting the Kalimah, Islam does not permit you to wage war against God's creation and do, in the name of God and His Messenger, the same evil acts which the oppressors and rebels of God perpetrate. You must therefore have the necessary strength to shoulder such heavy responsibility.

Rituals, a Training Course

The Prayer, Fasting, Almsgiving and Pilgrimage at their deepest level provide preparation and training for the assumption of just power. Just as governments train their armies, police forces and civil services before employing them to do their job, so does Islam, the Din given by Allah. It first trains all those who volunteer for service to God before allowing them to undertake Jihad and establish God's rule on earth.

There is one fundamental difference however. The work for which the secular governments employ their servants do not require qualities like fear of God, moral excellence and piety. Their employees can be adulterers, drunkards and liars, and it will not matter as long as they can carry out the task they have been given. But the work which Allah entrusts to His servants is wholly of a moral character. It is therefore essential that such men should be God-fearing and virtuous. Indeed, their training aims to make them morally so strong that when they rise to establish the caliphate of God on earth, they will be equal to this great task.

If they fight, they do not fight to acquire for themselves wealth, property and land, but to secure Allah's pleasure and for the benefit and well-being of His creation. If they gain victory, they must not become proud and arrogant; rather their heads should be bowed before their God. If they become rulers, they should not enslave people; rather they themselves should live as God's slaves, allow none to be a slave of anyone except God. If they acquire control over wealth, they should not fill their own pockets nor those of their relatives or their community; rather they should distribute these God-given treasures equitably among all His subjects according to their needs and circumstances.

No other method of training people to assume such great responsibilities exists except the *'Ibādāt* (acts of worship) that Allah has enjoined upon you: Salah, Sawm, Zakah and Hajj. Only when Islam has prepared its men does it tell them: Now you are the most pious slaves of God on earth. So go forward and fight; dislodge the rebels of God from the government and take over the powers of caliphate.

> You are the best community brought forth for mankind. You enjoin the doing of right and forbid the doing of wrong; and you believe in God (Āl 'Imrān 3: 110).

Governments Run by God-conscious People

Imagine in what a happy state God's creation will be where the army, police, judiciary, tax authorities and all other government functionaries are God-fearing and consider themselves accountable to Him in the Hereafter, where all government policies and laws are formulated on the basis of Divine guidance, where unjust actions have no place, where evil is quickly rectified by a government constantly ready to promote virtue with all its power and resources.

Such a government will quickly be able to reform the people; it will shut the door against oppression, exploitation, immorality and other prevalent vices; it will reform education to develop the right kind of thinking and attitudes. Once people have the chance to live in a just and fair, peaceful and moral society, eyes turned blind by long exposure to a godless leadership will, sooner or later, begin to perceive and recognize the Truth. Likewise, hearts furred up by vices surrounding them for centuries will become clear again and begin to see the Truth. No more, then, will people find any difficulty in understanding the simple truth that Allah alone is their God and they should serve no one else, and that the prophets who claimed to have brought His guidance were truthful.

Thoughts which today look extremely difficult to instil into the minds of people will penetrate automatically. Teachings which cannot be explained today through speeches and books will be understood immediately. For they will see with their own eyes the vast difference between a world run on man-made laws and one governed by Divine guidance. Submitting to the One God and accepting the truthfulness of His Prophet, blessings and peace be on him, will be very easy; to reject them will be almost impossible. I doubt that more than a handful of people in a thousand will display such great obstinacy as to reject the truth of Islam in preference to Disbelief. Who will choose a thorn as against a flower?

For a long time, brothers, you have been performing the various acts of worship without giving any thought to the ultimate purpose behind them. Never did you prepare yourselves for that purpose. But now, I say, you must understand that a heart devoid of any intention to undertake Jihad will find all ritual worship empty of meaning. Nor will those acts bring you any nearer to your God.

29

Central Importance of Jihad

Brothers in Islam! Why is Jihad so central to Islam? To understand this, let us first recollect the meanings of three keywords: Din, Shari'ah, and 'Ibadah.

> *Din* means obedience and submission.
> *Shar'ah* tells us how to obey and submit; it is the law.
> *'Ibadah* means worship and service.

Din, Shari'ah and 'Ibadah

Acknowledging that someone is your ruler to whom you must submit means that you have accepted his Din. He now becomes your sovereign and you become his subjects. The commandments and the codes that he gives you constitute the law or the Shari'ah which you must follow. Once you live in obedience to him according to the law laid down by him, you are serving and worshipping him: this is 'Ibadah. You, then, give him whatever he demands, obey whatever he orders, abstain from whatever he forbids, observe whatever limits he sets for your conduct, and follow whatever he instructs or decides in all your affairs.

Din, therefore, actually means the same thing as state and government; Shari'ah is the law of that state and government;

and 'Ibadah amounts to following and complying with that law. Whenever you accept someone as your ruler and submit to his orders, you have entered that person's Din. If you accept that Allah is your ruler, you have entered Allah's Din; if your ruler is some particular nation, you have entered that nation's Din; and if it is your own nation or your people, then you have entered the people's Din. To whatever you submit yourselves, you have entered its Din; and you are performing the 'Ibadah of the one whose laws you are following.

Duality of Din

It is necessary to spell out this point because, once you have grasped it, you can see that it is impossible for you to follow more than one Din at a time. Of various rulers, only one can rule your lives; of various systems of law, only one can become the law of your lives. And of the various objects of worship, it is only possible for you to worship one god.

You may object that this is not strictly true; as a matter of belief we can accept one ruler, even if in practice we obey another; we can worship one god, even if we submit to someone else; our hearts can believe one law, even if the affairs of our lives are regulated by another law.

In reply, I say: 'No doubt this can be done, and in fact it *is* being done; but this is *Shirk* – and this *Shirk* is sheer falsehood.' In reality, you are followers only of that being's Din whom you are actually obeying. Is it not then utter hypocrisy to call that being your ruler and to claim to belong to his Din whom you do not obey? What benefit will such belief give you if only your tongues and hearts subscribe to it? Is it not meaningless to assert that you have faith in his Shari'ah when all your affairs are conducted in violation of this Shari'ah and in fact you follow another Shari'ah? Is it not a pseudo-exercise to accept a certain being as your object of worship and bow your heads on the ground before him when in practice you give service to another being?

Only that being is your object of worship, and only him are you worshipping whose orders you obey, whose prohibitions you observe, whose limits you do not violate, whose code you follow in all your affairs, whose procedures regulate your transactions, whose decision you always seek and submit to, whose Shari'ah governs your dealings with other people, and on whose summons you surrender all your talents and powers, your hearts and brains, hands and feet, all your possessions, even your lives.

Whatever you say your beliefs are, it is your actual practice which constitutes the reality, mere lip-service carries no weight. If you obey a king's Din, Allah's Din will have no room in it. And if you submit to popular sovereignty, or to the Din of Britons or Germans, or to your nation and motherland, then again Allah's Din will have no place in it. But if, in reality, you are adherents of Allah's Din, there will be no room for any other Din.

Every Din Wants Power

A total Din, whatever its nature, wants power for itself; the prospect of sharing power is unthinkable. Whether it is popular sovereignty or monarchy, communism or Islam, or any other Din, it must govern to establish itself. A Din without power to govern is just like a building which exists in the mind only. But it is the building which actually exists, in which you actually live, that is important. Through its door you go in, through its door you come out. Its roof is above you, its walls surround you. You arrange your living pattern according to its shape and facilities.

What point is there, while living in a building whose architectural design obliges you to adopt certain living patterns, in pretending that you believe in a different sort of building altogether or that you are 'really' living therein. You cannot live in a building which exists only in your heads. In exactly the same way, there is no meaning in asserting that a certain Din is true while living your lives according to another Din. That Din alone is real and genuine whose authority is established on earth, whose laws are followed, and according to whose rules and regulations one's affairs of life are conducted. Let us look at some examples.

Popular Sovereignty

'Popular sovereignty' means that people of a country are its paramount sovereign; so it is a Din. Now their lives should be governed by a Shari' ah which people have themselves framed; and all the inhabitants of that country should obey and serve their own authority. How can this Din be established unless the sovereignty of people reigns supreme in the country, and unless a Shari'ah framed by people's representations is enforced? And if it is, there can be no room there for monarchy, for foreign rule, or for anyone else.

Monarchy

'Monarchy' means that a king is the paramount sovereign of a country; so it is a Din. Now he alone shall be obeyed and his Shari'ah alone enforced. If not, then it is futile to acknowledge the king as the sovereign and paramount ruler and his Shari'ah as the supreme law. If popular sovereignty is supreme or a foreign power takes over, no trace will be left of the monarchy nor will anyone be able to follow it.

British Rule

In India* the Din of the British prevails. It prevails because the Indian Penal Code and the Civil Procedure Code are enforced by British power. All your affairs are carried out within the

---

* In 1938–39 India was ruled by the British.

limits prescribed by the British and all of you bow your heads in obedience to their orders. As long as this Din prevails, no other Din, no matter how fervently you profess to follow it, can have any reality. And if the Indian Penal Code and the Civil Procedure Code ceased to operate and British orders were not obeyed, then 'Din of the British' would lose all meaning.

Din of Islam

Exactly similar is the position of the Din of Islam. This Din means that Allah alone is the Lord of everything on earth and He alone is the Sovereign. Thus, He alone must be obeyed and served, His Shari'ah alone must govern all affairs of our lives.

What does Allah's sovereignty imply? That His writ must run supreme in the world: legal judgements must be based on His Shari'ah, the police must operate according to His commandments, financial transactions must be carried out in conformity with His laws, taxes must be levied as directed by Him and spent as specified by Him, the Civil Service and the army must obey His code, people must devote their abilities, capacities, and efforts to fulfilling His desires. Further, Allah alone must be feared, His subjects must submit to Him only, and man must not serve anyone but Him.

Unless the Kingdom of God is established, these objectives cannot be realized. How can Allah's Din accept to co-exist with any other Din, when no other Din admits of such partnership? Like every other Din, Allah's Din, too, demands that all authority should genuinely and exclusively be vested in it. If it is not, the Din of Islam will not be there, and it will be futile to pretend that it is. This is the point which the Qur'ān has repeatedly stressed:

> And they were not enjoined anything but that they should serve God, making submission exclusively His, turning away [from all false gods] (al-Bayyinah 98: 5).

It is He who has sent forth His Messenger with the Guidance and the way of Truth, so that he makes it prevail over all ways [religions], however much Mushriks [who take gods beside God] may dislike it (al-Tawbah 9: 33).

And fight them, until there is no rebellion [against God], and all submission is to God alone (al-Anfāl 8: 39).

Authority [to lay down what is right and what is wrong] belongs only to God; He has commanded that you shall not serve any but Him (Yūsuf 12: 40).

So whoever hopes to meet his Lord, let him do righteous deeds, and let him not make anyone share in his Lord's service (al-Kahf 18: 111).

Have you not seen those who assert that they believe in what has been sent down to you, and what was sent down before you, and yet desire to summon one another to the rule of powers in rebellion against God, although they have been commanded to reject them . . . We have not sent any Messenger, but that he should be obeyed by God's leave (al-Nisā' 4: 60–4).

Read these Quranic Ayahs bearing in mind the true meanings of Din, Shari'ah, and 'Ibadah, and you will understand their message.

Jihad in Islam

The Din of Allah, like any other Din, does not allow that you merely believe in its truth and perform certain worship rites. If you are a true follower of Islam, you can neither submit to any other Din, nor can you make Islam a partner of it. If you believe Islam to be true, you have no alternative but to exert your utmost strength to make it prevail on earth: you either establish it or give your lives in this struggle.

By this criterion alone can be tested the sincerity of your faith. With a sincere belief, you will find it impossible even to sleep comfortably if you are made to live under another Din, not to speak of giving service to it, getting rich under it, or enjoying its comforts. Every moment you spend under another Din will be a bed of thorns; every morsel of food a poison.

Even if you passively accept to live under another Din, you are not a believer in the true sense of the term, no matter how assiduously you offer one Prayer after another, how many long hours you spend in meditation, how beautifully you explain the Qur'ān and how eruditely you write and speak on Islam. But, if some people actively serve another Din and fight its wars, no words are enough to describe their abominable behaviour. A day will soon come when they will meet their Maker and taste the wages of their sins. If they consider themselves Muslims, they are deluding themselves. With a little common sense, they could have understood how illogical it is to accept one Din as true and then, at the same time, agree to the dominance of another contrary Din, or actively work for it. Fire and water may exist together, but not such conduct with faith in Allah.

All that the Qur'ān says in this regard cannot be reproduced here, but I cite a few Ayahs:

> Do men think that they will be left to say, 'We believe', and they will not be tested? And, indeed, We tested those who were before them. God will surely mark out those who speak truly, and He will surely mark out the liars (al-'Ankabūt 29: 2–3).

> And some men there are who say, 'We believe in God', but whenever they are made to suffer in God's cause, they take the persecution by man as it were God's punishment. And, then, if help comes from your Lord, they will say, 'We have always been with you.' What, is not God fully aware of what is in the hearts of all beings? God will surely mark out who believe, and He will surely mark out the hypocrites (al-'Ankabūt 29: 10–11).

And God is not such that He will leave the believers in the state in which you are, till He shall distinguish the bad from the good (Āl 'Imrān 3: 179).

Do you think you would be left [alone] while God has not yet seen which of you have struggled, and taken not – apart from God and His Messenger and the believers – any helper (al-Tawbah 9: 16).

Have you not seen those who would be friends with people with whom God is angry? They are neither of you nor of them . . . Those are Satan's party. Why, it is those, Satan's party, who are the losers. Surely, those who oppose God and His Messenger [work against the establishment of the Religion of Truth], those are among the most abject. God has ordained, 'I shall surely prevail, I and My Messengers.' Surely God is All-strong, All-mighty (al-Mujādalah 58: 14–21).

Recognizing True Believers

True believers carry only one identification: all their efforts are directed to eradicating every false Din – and every Din other than Allah's is false – and establishing in its place the true Din. They live, suffer losses, and die in His cause. Whether they succeed or fail matters little. On the contrary, if they reconcile themselves to the domination of a false way of life or help make it dominant, they are liars if they claim to possess Iman.

Change Only Through Struggle

People who use the difficulty of establishing the true Din as a pretext for not trying to do so have their answer in the Qur'ān. Obviously, whenever you rise to establish the true Din, some false Din is already in a position of power, controlling all resources. Otherwise there would, by definition, be nothing to topple. It is therefore equally obvious that the replacement of this false Din by the true Din will always be a long and hard struggle. It cannot be accomplished, now or ever, easily and without any sacrifice. It is impossible to claim that you want the establishment of true Din while at the same time continuing to tolerate those parts of the false Din which appear to be of benefit to you personally. True Din can only be established precisely when people are prepared to give up the benefits and privileges they enjoy under the false Din.

Jihād fī sabīli 'llāh is never easy. It is meant only for those who have the will to struggle for their cause; and such people are always few in number. Let those who claim to follow the true Din but are not prepared to make any sacrifice continue to serve their self-interests. While sacrifices are being made in the cause of Truth, such people are nowhere in evidence; when the battle is won, they will appear as if from nowhere, saying: *'Innā kunnā ma'akum'* (we have always been with you; now come and give us our share).

Let us not be like those who claim to believe in Allah, but give neither time, money, nor lives for the sake of His Din. Let us come forward and fight in Allah's cause with whatever we possess.

Preface
to the Eighth Reprint

This collection of my Friday addresses was first published in November, 1940. Since then, until November, 1951, 20,000 copies have been printed in seven editions during the past eleven years. During this entire period, no one saw anything erroneous or evil in it. However, when some Ulama for reasons best known to themselves became displeased and angry with me and the Jama'at Islami, they were quick to detect a few grave 'errors' in this book, as they found in my other writings.

Only Allah knows whether these Muftis [who issue legal edicts] read the book themselves or put someone else on the job of reading it and extracting some sentences which could provide them with the ammunition to issue their *fatwa* (edicts) against me. Be that as it may, they could find only four objectionable sentences in the whole book. In the nineteenth address, the following sentences drew their wrath.

. . . without Almsgiving, even Salah, Sawm, and Iman have no meaning and lose their credibility.

Those who disregard these two fundamental teachings [the Prayer and Almsgiving] are not true in their profession of faith.

It [the Qur'ān] states beyond doubt that the affirmation of Kalimah Tayyibah has no weight unless accompanied by the performance of the Prayer and the giving of the Alms.

In the twenty-fifth address, they have selected the following sentences:

As for those who never bother to think about performing the Hajj at all, but who nonetheless manage to travel all over the world, perhaps even passing within a few hours' journeying time of Makka on their way to Europe – such people are certainly not Muslims. They lie if they call themselves Muslims, and people who consider them Muslims are ignorant of the Qur'ān.

These sentences have been used to decree that I am a Kharjite and Mu'tazalite, that I, as against the accepted position of *Ahl Sunnah,* consider deeds to be part of faith, and excommunicate the non-practising Muslims.

Surprisingly, close to these sentences were others which not only explained my true intent but also refuted these allegations. The so-called Muftis, however, either failed to see them or deliberately ignored them because they did not serve their purpose.

For example, take the first sentence and read it with the sentence which precedes it:

After the death of the Prophet, blessings and peace be on him, some tribes refused to give Zakah. Abu Bakr declared war on them, as if they had disowned Islam and became Unbelievers, even though they performed the Prayer and professed faith in Allah and the Messenger. For, they were like a rotten limb. Islam is an integral whole of which Almsgiving is an essential part; without Almsgiving, even Salah, Sawm and Iman have no meaning and lose their credibility.

Similarly, just before their last chosen sentence too, I referred to one Quranic verse, two Hadith, one verdict of 'Umar, all of which endorsed my position. However, their selective eye passed them over. Such are the tricks played by people who are considered great teachers of Islam and experts in purifying souls!

Again, in this very book, there is one whole address [the ninth] which explains what type of Iman is my subject. One type is the 'legal' Islam which is dealt with by the jurists and philosophers. This definition of Islam ensures that no one can be expelled from the fold of Islam and deprived of those rights which Islam grants him, until he violates certain minimum necessary conditions for being Muslim. The other is the 'real' and 'true' Islam and Iman; on this basis a man will be judged in the Hereafter.

Having differentiated between the two, I have explained that the objective of various prophets was never to produce the first type of Muslims. Rather the prophets' mission was to inculcate the real Iman, full of sincerity, obedience, devotion, and loyalty. I have asked Muslims not to be content with that Islam which merely ensures to keep them on its boundary so that they cannot be called Unbelievers. Rather they should cultivate that Islam which would ensure that they are accepted as sincere and loyal believers in the sight of God. Had the jurists read this discussion, they would have understood the purpose behind this book, and every other word at least would have told them the same story.

But they, perhaps, were not at all concerned with the intent of the author. From the very outset, they were searching for something which, torn out of context, could be used to issue a *fatwa*. For them, perhaps, a *fatwa* is not a responsible religious edict which requires that the truth be investigated, but a whip with which to lash those against whom they feel animosity, whenever the need be.

Even the least intellectual integrity requires that one understands the subject of a book before interpreting any of its particular parts. This book is not a book of *fiqh* (law) or *kalām* (philosophical theology); nor is its language that of a legal edict. Its purpose is not to define those minimum conditions going beyond which may justify that one be declared to have gone out of the pale of Islam. This is a book of admonition and exhortation, of advice and counsel. Its purpose is to inspire people to obey God, to refrain from disobeying Him, and to be sincere to Him.

This being my purpose, would the Muftis have advised me to convince the Muslims that the Prayer, Fasting, Hajj, Zakah were all an unnecessary appendage, and that they could remain Muslims without them?

My position on the relationship between faith and deeds and the conditions for the excommunication of Muslims has been fully explained in other articles that I have written on this very subject. Determining that position from certain stray sentences in the *Khuṭubāt* rather than from my *Tafhimāt*, Volume 2, can hardly be considered an honest approach.

Abul A'la
16 August, [19]52

Index

THE QURANIC VERSES

al-Baqarah

2: 2–3	200, 225
2: 13	248
2: 43	200
2: 45	149
2: 61	64
2: 85	199
2: 124	249
2: 125	228
2: 128	248
2: 129	256
2: 143	176
2: 170	97
2: 177	201, 229
2: 183	183, 186
2: 195	226
2: 197	257, 259
2: 198	257, 259
2: 200	257
2: 208	34
2: 219	229
2: 256	209
2: 256–7	120
2: 258	246
2: 262–3	227
2: 264	213, 227
2: 267	211, 228, 231
2: 268	226
2: 271	228
2: 272	212, 227
2: 276	221
2: 280	229

Āl 'Imrān

3: 19	34, 125
3: 64	94
3: 83	94, 127
3: 85	34, 126
3: 92	109, 210, 226
3: 96–7	250
3: 97	256, 261
3: 110	176, 292
3: 133	212
3: 179	302
3: 190–1	224

al-Nisā'

4: 5	228
4: 36	230
4: 42	149
4: 60–4	300
4: 103	223
4: 136	25, 34

al-Mā'idah

5: 3	47
5: 12	199
5: 41	34
5: 44	67, 93
5: 55–6	201

5: 66	35, 64	*Ibrāhīm*	
5: 92	123	14: 24–7	77
5: 104–5	97	14: 27	82
		14: 35–7	251
al-An'ām			
6: 57	95	*al-Isrā '*	
6: 65	133	17: 26	229
6: 79–80	246	17: 29	229
6: 116	99		
6: 141	231	*al-Kahf*	
6: 163–4	111	18: 28	224
		18: 111	300
al-A'rāf			
7: 28	258	*Maryam*	
7: 31	258	19: 31	200
7: 35	128	19: 41–5	246
7:96	35	19: 55	199
7: 156	199		
		ṬāHā	
al-Anfāl		20: 1–2	64
8: 39	127, 176, 300		
8: 45	223	*al-Anbiyā '*	
		21: 37	219
al-Tawbah		21: 53	97
9: 11	202	21: 57–70	246
9: 16	302	21: 73	198
9: 33	127, 300		
9: 34	213	*al-Ḥajj*	
9: 34–5	232	22: 25	278
9: 37	259	22: 26–8	252
9: 44–5	214	22: 28	263
9: 54	214	22: 36	258
9: 60	232	22: 37	258
9: 67	214	22: 40–1	203
9: 71	202		
9: 98	214	*al-Nūr*	
9: 103	232	24: 22	211
9: 111	76	24: 46–52	105
		24:54	123
Yūnus		24:55	177
10: 79	97	24:63	124
Hūd		*al-Furqān*	
11:52	35	25: 43–4	96
		25: 67	229
Yūsuf			
12:40	137, 300		

al-Qaṣaṣ
28: 50 95

al-'Ankabūt
29: 2–3 301
29: 10–11 301
29: 45 147,
29: 67 250

al-Rūm
30: 39 221

Luqmān
31: 21–3 98

al-Ṣāffāt
37: 99–111 248

Fuṣṣilat
41: 6–7 205

Zukhruf
43: 23–5 98

Muḥammad
47: 38 214

al-Ḥujurāt
49:13 55
49: 15 33, 34

al-Dhāriyāt
51: 19 230
51: 56 135

al-Ḥadīd
57: 7 34

al-Mujādalah
58: 14–21 302

al-Ḥashr
59:9 210

al-Jumu'ah
62: 10 147

al-Munāfiqūn
63: 9 212

al-Taghābun
64: 16 226

al-Dahr
76: 8–9 211
76: 8–10 230

al-Bayyinah
98: 5 126, 299

al-Mā'ūn
107: 1–5 34

CPSIA information can be obtained
at www.ICGtesting.com
Printed in the USA
LVOW12s0852111117

555862LV00001B/1/P